Human–AI Teaming

STATE-OF-THE-ART AND RESEARCH NEEDS

Committee on Human-System Integration Research Topics
for the 711th Human Performance Wing
of the Air Force Research Laboratory

Board on Human-Systems Integration
Division of Behavioral and Social Sciences and Education

A Consensus Study Report of

The National Academies of
SCIENCES • ENGINEERING • MEDICINE

THE NATIONAL ACADEMIES PRESS
Washington, DC
www.nap.edu

THE NATIONAL ACADEMIES PRESS   **500 Fifth Street, NW**   **Washington, DC 20001**

This activity was supported by contract number WBSRA-21-10-NAS between the National Academy of Sciences and the Wright Brothers Institute as a subcontract to the Air Force Research Laboratory. Any opinions, findings, conclusions, or recommendations expressed in this publication do not necessarily reflect the views of any organization or agency that provided support for the project. Also supporting the Committee's work are the Board on Human-System Integration core sponsorship grants with the National Aeronautics and Space Administration, U.S. Army Research Laboratory, the Human Factors and Ergonomics Society, and the Society for Human Resource Management.

International Standard Book Number-13: 978-0-309-27017-5
International Standard Book Number-10: 0-309-27017-0
Digital Object Identifier: https://doi.org/10.17226/26355

Additional copies of this publication are available from the National Academies Press, 500 Fifth Street, NW, Keck 360, Washington, DC 20001; (800) 624-6242 or (202) 334-3313; http://www.nap.edu.

Copyright 2022 by the National Academy of Sciences. All rights reserved.

Printed in the United States of America

Suggested citation: National Academies of Sciences, Engineering, and Medicine. 2022. *Human-AI Teaming: State-of-the-Art and Research Needs*. Washington, DC: The National Academies Press. https://doi.org/10.17226/26355.

The National Academies of
SCIENCES · ENGINEERING · MEDICINE

The **National Academy of Sciences** was established in 1863 by an Act of Congress, signed by President Lincoln, as a private, nongovernmental institution to advise the nation on issues related to science and technology. Members are elected by their peers for outstanding contributions to research. Dr. Marcia McNutt is president.

The **National Academy of Engineering** was established in 1964 under the charter of the National Academy of Sciences to bring the practices of engineering to advising the nation. Members are elected by their peers for extraordinary contributions to engineering. Dr. John L. Anderson is president.

The **National Academy of Medicine** (formerly the Institute of Medicine) was established in 1970 under the charter of the National Academy of Sciences to advise the nation on medical and health issues. Members are elected by their peers for distinguished contributions to medicine and health. Dr. Victor J. Dzau is president.

The three Academies work together as the **National Academies of Sciences, Engineering, and Medicine** to provide independent, objective analysis and advice to the nation and conduct other activities to solve complex problems and inform public policy decisions. The National Academies also encourage education and research, recognize outstanding contributions to knowledge, and increase public understanding in matters of science, engineering, and medicine.

Learn more about the National Academies of Sciences, Engineering, and Medicine at **www.nationalacademies.org**.

The National Academies of
SCIENCES · ENGINEERING · MEDICINE

Consensus Study Reports published by the National Academies of Sciences, Engineering, and Medicine document the evidence-based consensus on the study's statement of task by an authoring committee of experts. Reports typically include findings, conclusions, and recommendations based on information gathered by the committee and the committee's deliberations. Each report has been subjected to a rigorous and independent peer-review process and it represents the position of the National Academies on the statement of task.

Proceedings published by the National Academies of Sciences, Engineering, and Medicine chronicle the presentations and discussions at a workshop, symposium, or other event convened by the National Academies. The statements and opinions contained in proceedings are those of the participants and are not endorsed by other participants, the planning committee, or the National Academies.

For information about other products and activities of the National Academies, please visit www.nationalacademies.org/about/whatwedo.

COMMITTEE ON HUMAN-SYSTEM INTEGRATION RESEARCH TOPICS FOR THE 711TH HUMAN PERFORMANCE WING OF THE AIR FORCE RESEARCH LABORATORY

MICA R. ENDSLEY (*Chair*), SA Technologies
BARRETT S. CALDWELL, Purdue University
ERIN K. CHIOU, Arizona State University
NANCY J. COOKE, Arizona State University
MARY L. CUMMINGS, Duke University
CLEOTILDE GONZALEZ, Carnegie Mellon University
JOHN D. LEE, University of Wisconsin-Madison
NATHAN J. MCNEESE, Clemson University
CHRISTOPHER MILLER, Smart Information Flow Technologies
EMILIE ROTH, Roth Cognitive Engineering
WILLIAM B. ROUSE, NAE, Georgetown University

Staff

DANIEL TALMAGE, *Study Director*

BOARD ON HUMAN-SYSTEMS INTEGRATION

FREDERICK OSWALD (*Chair*), Department of Psychology, Rice University
JAMES BAGIAN, NAE/NAM, Institute for Healthcare Policy and Innovation, University of Michigan, Ann Arbor
DIANA BURLEY, Graduate School of Education and Human Development, George Washington University
BARBARA DOSHER, NAS, School of Social Sciences, University of California, Irvine
MICA ENDSLEY, SA Technologies, Mesa, Arizona
EDMOND ISRAELSKI, AbbVie, North Chicago, Illinois
JOHN LOCKETT, U.S. Army Research Laboratory (Retired)
NAJMEDIN MESHKATI, Viterbi School of Engineering, University of Southern California
EMILIE ROTH, Roth Cognitive Engineering, Stanford, California
WILLIAM J. STRICKLAND, Human Resources Research Organization, Alexandria, Virginia
MATTHEW WEINGER, Vanderbilt University Medical Center

Staff

MARY ELLEN O'CONNELL, *Interim Director*
TOBY M. WARDEN, *Director* (Until 5/25/2021)

Preface

Artificial intelligence (AI) is being proposed as a force multiplier for the military. AI brings its own unique challenges, however, which must be balanced with effective human oversight, particularly in operations with high-consequence outcomes. AI therefore needs to work effectively as a part of a distributed team. This report addresses the state-of-the-art in human-AI teaming and establishes a framework for future research to meet the goal of effective use of AI for future defense operations.

I wish to express my deep appreciation to the members of the committee for their diligent and dedicated contributions. The committee's expertise and knowledge were indispensable throughout our deliberations and the writing of the report. Their efforts, which often required working nights and weekends, are particularly notable given the incredibly challenging year. I cannot thank them enough. On behalf of the entire committee, I also wish to thank the National Academies of Sciences, Engineering, and Medicine staff for their outstanding support and guidance. I am also deeply appreciative to Heather Kreidler for her writing and fact checking. The report benefited deeply from the editing skills of Susan Debad. Additionally, I want to express our sincere gratitude to everyone who contributed their time, expertise, and experiences to our committee, especially all the workshop presenters and attendees. The presentations, resources, and insights contributed immensely to our deliberations. Finally, I wish to thank the Air Force Research Laboratory for their partnership and forthright participation throughout this process. I offer this report in the spirit of that partnership and believe that the research areas discussed in the report will be useful to the sponsor as they move forward.

Mica Endsley, *Chair*
Committee on Human-System Integration Research Topics for the
711th Human Performance Wing of the Air Force Research Laboratory

Acknowledgment of Reviewers

This Consensus Study Report was reviewed in draft form by individuals chosen for their diverse perspectives and technical expertise. The purpose of this independent review is to provide candid and critical comments that will assist the National Academies of Sciences, Engineering, and Medicine in making each published report as sound as possible and to ensure that it meets the institutional standards for objectivity, evidence, and responsiveness to the study charge. The review comments and draft manuscript remain confidential to protect the integrity of the deliberative process.

We thank the following individuals for their review of this report:

John Allspaw, Principal, Adaptive Capacity Labs, LLC, New York, New York
Ellen J. Bass, Department of Health Systems and Sciences Research, College of Nursing and Health Professions, and Department of Systems and Information Engineering, College of Computing and Informatics, Drexel University
Ann Bisantz, Department of Industrial and Systems Engineering, University at Buffalo, The State University of New York
Michael Coovert, Department of Psychology, University of South Florida
Cindy Dominguez, Principal Cognitive Scientist, The Mitre Corporation. Exeter, New Hampshire
Stephen M. Fiore, Cognitive Sciences, Department of Philosophy, University of Central Florida
Jamie C. Gorman, School of Psychology, Georgia Institute of Technology
Julie A. Shah, Interactive Robotics Group, Computer Science and Artificial Intelligence Laboratory, Massachusetts Institute of Technology
James C. Spohrer, Board of Directors, International Society of Service Innovation Professionals (ISSIP), San Jose, California

Although the reviewers listed above have provided many constructive comments and suggestions, they were not asked to endorse the conclusions or recommendations of this report nor did they see the final draft before its release. The review of this report was overseen by Robert F. Sproull, Adjunct Professor, Manning College of Information & Computer Sciences, University of Massachusetts at Amherst and Julie J.C.H. Ryan, Chief Executive Officer, Wyndrose Technical Group. They were responsible for making certain that an independent examination of this report was carried out in accordance with the standards of the National Academies and that all review comments were carefully considered. Responsibility for the final content of the report rests entirely with the authoring committee and the National Academies.

Contents

SUMMARY   1

1. INTRODUCTION   5
   Study Background and Charge to the Committee, 6
   Committee Approach, 7
   Automation and AI, 7
   Limits of AI, 8
   Effect of AI on Human Performance, 9
   Report Structure and Summary, 10

2. HUMAN-AI TEAMING METHODS AND MODELS   11
   Teams, 11
   Human-AI Teaming Models and Perspectives, 12
   Should Humans Team with AI?, 14
   Improved Models for Human-AI Teams, 16
   Key Challenges and Research Gaps, 17
   Research Needs, 17
   Summary, 18

3. HUMAN-AI TEAMING PROCESSES AND EFFECTIVENESS   19
   What Does It Mean for AI to Be a Teammate?, 19
   Processes and Characteristics of Effective Human-AI Teams, 20
       Team Heterogeneity, 20
       Shared Cognition, 21
       Communication and Coordination, 22
       Social Intelligence, 22
       Other Features of Effective Teams, 23
   Key Challenges and Research Gaps, 23
   Research Needs, 23
   Summary, 24

| 4 | SITUATION AWARENESS IN HUMAN-AI TEAMS | 25 |

Situation Awareness in Multi-Domain Operations, 25
    Key Challenges and Research Gaps, 27
    Research Needs, 27
Shared SA in Human-AI Teams, 27
    Key Challenges and Research Gaps, 29
    Research Needs, 29
Summary, 30

| 5 | AI TRANSPARENCY AND EXPLAINABILITY | 31 |

Display Transparency, 34
    Key Challenges and Research Gaps, 35
    Research Needs, 35
AI Explainability, 36
    Key Challenges and Research Gaps, 37
    Research Needs, 38
Summary, 40

| 6 | HUMAN-AI TEAM INTERACTION | 41 |

Level of Automation, 41
    Key Challenges and Research Gaps, 44
    Research Needs, 44
AI Dynamics and Temporality, 44
    Key Challenges and Research Gaps, 45
    Research Needs, 45
Granularity of Control, 46
    Key Challenges and Research Gaps, 46
    Research Needs, 46
Other Human-AI Team Interaction Issues, 47
    Key Challenges and Research Gaps, 47
    Research Needs, 47
Summary, 48

| 7 | TRUSTING AI TEAMMATES | 49 |

Trust Frameworks Past and Present, 49
Trusting AI in Complex Work Environments, 51
Key Challenges and Research Gaps, 51
Research Needs, 52
Summary, 55

| 8 | IDENTIFICATION AND MITIGATION OF BIAS IN HUMAN-AI TEAMS | 57 |

Human Biases, 57
AI Biases, 57
Human-AI Team Bias, 59
Key Challenges and Research Gaps, 60
Research Needs, 60
Summary, 61

9	**TRAINING HUMAN-AI TEAMS**	63
	Human-Human Team Training to Inform Human-AI Team Training, 63	
	Strategies for Team Training, 64	
	The Use of Simulation, 64	
	Training Content: Taskwork and Teamwork, 65	
	Key Challenges and Research Gaps, 65	
	Research Needs, 66	
	Summary, 67	
10	**HSI PROCESSES AND MEASURES OF HUMAN-AI TEAM COLLABORATION AND PERFORMANCE**	69
	Taking an HSI Perspective in Human-AI Team Design and Implementation, 69	
	Key Challenges and Research Gaps, 70	
	Research Needs, 70	
	Requirements for Research in Human-AI Team Development, 71	
	Key Challenges and Research Gaps, 71	
	Research Needs, 71	
	Research Team Competencies, 72	
	Key Challenges and Research Gaps, 73	
	Research Needs, 73	
	HSI Considerations for Human-AI Teams, 73	
	Key Challenges and Research Gaps, 75	
	Research Needs, 75	
	Testing, Evaluation, Verification, and Validation of Human-AI Teams, 75	
	Key Challenges and Research Gaps, 77	
	Research Needs, 77	
	Human-AI Team Research Testbeds, 77	
	Key Challenges and Research Gaps, 78	
	Research Needs, 78	
	Human-AI Team Measures and Metrics, 78	
	Key Challenges and Research Gaps, 80	
	Research Needs, 80	
	Agile Software Development and HSI, 81	
	Key Challenges and Research Gaps, 82	
	Research Needs, 82	
	Summary, 83	
11	**CONCLUSIONS**	85
	REFERENCES	91
	APPENDIXES	
A	Committee Biographies	115
B	Human-AI Teaming Workshop Agenda	119
C	Definitions	121

Summary

The military is investing in artificial intelligence (AI) as a tool that can potentially play a critical role in supporting command and control for future multi-domain operations (MDO) by boosting the processing rate of a wide variety of data inputs, automating mission planning, and creating faster predictive targeting and systems maintenance. Achieving this goal requires that the AI system be both reliable and robust across a wide variety of potential future missions, and that it works well as a teammate with humans. This report examines the factors that are relevant to the design and implementation of AI systems with respect to human operations, and it recommends needed research for achieving successful performance across the human-AI team.

Although AI has many potential benefits, it has also been shown to suffer from a number of challenges for successful performance in complex, real-world environments such as military operations, including brittleness, perceptual limitations, hidden biases, and lack of a model of causation important for understanding and predicting future events. These limitations mean that, for the foreseeable future, AI will remain inadequate for operating on its own in many complex and novel situations for the foreseeable future, and that humans will need to carefully manage AI systems to achieve their desired utility.

Research over the past 30 years has demonstrated, however, that people are significantly challenged in performing as successful monitors of complex automation, including AI systems. People can suffer from poor understanding of what the systems are doing, high workload when trying to interact with AI systems, poor situation awareness (SA) and performance deficits when intervention is needed, biases in decision making based on system inputs, and degradation of manual skills. These numerous challenges will continue to create problems in terms of human performance, even with more capable AI-based automation.

Therefore, effective human-AI teams capable of taking advantage of the unique abilities of both humans and AI, while overcoming the known challenges and limitations of each team member, need to be developed. An effective human-AI team ultimately augments human capabilities and raises performance beyond that of either entity. To this end, the committee has developed an interrelated set of research objectives that are presented to focus around the development of effective human-AI teams, based on improvements in models and metrics for human-AI teams (Chapter 2), team processes (Chapter 3), SA (Chapter 4), AI transparency and explainability (Chapter 5), human-AI interaction approaches (Chapter 6), trust (Chapter 7), reduction of human and AI bias (Chapter 8), and training (Chapter 9), supported by a foundation of human-systems integration (HSI) processes (Chapter 10). The report ends with a concluding chapter summarizing human-AI teaming research objectives aligned along near-, mid-, and far-term objectives. Each chapter has a summary of research objectives that have been developed by the committee for the sponsor.

HUMAN-AI TEAM MODELS

The committee finds that there is significant value in considering the human and AI as a team. This team construct fosters a recognition of the need to consider the interrelated roles of each team member, and it places emphasis on the value of team interactions, including communication and coordination, for boosting their combined performance. In such team arrangements, the committee believes that, in general, the human should have authority over the AI system, for both ethical and practical reasons. Improved computational models of human-AI teams are called for that consider the interrelated, dynamically evolving, distributed, and adaptive collaborative tasks and conditions that are also needed for networked command and control systems for MDO, and that are predictive within the design trade space. Improved metrics for human-AI teaming are needed that consider the team's ability to manage interdependencies and dynamic role assignments, that reduce uncertainty, and that improve the ability of the AI system to deliver capabilities that are in line with expectations of warfighters.

While it is assumed that human-AI teams will be more effective than either humans or AI systems operating alone, in the committee's judgment this will not be the case unless humans can (1) understand and predict the behaviors of the AI system (see Chapters 4 and 5); (2) develop appropriate trust relationships with an AI system (see Chapter 7); (3) make accurate decisions based on input from the AI system (see Chapter 8); and (4) exert control over the system in a timely and appropriate manner (see Chapter 6).

HUMAN-AI TEAM PROCESSES

Supporting humans and AI systems as teammates relies on a carefully designed system with the capability for both taskwork and teamwork. Along this line, research is needed to improve team effectiveness in long-term, distributed, and agile human-AI teams through improved team assembly, goal alignment, communication, coordination, social intelligence, and the development of a new human-AI language (see Chapter 3). This research can leverage the large body of existing work on human-human teaming, but the committee recognizes that new research is needed to better understand and support effective team processes between humans and AI systems. In addition, the committee believes that research should examine the potential for an AI system to boost team performance by serving as a team coordinator, orchestrator, or human-resource manager.

SITUATION AWARENESS

It is widely recognized that human situation awareness (SA) is critical for effective MDO performance, including for the oversight of AI systems. Methodologies for supporting individual and team SA in command and control operations need to be extended to MDO, and methods for using AI to support information integration, prioritization, and routing across the joint battle space are needed, as well as for improving resilience to adversarial attacks on SA. Methods for improving human SA of AI systems need to be developed that consider diverse types of applications, timescales of operations, and the changing capabilities associated with machine learning (ML)-based AI systems (see Chapter 4). In addition, research directed at creating shared SA within the human-AI team deserves attention. The degree to which AI systems need to have both self-awareness and awareness of their human teammates needs to be explored, to determine the benefit for overall team performance. Finally, future AI systems will need to possess integrated situation models to appropriately understand the current situation and to project future situations for decision making. AI models of the dynamic task environment will be needed that can work with humans to align or deconflict goals and to synchronize situation models, decisions, function allocations, task prioritizations, and plans to achieve coordinated and approved actions.

AI TRANSPARENCY AND EXPLAINABILITY

Improved AI system transparency and explainability (see Chapter 5) are key to achieving improved human SA, as well as trust. Real-time transparency is critical for supporting understanding and predictability of AI systems and has been found to significantly compensate for out-of-the-loop performance deficits. Research is needed to better define the information requirements and methods for achieving transparency of ML-based AI systems, as well as to define when such information should be provided to meet SA needs without overloading the human. Improved visualization of explanations from ML-based AI systems needs further exploration, as well as research on the value of machine personae. Further, the relationship between AI explainability and trust would benefit from further research, to inform improved, multi-factor models of how explanations can foster trust and trust-influenced decisions. Effective mechanisms to adapt explanations to receivers' needs, prior knowledge and assumptions, and cognitive and emotional states need to be developed. The committee also suggests that research be directed at determining whether explanations of human reasoning could likewise improve AI system and human-AI team performance.

HUMAN-AI TEAM INTERACTION

Interaction mechanisms and strategies within the human-AI team are critical to team effectiveness, including the ability to support flexible assignments of levels of automation (LOAs) across functions over time. Research is needed to determine improved methods for supporting collaboration between humans and AI systems in shared functions, to support human operators working with AI systems at multiple LOAs, and to determine methods for maintaining or regaining SA when working with AI systems at high LOAs (i.e., on-the-loop control). Research is also needed to determine new requirements to support dynamic functional assignments across human-AI teams, and to determine the best methods for supporting dynamic transitions in LOAs over time, including when such transitions should occur, who should activate them, and how they should occur, to maintain optimal human-AI team performance. The committee suggests that research also be conducted on Playbook control methodologies (defined in Chapter 6), extending it to MDO tasks and human-AI teaming applications. Finally, research directed at a better understanding and prediction of emergent human-AI interactions, and on a better understanding of the effects of interaction design decisions on skill retention, training requirements, job satisfaction, and overall human-AI team resilience would be beneficial.

TRUST

Trust in AI is recognized as a foundational factor associated with use of AI systems. It would benefit future research to better document the decision context and goals involved in the teaming environment (detailed in Chapter 7), to advance understanding of how broader sociotechnical factors affect trust in human-AI teams. Interaction structures that extend beyond supervisory control arrangements would also benefit from further study, particularly to understand the effect of AI directability on the trust relationship. The team lens is useful here for identifying novel interaction structures with AI teammates. Improved measures of trust are needed that draw on the importance of cooperation, and that separate the concept of distrust from trust. Finally, dynamic models of trust are needed that capture how trust evolves and affects performance outcomes in various human-AI team contexts. This research would do well to examine trust-enabled outcomes that emerge from dyadic team interactions and extend that work into how trust evolves in larger teams and multi-echelon networks.

BIAS

The potential for bias in AI systems, often hidden, can be introduced through the development of its algorithms as well as through systemic biases in training sets, among other factors (see Chapter 8). Further, humans can suffer from several well-known decision biases. Of particular import, human decision making can be directly affected by the accuracy of the AI system, creating a human-AI team bias; therefore, humans cannot be viewed as independent adjudicators of AI recommendations. Research is needed to better understand the interdependencies between human and AI decision-making biases, how these evolve over time, and methods for detecting and preventing bias with ML-based AI. Research is also needed to detect and prevent potential adversarial attacks that may attempt to take advantage of these biases.

TRAINING

Training of the human-AI team will be needed to develop the appropriate team constructs and skills necessary for effective performance (see Chapter 9). Directed research is needed to determine what, when, why, and how to best train human-AI teams, taking into consideration various team compositions and sizes. Existing training methodologies can be explored to see whether they can be adapted to human-AI teaming. In addition, training may be needed to better calibrate human expectations of AI teammates and to foster appropriate levels of trust. Specific platforms will be necessary to develop and test human-AI teamwork procedures.

HSI PROCESSES AND MEASURES

Finally, achieving the successful development of an AI system that can function as a good teammate will require advances in HSI processes and measures (see Chapter 10). Good HSI practice will be key to the design, development, and testing of new AI systems, particularity with respect to system development based on agile or DevOps practices. New HSI design and testing methods for effective human-AI teams will also be needed, including an improved ability to determine requirements for human-AI teams, particularly those that involve ML (see Chapter 10). Improved approaches for multi-disciplinary AI development teams are needed that include human factors engineers, sociotechnical researchers, systems engineers, and computer scientists. New teams, methods, and tools centered around AI lifecycle testing and auditability, as well as AI cyber vulnerability, will also be needed. Methods for testing and verification of evolving AI systems need to be developed to detect AI system blind spots and edge cases and to consider brittleness. New human-AI testbeds to support research and development activities by these new teams will also be important. Finally, improved metrics for human-AI teaming may be needed, specifically regarding matters of trust, mental models, and explanation quality.

CONCLUSION

In total, 57 research objectives are presented to address the many challenges for effective human-AI teaming. These research objectives are divided into near term (1–5 years), mid-term (6–10 years), and far term (10–15 years) priorities. This integrated set of research objectives will achieve significant advances in human-AI teaming competence. These objectives are fundamental prerequisites to the safe introduction of AI into critical operations such as MDO, and they create a framework for better understanding and supporting the effective use of AI systems.

1

Introduction

The military is moving toward multi-domain operations (MDO), which involve dynamic and distributed combinations of actions across the traditionally separate air, land, maritime, space, and cyberspace domains, as well as the information domain and the electromagnetic spectrum domain, to achieve synergistic and combined effects with improved mission outcomes. The goal of MDO command and control (MDC2), also called joint all-domain command and control (JADC2), is to achieve operational and informational advantages by "connecting distributed sensors, shooters, and data from all domains to joint forces, enabling coordinated exercise of authority to integrate planning and synchronize convergence in time, space, and purpose" (USAF, 2020, p. 6). MDO is representative of a wide body of research that considers not only the behaviors and performance of teams, but also interrelated teams of teams (or multi-team systems) (Marks et al., 2005; Schraagen et al., 2021; Zaccaro and DeChurch, 2011).

A key facet of MDO is the need to accelerate and increase the military's ability to develop timely, decision-quality information, integrated across domains, which includes the ability to rapidly understand relationships between information from different domains. The development of rapid, cross-domain situation awareness (SA) is critical to effective planning and decision making, to optimize the use of available military resources. SA is also important for monitoring across operations (e.g., feedback on effects, synchronization, or tempo), which is needed for mission control and dynamic replanning (see NASEM, 2018, 2021a, and 2021b for more information on MDC2).

Artificial intelligence (AI) is seen as a tool that can potentially play a critical role in supporting the military's objectives for MDC2. AI can significantly boost the ability to process the massively increasing volume of intelligence, surveillance, and reconnaissance data generated each year (Cook, 2021), automate the mission-planning process, and create faster predictive targeting and systems maintenance (Hill, 2021). Achieving this goal, however, requires that the AI systems be highly reliable and robust within the broad range of missions and conditions in which they might be employed, and that these systems operate seamlessly within a much larger and more complex set of military systems and human operations (USAF, 2015).

The goal of this report is to examine the factors relevant to the design and implementation of AI systems with respect to their operations with humans, and to recommend necessary research for achieving successful performance across the joint human-AI team, particularly with regard to MDO, although many research objectives apply to human-AI teaming across various military and non-military contexts.

STUDY BACKGROUND AND CHARGE TO THE COMMITTEE

The Air Force Research Laboratory (AFRL), 711th Human Performance Wing, sought the assistance of the National Academies of Sciences, Engineering, and Medicine to examine the requirements for appropriate use of AI in future operations. The AFRL was particularly concerned about the state of the research base, to support the design of future systems by promoting effective human performance when AI is a part of the system. In considering the integration of AI into future operations, the AFRL takes a systems approach, which recognizes that people, technology, and operational systems such as policies, procedures, structures, and informational flows can affect each other and overall mission performance. Therefore, determining the methods and infrastructure that will allow humans to effectively and efficiently interact with AI is fundamental to the USAF's goals. The committee's overall task was to examine the state of research on human-AI teaming and to determine gaps and future research priorities. The committee's full statement of task is shown in Box 1.1.

To address this charge, an independent committee with a broad range of expertise was appointed, including individuals with backgrounds in human factors, cognitive engineering, human-computer interaction, industrial-organizational psychology, and AI, as well as experts in military operations related to human-AI teaming. Brief biographies of the 11 committee members are presented in Appendix A.

BOX 1.1
Statement of Task

The National Academies of Sciences, Engineering, and Medicine will convene an ad hoc committee to recommend promising research opportunities and design considerations to inform the 2021 strategic research agenda of the 711th Human Performance Wing (711 HPW) of the Air Force Research Laboratory (AFRL). The committee will explore critical human-systems integration issues for designing autonomous agents having greater transparency and intelligibility to support effective joint human-machine decision making and performance in multi-domain command and control operations. The committee will convene a public workshop as the primary source of information for its work.

The workshop, developed with input related to current AFRL 711th Human Performance Wing research priority areas, will examine the understanding of effective team performance in human interaction with artificial intelligence (AI) in the context of warfighter-centered designs and systems.

With attention to multi-domain command and control operations, the committee will:

- Identify key human-systems integration design considerations, methods, approaches, and associated research aimed at warfighter systems that incorporate human-AI teaming;
- Identify gaps in knowledge on effective human-machine teaming necessary to achieve future Air Force mission capability; and
- Identify promising human-systems integration and human factors research opportunities that would accelerate mission capability development.

With respect to the identification of research opportunities, the areas of human robot interaction and manned-unmanned aircraft teaming will not be examined. Additionally, the committee's primary focus will be the human effectiveness component of human-AI teaming rather than the computer science and software dimensions.

COMMITTEE APPROACH

The committee was to complete its work as a "fast-track" consensus committee, with a formal report of its findings provided within nine months of its inception in May of 2021. Its process was to

- Review the available research literature on human-automation integration, AI performance and limitations, human teaming, and human-AI interaction to include models and approaches, AI transparency and explainability, shared SA and mental models, trust and bias, communication and collaboration, measures and metrics, and human-systems integration processes for addressing human-AI teaming;
- Host a virtual workshop, Human-AI Teaming for Warfighter-Centered Design, July 28–29, 2021, to gather data on relevant research efforts;
- Conduct a series of virtual online meetings to support committee deliberations and discussions;
- Identify major findings, research gaps, and research needs, based on the workshop and research literature; and
- Prioritize research needs for advancing the state of knowledge on human-AI teaming.

AUTOMATION AND AI

The work of the committee was largely influenced by the extant research base on human-automation interaction developed over the past 40 years, in addition to research on human interaction with autonomous and semi-autonomous systems, as well as AI in its many forms.

Automation, as used in this report, is defined as a technology that performs tasks independently, without continuous input from an operator (Groover, 2020). Automation can be fixed (mechanical) or programmable (based on defined rules and feedback loops), either via a static set of software commands or via flexible, rapid customization by a human operator. Tasks may be fully automated (autonomous) or semi-automated, requiring human oversight and control for portions of the task. Automation is also defined as "the execution by a machine agent of a function that was previously carried out by a human. What is considered automation will, therefore, change with time" (Parasuraman and Riley, 1997, p. 231).

Autonomous systems have a set of intelligence-based capabilities that can respond to situations that were not explicitly programmed or were not anticipated in the design (i.e., systems that can generate decision-based responses) (USAF, 2013). Autonomous systems have a certain amount of self-government and self-directed behavior, and they can serve as human proxies for decisions (USAF, 2015). Systems may be fully autonomous or partially autonomous. Partially autonomous systems require human actions or inputs for portions of the task.

AI seeks to provide intellectual processes similar to those of humans, including the "ability to reason, discover meaning, generalize, or learn from past experience" (Copeland, 2021). AI systems may be applied to parts of a task (e.g., perception and categorization, natural language understanding, problem solving, reasoning, or system control), or to a combination of task-related actions. AI software approaches may involve symbolic approaches (e.g., rule-based or case-based reasoning), often in the form of decision-support systems; or AI software may apply other advanced algorithms, such as Bayesian belief-nets, fuzzy systems, and connectionist or machine learning (ML)-based approaches (e.g., logistic regression, neural networks, deep learning, or decision trees). AI software may also incorporate hybrid architectures that include more than one algorithmic approach.

In the body of this report, the term AI is used to describe a form of highly capable automation directed at highly perceptual and cognitive tasks. AI potentially improves upon previous forms of automation in its ability to sense and interpret situations, adapt to changes in conditions and the environment, prioritize and optimize based on changes in goals, and refine its abilities through learning. These abilities of AI are often only aspirational, however, and today, many systems built with AI software fall short of these capabilities. Although many autonomous or semi-autonomous systems may employ AI, in other cases AI may merely enhance or facilitate operations that are conducted by humans. As such, many of the committee's findings are based on the research on human-automation interaction and human-autonomy interaction, with additional research objectives made where further extensions are needed to deal with unique aspects of AI systems (e.g., challenges associated with ML-based AI).

It should be noted that AI is currently being used for many different types of functions—from object recognition to decision making to automated control loop execution—and may have different levels of reliability and capabilities over time. Further, in many cases, AI software may not be stand-alone, but may be embedded within a more complex system with which humans interact. While recognizing these differences, throughout this report the committee will refer to AI software or systems with respect to the features and factors that will be important for its successful integration with humans as part of a larger sociotechnical system.

AI software is thought to be potentially beneficial for military operations due to AI's ability to (1) execute tasks very quickly, advantaging time-critical mission applications; (2) enhance precision-strike capabilities by automating the processing of intelligence, surveillance and reconnaissance data, target recognition, tracking, selection, and engagement; (3) improve coordination of forces across a distributed network; (4) improve the ability to operate in anti-access/area denial areas where human control opportunities may be limited; (5) increase persistence of operations over time; (6) increase the speed and accuracy of SA and decision making, thus improving lethality and deterrence; and (7) provide enhanced endurance over time (Konaev et al., 2020). These gains will not be possible, however, unless the military pays careful attention to the creation of robust AI applications that emphasize safety and security and are well integrated with the warfighter (Konaev et al., 2020).

LIMITS OF AI

Although there is a tendency among many to view AI as highly capable in comparison to humans (National Security Commission on Artificial Intelligence, 2021), in reality, AI software is subject to a number of performance limitations. This list is not meant to be exhaustive, and likely will change over time, but it points out many of the larger challenges associated with current AI software approaches.

- *Brittleness*: AI will only be capable of performing well in situations that are covered by its programming or its training data (Woods, 2016). When new classes of situations are encountered that require behaviors different from what the AI system has previously learned, it may perform poorly by over-generalizing from previous training. Even if an AI system can learn in real time, such training requires time and repeated experiences, as well as meaningful feedback on decision results, potentially causing performance deficits during the learning cycle.
- *Perceptual limitations*: Though improvements have been made, many AI algorithms continue to struggle with reliable and accurate object recognition in "noisy" environments, as well as with natural language processing (Akhtar and Mian, 2018; Alcorn et al., 2019; Yadav, Patel, and Shah, 2021). The use of AI for higher-order cognitive processes can be undermined if information inputs are not registered correctly.
- *Hidden biases*: AI software may incorporate many hidden biases that can result from being created using a limited set of training data, or from biases within that data itself (Ferrer et al., 2021; Howard and Borenstein, 2018). Because ML-based AI software is often opaque (i.e., the features and logic used are not easily subject to human inspection), these biases may go undetected.
- *No model of causation*: ML-based AI is based on simple pattern recognition; the underlying system has no causal mode (Pearl and Mackenzie, 2018). Because AI cannot use reason to understand cause and effect, it cannot predict future events, simulate the effects of potential actions, reflect on past actions, or learn when to generalize to new situations. Causality has been highlighted as a major research challenge for AI systems (Littman et al., 2021).

In the committee's judgment, although AI software is capable of rapidly processing large volumes of data for known types of events or situations, the limitations of this software means that, for the foreseeable future, AI will remain inadequate for recognizing and operating in most novel situations. The performance of an AI system could be suboptimal due to unknown biases or limitations in its training data, or the presence of challenges for which no clear "correct response" is known (e.g., cyber operations in which the outcome of an action has not been previously observed). Use of AI in the military context also introduces the particular challenge posed by adversaries who might try to accentuate and exploit the vulnerabilities of AI.

EFFECT OF AI ON HUMAN PERFORMANCE

Automation is known to create challenges for people who must interact with or oversee its performance, and these challenges are also applicable to AI systems.

- *Automation confusion*: "Poor operator understanding of system functioning is a common problem with automation, leading to inaccurate expectations of system behavior and inappropriate interactions with the automation" (Endsley, 2019, p. 3; see also Sarter and Woods, 1994; Wiener and Curry, 1980). "This is largely due to the fact that automation is inherently complex, and its operations are often not fully understood even by [people] with extensive experience using it" (Endsley, 2019, p. 3; see also Federal Aviation Administration Human Factors Team, 1996; McClumpha and James, 1994). Developing a correct mental model of how an automation works is a major challenge. Furthermore, as people transition from directly performing a task to interacting with automation to accomplish that task, cognitive workload often increases (Hancock and Verwey, 1997; Warm, Dember, and Hancock, 1996; Wiener, 1985).
- *Irony of automation*: When automation is working correctly, people can easily become bored or occupied with other tasks and fail to attend well to automation performance. Periodically, however, high workload spikes will occur, overstretching human performance (Bainbridge, 1983).
- *Poor SA and out-of-the-loop performance degradation*: People working with automation can become out-of-the-loop, meaning slower to identify a problem with system performance and slower to understand a detected problem (Moray, 1986; Wiener and Curry, 1980; Young, 1969). The out-of-the-loop problem results from lower SA (both of the automation and of the state of the system and environment) when people oversee automated systems compared to when they perform tasks manually (Endsley and Kiris, 1995). The out-of-the-loop problem can result in catastrophic consequences in novel or unexpected situations (Sebok and Wickens, 2017; Wickens, 1995).
- *Human decision biasing*: Research has shown that when the recommendations of an automated decision-support system are correct, the automation can improve human performance; however, when an automated system's recommendations are incorrect, people overseeing the system are more likely to make the same error (Layton, Smith, and McCoy, 1994; Olson and Sarter, 1999; Yeh, Wickens, and Seagull, 1999). That is, human decision making is not independent, but can be biased by errors made by automation (Endsley and Jones, 2012).
- *Degradation of manual skills*: To effectively oversee automation, people need to remain highly skilled at performing tasks manually, including understanding the cues important for decision making. However, these skills can atrophy if they are not used when tasks become automated (Casner et al., 2014; Young, Fanjoy, and Suckow, 2006). Further, people who are new to tasks may be unable to form the necessary skill sets if they only oversee automation. This loss of skills will be particularly detrimental if computer systems are compromised by a cyber attack (Ackerman and Stavridis, 2021; Hallaq et al., 2017), or if a rapidly changing adversarial situation is encountered for which the automation is not suited (Nelson, Biggio, and Laskov, 2011).

Because AI systems are incapable of adequate performance in novel situations, it will be necessary for substantial portions of certain tasks to be performed by humans, for the foreseeable future. However, the many challenges for human interactions with automated systems will continue, even with more capable automation based on AI. Therefore, in the committee's judgment, the design and development of effective human-AI teams that can take advantage of the unique capabilities of both people and AI while overcoming the known challenges and limitations of both is an important future research focus.

REPORT STRUCTURE AND SUMMARY

In this report, the committee will examine the role of AI in military operations and MDC2 with respect to that of human decision makers. The report is divided into 11 interrelated chapters, as illustrated in Figure 1-1. The current chapter provides an overview of the problem and the charge to the committee, as described in the statement of task (Box 1.1). Chapter 2 examines teaming strategies and roles for humans and AI, and the effects of these approaches for overall mission performance. Chapter 3 discusses the requirements and processes for effective human-AI teamwork. Chapter 4 focuses on supporting human SA and shared SA in human-AI teams, followed by Chapter 5, which discusses requirements for AI display transparency and explainability. Chapter 6 addresses human-AI interaction design. Chapter 7 focuses on human trust in AI in team contexts. Chapter 8 examines the interactions between AI biases and inaccuracies and human decision biases, as well as methods for addressing them. Chapter 9 focuses on issues related to training human-AI teams. Chapter 10 addresses the overall human-systems integration development and testing process, including measures and metrics of human-AI collaboration. Chapter 11 provides a summary of the committee's conclusions and a prioritized list of research objectives. As illustrated in Figure 1-1, however, these topics are highly interrelated, and so the committee's research objectives are best viewed within that light.

Appendix A contains the committee members' biographies. The agendas and speakers from the data-gathering workshops and open meetings held to fulfill the statement of task are presented in Appendix B. Appendix C provides definitions of the technical terms used in this report.

Throughout the report, the discussion of human-AI teams is pertinent to not only single human-AI teams, but also to multi-team systems that may include AI in various places, at various times, and acting in a variety of roles. It should be noted that many of the research needs discussed in this report that are relevant to human-AI teaming apply to many contexts as well as MDO. Specific concerns for MDO are also discussed throughout the report.

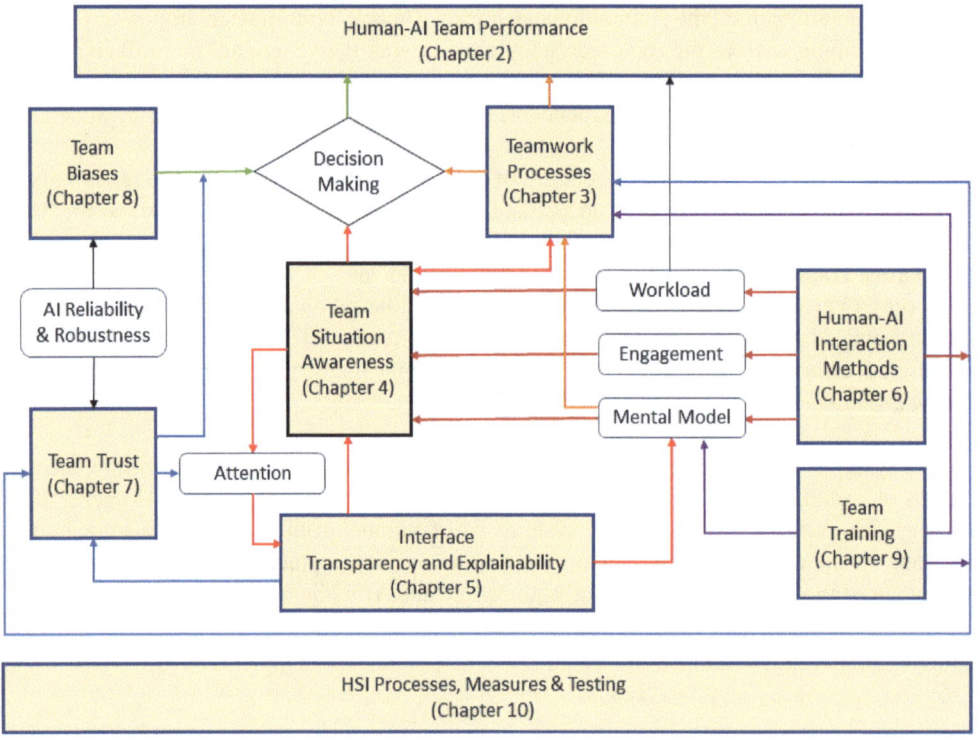

FIGURE 1-1 Topics contributing to effective human-AI teaming.
SOURCE: Based on the human-autonomy system oversight model, Endsley, 2017.

2

Human-AI Teaming Methods and Models

There is a rich history of research on human-human teams and human-automation teams across military and civilian domains, including healthcare, manufacturing, process control, emergency response, engineering, and design. Across these and other domains, teams are recognized for the ability to coordinate and perform multiple roles beyond the skills or capabilities of a single individual (Salas, Cooke, and Rosen, 2008; Tsifetakis and Kontogiannis, 2019). This chapter reviews the findings of team research, suggests implications for human-AI teaming, and addresses several associated challenges. Although there are also important ethical considerations around the development of AI systems (Defense Innovation Board, 2019; Flathmann et al., 2021; Hagendorff, 2020; Montréal Responsible AI Declaration Steering Committee, 2018), this report will primarily focus on the development of effective AI systems for supporting human control and interaction to achieve mission goals.

TEAMS

Field-based studies of the long-term dynamics of military teams and operations, as well as team development and training, have been performed since the 1950s and 1960s (Goodwin, Blacksmith, and Coats, 2018; McGrath, 1984; Morgan, Salas, and Glickman, 1993). Nuclear submarine crews, Antarctic research deployments, and undersea research facilities have also been studied (Driskell, Salas, and Driskell, 2018; Gunderson, 1973; Radloff and Helmreich, 1968). Broader examinations of team processes and dynamics, such as McGrath (1984) and Sundstrom, DeMeuse, and Futrell (1990), describe military teams as a particular application of action/performance teams, with the distinguishing characteristics of skilled specialist roles, focused performance events, and improvisation due to the dynamics and unpredictable nature of tasks. In a review of team-studies literature, Salas, Bowers, and Cannon-Bowers (1995) define teams as including two or more individuals with common goals, role assignments, and interdependence. Additional team characteristics include decision making within a task context, specialized task-related knowledge and skills, and performance within the task-context constraints of time pressure, workload, and other conditions. The concept of mental models is an important element of task-related knowledge. Mental models refer to a team member's organized information and perception of current states, situational dynamics, and contextual cues. Individual mental models allow for anticipation and prediction of future task conditions. Mental models that are shared among team members allow team members to anticipate and predict the needs and processes of other team members that are important for supporting mutual coordination (Goodwin, Blacksmith, and Coats, 2018). The shared mental models of team members often strongly affect performance in terms of understanding each other's roles and predicted behaviors. The way team members are trained and aided to become effectively performing teams is of particular importance, and it is an area where AI has great potential (see Chapter 9).

Teams are created to perform a variety of tasks that require the coordination of multiple interdependent individuals (Cooke et al., 2007), and this definition does not require all team members to be human (see Chapter 3). Further, the performance of a team is not decomposable to, or an aggregation of, individual performances. This description emphasizes the interdependence of team members (Salas, Bowers, and Cannon-Bowers, 1995; Tsifetakis and Kontogiannis, 2019).

Task demands and team composition often vary over time. Current and future human-AI teaming military tasks will similarly be characterized primarily by their dynamic nature. The specific types of tasks and activities that a team performs must be accompanied by the component elements of a team, such as interdependent roles and expectations, support from other team members, common understandings, effective interactions, and mutual trust in others' capabilities and performance (Cooke, 2018).

Relevant team characteristics include dimensions of team membership and team configurations (e.g., human-human, human-non-human, human-AI, or combinations thereof), sources of information and instruction, superordinate goals and priorities, and interdependence of teammate goals, as well as factors such as team cohesion, communication, and coordination (see Chapter 3). Further, teammates also perform their roles with a certain amount of operational independence or autonomy. When used in this sense, autonomy is not synonymous with AI; it refers to a dynamic functional state. The degree to which a human or AI system is autonomous is an operational question of independent function, addressing two performance-related queries: *autonomy from whom*, and *autonomy to do what* (Caldwell and Onken, 2011). In other words, a human who is ordered to perform an action only upon receiving an order to do so is acting with low autonomy for that action. A system that automatically goes into shutdown mode when detecting specific onboard conditions, such as a piece of space hardware going into "safe mode," is demonstrating high autonomy to protect critical performance capability (see Chapter 5).

HUMAN-AI TEAMING MODELS AND PERSPECTIVES

The use of AI in future military systems requires that humans can effectively control any systems that could potentially have lethal outcomes. The Department of Defense (DOD) stipulates that lethal autonomous weapons systems be designed to "allow commanders and operators to exercise appropriate levels of human judgment over the use of force" (DOD, 2012, p. 2). This does not require real-time control, "but rather broader human involvement in decisions about how, when, where, and why the weapon will be employed" (CRS, 2020, p. 2). This stipulation also requires the human-AI interface be readily understandable to trained operators and that adequate training be provided. In the committee's opinion, because the employment of force may follow from a wide variety of AI actions and recommendations in the multi-domain operations (MDO) context, this places considerable focus on the need for effective human understanding of and control over AI systems.

A recent review of AI in military systems found that "failure to advance reliable, trustworthy, and resilient AI systems could adversely affect deterrence, military effectiveness, and interoperability" (Konaev et al., 2020, p. 6). In addition, the National Security Commission on Artificial Intelligence recently stated:

> to establish justified confidence, the government should focus on ensuring that its AI systems are robust and reliable, including through research and development (R&D) investments in AI security and *advancing human-AI teaming through a sustained initiative led by the national research labs*. It should also enhance DOD's testing and evaluation capabilities as AI-enabled systems grow in number, scope, and complexity. Senior-level responsible AI leads should be appointed across the government to improve executive leadership and policy oversight (Schmidt et al., 2021, p. 11).

These reviews have increased the focus on the importance of human-AI teaming for military operations. A human-AI team is defined as "one or more people and one or more AI systems requiring collaboration and coordination to achieve successful task completion" (Cuevas et al., 2007, p. 64). Similarly, McNeese et al. (2018) define a human-autonomy team as a team in which humans and autonomous agents function as coordinated units;

this is also applicable to human-AI teams. The consideration of AI as a teammate to human operators goes back several decades (Taylor and Reising, 1995). Recent work by the National Aeronautics and Space Administration posits three major tenets for human-autonomy teams: (1) bi-directional communication about mission goals and rationale; (2) transparency regarding what the automation is doing and why; and (3) operator-directed interfaces for dynamic function allocation (Brandt et al., 2017; Shively et al., 2017). In Forbus's (2016) discussion of the need for AI to develop as a social organism to work effectively with humans, he states that AI must (1) have autonomy, including needs and drives to improve, and have good relationships with humans; (2) be capable of having a "shared focus" with humans; (3) be capable of natural language understanding to build shared situation awareness and formulate joint plans with humans; (4) learn to build models of the intentions of others; and (5) interact with others, including by helping and teaching. Other researchers stress the importance of both team cognition and collective intelligence for human teaming with autonomous systems (Canonico, Flathmann, and McNeese, 2019). Johnson and Vera (2019) also highlight the importance of team intelligence, which they define as "knowledge, skills, and strategies with respect to managing interdependence" in teams (p. 18). (See O'Neill et al., 2020 for a literature review on human-autonomy teaming.)

A North Atlantic Treaty Organization (NATO) working group focused on the importance of meaningful control over AI systems. "Meaningful human control can be described as the ability to make timely, informed choices to influence AI-based systems that enable the best possible operational outcomes" (Boardman and Butcher, 2019, p. 7-1). Meaningful human control includes both freedom of choice for the human and sufficient human understanding of the situation and system. Boardman and Butcher (2019) concluded that, to have meaningful control, the human must have (1) freedom of choice; (2) the ability to impact the behavior of the system; (3) time to engage with the system and alter its behavior; (4) sufficient situation understanding; and (5) the ability to predict the behavior of the system and the effects of the environment.

Wynne and Lyons (2018) noted the importance of understanding how humans perceive autonomous partners. They employ the term "autonomous agent teammate-likeness," which they define as "the extent to which a human operator perceives and identifies an autonomous, intelligent agent partner as a highly altruistic, benevolent, interdependent, emotive, communicative and synchronized agentic teammate, rather than simply an instrumental tool" (p. 355). Factors such as perceived agency, the ability to communicate, the presence of shared mental models to direct information sharing, and shared intent contribute to the willingness of humans to consider an AI system as a teammate (Lyons et al., 2021). "Effective team processes can: (1) signal shared intent toward collective goals, (2) promote team cognition in support of the development and maintenance of shared mental models, and (3) promote aiding and performance monitoring via communication" (Lyons et al., 2021, p. 5). Lyons et al. (2021) conclude that "the challenges of human-autonomy teaming rest in developing (1) team-based affordances for fostering shared awareness and collective motivation, (2) an understanding of the types of tasks and interactions that stand to benefit from social cueing, and (3) developing techniques for using these cues to enhance [human-autonomy team] performance" (p. 5).

There are multiple ways of combining humans and AI into teams, including humans supervising an AI system that is serving as an aide or helper, humans collaborating with an AI system as equal teammates, and an AI system acting as a limiter of human performance (Endsley, 2017). It should also be recognized that AI systems may play a variety of roles, ranging from decision-support tool to assistant, collaborator, coach, trainer, or mediator. Within the human-AI teaming literature, it is generally accepted that the human should be in charge of the team, for reasons that are both ethical and practical (Boardman and Butcher, 2019; Bryson and Theodorou, 2019; Shneiderman, 2020; Taylor and Reising, 1995). Not only are humans legally and morally responsible and accountable for their actions, they also function more effectively when their level of engagement is high (Endsley and Jones, 2012). While it is assumed that human-AI teams will be more effective than either humans or AI systems operating alone, in the committee's judgment this will not be the case unless humans can (1) understand and predict the behaviors of the AI system (see Chapters 4 and 5); (2) develop appropriate trust relationships with the AI system (see Chapter 7); (3) make accurate decisions based on input from the AI system (see Chapter 8); and (4) exert control over the AI system in a timely and appropriate manner (see Chapter 6).

SHOULD HUMANS TEAM WITH AI?

As an alternative perspective, Shneiderman (2021) argues against using the "teaming" metaphor in the design of AI systems, stating, "A perfect teammate, buddy, assistant, or sidekick sounds appealing, but can designers deliver on this image or will users be misled, deceived, and disappointed?". He argues that alternative metaphors, such as supertools, tele-bots, or active appliances, are preferable because they more effectively communicate that the AI system is in the service of the human(s)' goals, with the human(s) remaining in control. By leveraging such alternative metaphors, it is possible to convey the benefits of the teaming metaphor, such as helpfulness, while broadening the options for how that help could be provided and avoiding unrealistic expectations that may arise when an AI agent is referred to as a teammate. Similar points have been made by others (Groom and Nass, 2007; Klein, Feltovich, and Woods, 2005).

While these arguments have merit, this committee strongly feels that there are important benefits to adopting the teaming metaphor for research and design, especially as AI systems grow in capability and autonomy. While current AI systems fall substantially short of the criteria for an effective teammate, there is value in highlighting what those criteria are and striving to build AI systems that can meet them. While Shneiderman (2021) argues against classifying a non-human as a teammate, the military already has a long history of humans working with birds and non-human mammals; thus, the committee rejects the notion that all members of a military team must be human. Instead, we focus on functional considerations of what individual actors (regardless of type) must *do, need to know,* and *contribute* to be considered effective team members. McGrath describes teams as co-acting agents with a shared mission and task-oriented goals, and distinguishes various typologies of teams, ranging from naturally occurring, long-duration standing crews to dynamic, problem-solving teams purposefully created for mission-specific functions (McGrath, 1984, 1990). To adapt to changing environmental and task conditions, teams, according to McGrath's definition, require the effective (and effectively integrated) performance of each team member. Thus, the use of the teaming metaphor is based on the coordination and interdependence that needs to occur in a dynamic setting.

Landmark studies of military tactical teams during training provide a fundamental assessment of the behavior and performance attributes of successfully performing teams (Oser et al., 1989; Salas, Bowers, and Cannon-Bowers, 1995). The most successful teams demonstrated clear, effective, and assistance-based communications, as well as the ability to identify and begin additional tasks when needed. Team performance, then, represents not only interdependent performance, but also temporal and functional performance alignment and communication to support that alignment.

Further, AI is essentially different from other forms of technology with which humans interact. In multiple task settings, humans can develop synergistic interactions with tools that enhance their own task performance, but these interactions do not constitute a team. Salas et al. (1992) explicitly define a team as a group whose members are inherently interdependent in carrying out a common goal. Although an infantry soldier may rely heavily on a gun, helmet, or map for improved performance, these tools do not represent team members with interdependent capabilities or shared understandings. Likewise, an assemblage of humans, individually and independently providing information to a superior officer and receiving individual orders for next actions, also would not be characterized as a team. These types of exclusions imply some important considerations for future studies of human-AI team dynamics. For an AI system to be a part of a team, it must be capable of interdependence in its operations, as well as a degree of autonomy in its execution (Reyes, Dinh, and Salas, 2019).

For this reason, the committee feels that there is considerable value in the team metaphor. First, it is possible for a human-AI unit to meet the definition of a team, with interdependent capabilities, contributions, and roles in the performance of a complex task beyond the capacity of a single agent. Second, by considering humans and AI as teammates, the value of team interactions in producing performance superior to that of independent individuals can be brought to bear, including an improved ability to adapt to changing demands and to provide each other with mutual support and back-up. Third, it has been noted that the need for team coordination increases as the capabilities of a technology or agent increase, as is the case with AI systems (Johnson, Vignatti, and Duran, 2020). Finally, the committee rejects the assumption that defining a person and an AI system as a team implies that those agents are equivalent in their agency, functionality, capabilities, responsibilities, or authority. Additional discussion of the processes and capabilities associated with shared mental models is provided in Chapter 3.

Frameworks to describe information and task coordination at higher levels of aggregation, such as Malone's collective intelligence (Malone, 2018; Malone and Crowston, 2001), or Miller's supranational systems level of living systems (Miller and Miller, 1991), further elaborate the need to allocate functions of cognitive processing, information flow, and task coordination beyond the scope or capability of individuals. As an example, the coordinated humanitarian aid and disaster response after the Surfside condominium collapse in Florida in 2021 included the interdependent roles of humans, from military and local law enforcement agencies, with trained search-and-rescue dogs and uninhabited flight vehicles requiring manual post-flight processing (Murphy, 2021). From an operational standpoint, these operations support a metaphor of human-AI teaming as the joint activity of multiple, heterogenous actors with coordination requirements. Murphy's analysis underscores the importance of distinguishing team member *functions* from the *attributes* of specific actors. For example, for a dog or a drone to be seen as an important part of a disaster response team, it should not be assumed that the dog or drone must perform the search function exactly the same way a human would, using the same perceptual cues (Burke et al., 2004; Murphy, 2021). Stipulating that AI teammates must function as though they were equivalently capable humans contradicts extant research on the performance of various types of groups and teams.

Simplifying assumptions about the nature of effective human-human *task* coordination, including studies of military teams, often underestimate the *teamwork* functions necessary for mission-essential competencies and appropriate team performance outcomes (Alliger et al., 2007; Salas, Bowers, and Cannon-Bowers, 1995). Teamwork is defined as an interrelated set of knowledge, skills, and attitudes that enables teams to perform in a coordinated, adaptive manner. Teamwork includes an understanding of roles, responsibilities, interdependencies, interaction patterns, communications, and information flow (Cannon-Bowers, Salas, and Converse, 1993). Teamwork is often contrasted with taskwork, which focuses on the activities, skills, and knowledge associated with performing the tasks required for a job (i.e., operating procedures, capabilities, and limitations of equipment and technology; task procedures, strategies, constraints; relationships between components; and likely contingencies and scenarios) (Cannon-Bowers, Salas, and Converse, 1993). The use of AI capabilities in these contexts extends the work of prior authors, such as Hutchins (1990), who emphasize the growing role of information technologies to support the communication and coordination of distributed expertise and to provide dynamic, current updates of a situation.

Across much of teamwork research, coordination is defined as "managing dependencies between activities" (Malone and Crowston, 2001, p. 10), while the related concept of groupwork highlights not only member characteristics, but also local situations, tasks, and organizational contexts (Olson and Olson, 2001) (see Chapter 3 and Marks, Mathieu, and Zaccaro, 2001 for a discussion of team processes). The process of coordinating between team members involves using distributed expertise and technologies to manage time constraints, resolve uncertainty, and support shared information needs (Cannon-Bowers, Salas, and Converse, 1993; Hutchins, 1990; Malone, 2018). Based on these considerations, in the committee's opinion the dynamic, performance-based contexts, tasks, and timescales of MDO present a major challenge for defining and evaluating effective human-AI teaming configurations.

The terms "human supervisory control" and "levels of automation" (Sheridan, 1988, 1992, 2011; Sheridan and Verplank, 1978), originally used as general descriptions of human-automation interactions, have been inaccurately interpreted to imply a conflict between human and AI control (see Chapter 6). Roethlisberger and Dickson (1934) used the term supervisory control to describe differences in function allocation between human workers in a production team. In supervisory control, the human handles high-level tasks, decides on overall system goals, and monitors the system "to determine whether operations are normal and proceeding as desired, and to diagnose difficulties and intervene in the case of abnormality or undesirable outcomes" (Sheridan and Johannsen, 1976, p. v). Determination of appropriate task functions and evaluations of appropriate performance (both quantity and quality) are traditionally considered to be elements of human supervisory responsibility. Assignments of control and responsibility between humans and automation include determinations of who should be assigned which tasks and where responsibility should lie in cases of performance breakdown. Equal participation or distinct independence of action or decision making by all team members is never assumed.

IMPROVED MODELS FOR HUMAN-AI TEAMS

The use of the term *"model"* here is deliberately ambiguous, as it can relate alternatively to computational descriptions of performance dynamics, theoretical constructs of required components and processes, or best practices demonstrated from operational experience. In the committee's judgment, while there has been some work, particularly using descriptive models, to describe the elements and factors relevant to human-AI teaming, to date none of these efforts has progressed toward computational models or quantifications of the relative importance of team characteristics, processes, or other factors. Further, in the committee's opinion, teaming models need to be informed by an understanding of the real-world demands and needs associated with military command and control operations.

Studies conducted in the New Command and Control Concepts and Capabilities (NATO SAS-050) program examined the evolution from traditional command and control to network-enabled capability paradigms (Stanton, Baber, and Harris, 2008; Walker et al., 2009), reinforcing similar research conducted in the U.S. military context (Bolstad et al., 2002; Burns, Bryant, and Chalmers, 2005; Cooke et al., 2007; Graham et al., 2004; Kott, 2008; Moore et al., 2003; Riley et al., 2006). These studies, while not specifically focused on incorporating AI systems as functional team members, strongly emphasize that information distribution, patterns of interaction, and allocation of decision rights are crucial to coordinating the expertise of team members to achieve effective task execution. The results of these studies and others addressing network-enabled capability and mission-essential competencies in the military environment (Alliger et al., 2007; Bennett et al., 2017), provide important insights and research priorities for the development of human-AI teams, as well as for both human warfighter training and the creation of simulations that could be used in human-AI development and performance testing (McDermott et al., 2018).

As described above, teams exist as, and are trained to function as, integrated systems—not simply as aggregated components (Burke et al., 2004; Salas, Bowers, and Cannon-Bowers, 1995; Tsifetakis and Kontogiannis, 2019). Feedback-based mechanisms that allow team members to monitor and assess task performance, and opportunities to improve skills through ongoing practice, are important mechanisms to improve the performance of human team members (Salas et al., 1992; Sottilare et al., 2017; Swezey and Salas, 1992). Communication and support behaviors between team members represent feedback-based processes for developing shared experience on which mutual trust is based (Cuevas et al., 2007). Human-AI interactions present an opportunity for humans (and AI systems) to develop and calibrate mutual understanding and expectations of how other team members will function, across a range of task scenarios and environmental constraints.

In the committee's opinion, another key challenge lies in the development of AI systems that can function in the challenging real-world complexity of MDO, which may be very different from laboratory scenarios, and the use of metrics to quantify system performance. For example, the explainability and transparency of AI systems performing tasks as a part of human-AI teams is one of the most important AI design challenges (see Chapter 5) and highlights the differences between sandbox-based research and real-world applications (see Chapter 10).

From a computer science perspective, the explainability and transparency of a machine learning (ML) algorithm is often based on its ability to be queried by a computer scientist in a post-hoc examination (Bhatt et al., 2020; Burkart and Huber, 2021). However, many ML-based AI systems are especially brittle in the face of unanticipated data in training sets, or when training sets do not apply to the real-world context of application. More importantly, post-hoc querying by a computer scientist to assess an AI system's team performance is in no way equivalent to real-time understanding by human members of a human-AI team, who may be facing life-and-death decisions and experiencing significant uncertainty and time constraints. Therefore, the committee believes that measures of AI explainability derived in research environments may not generalize well to the levels of explainability necessary in real-world MDO.

Resolution of uncertainty and reduction of entropy are essential intelligence functions associated with any complex, dynamic, evolving task. The nature of these tasks often precludes training under relevant real-world conditions. In the committee's judgment it is therefore highly unlikely that future generations of AI systems will be able to address such unstructured challenges within mission-relevant time constraints. The higher the proposed or expected level of autonomous capability of AI systems, the greater the frustration and distrust of real-world users asked to rely on such systems, regardless of the results of testing in a constrained research context. Thus, the committee emphasizes the importance of computational and functional models of AI systems relevant to real-world challenges of MDO, as opposed to those developed using traditional assessments in research settings.

KEY CHALLENGES AND RESEARCH GAPS

The committee finds four key challenges in the development of effective models and measures for human-AI teams.

- Existing human-AI research is severely limited in terms of the conceptualizations of functions, metrics, and performance-process outcomes associated with dynamically evolving, distributed, and adaptive collaborative tasks. Research programs that focus primarily on the independent performance of AI systems generally fail to consider the functionality that AI must provide within the context of dynamic, adaptive, and collaborative teams. Research should specifically consider the dynamic process factors and timing constraints involved when human-AI team members address uncertainties in task progress or the evolution of performance over work sessions, shifts, task episodes, software updates, and longer time horizons (see Goodwin, Blacksmith, and Coats, 2018).
- Many measures of team performance do not address the real-world performance demands of complex and dynamic MDO tasks, which often have high consequences and low tolerance for either delay or information input classification errors. These challenges are multiplied when researchers do not understand, value, or weight the cost of timely, high-confidence resolution of crucial sources of uncertainty in the entropic fog of war.
- Currently, human-AI team performance evaluation does not adequately address the role of AI systems in providing support and coordination as an effective and trusted teammate. These performance evaluation considerations are needed for model-optimization criteria and/or as skill assessments of AI performance in real-world tasks. One operational example illustrating the trust that is needed in an AI system is whether the system performs as promised, with degradations in trust occurring due to violations of promised functional capabilities (Bhatti et al., 2021; Demir et al., 2021).
- Descriptive models of human-AI team performance need to be extended into computational models that can predict the relative value of teaming compositions, processes, knowledge structures, interface mechanisms, and other characteristics.

RESEARCH NEEDS

The committee recommends addressing four major research objectives to improve human-AI teaming performance.

Research Objective 2-1: Human-AI Team Effectiveness Metrics. Research is needed to define metrics describing how AI systems help to manage dependencies between themselves and other team members performing mutually supportive, dynamic, adaptive, and collaborative tasks, within relevant functions. It is advisable that this research consider the limits of how and when an AI system is fixed, meaning unable to recognize the functional roles required and how its capabilities might support those roles. Further, metrics associated with the flexibility of an AI system to adjust its role and contributions to team needs are needed, similar to those metrics assessed in human-only, network-enabled capability teams (Stanton, Baber, and Harris, 2008; Walker et al., 2009). These metrics would best be considered components and figures of merit in the performance specifications and skill-evaluation scores associated with AI systems, similar to skills assessments for human warfighters. This research should specifically consider the different timing constraints on the team members as well as the evolution of performance over work sessions, shifts, software updates, and longer time horizons.

Research Objective 2-2: AI Uncertainty Resolution. The capability of the AI to resolve temporal and operational uncertainty in situation, role, and plan needs to be quantified. This includes the time to resolve uncertainty (TRU) in situation assessments, in the required AI role in the current network-enabled capability/multi-domain operations configuration, and in the required AI role in updated plans for action. These TRU measures can be integrated with existing network-enabled capability studies of combat estimates or other high-fidelity simulations/synthetic environments (Goodwin, Blacksmith, and Coats, 2018). Even if an AI system has high confidence assessments and good post-hoc explainability, its role in a dynamic human-AI team is extremely limited if the TRU is large, especially compared to the time available for decision making and performance (Caldwell and Wang, 2009). Thus, the committee suggests that modeling emphasize TRU rates and the ratio of TRU to time available as parameters to minimize, in a variety of dynamic contexts with varying situation and information entropy and uncertainty levels.[1]

Research Objective 2-3: AI Over-Promise Rate. The ability of an AI system to appropriately calibrate and execute its expected functions needs to be quantified. The ability of the AI system to deliver as promised contributes to human trust of autonomous systems (Sheridan and Parasuraman, 2005). Trust of others, either human team members or AI systems, is an experiential, asymmetric process based on whether the actor meets/exceeds or falls short of performance demands compared to performance expectations. For example, an analog watch has a limited range of functions and performance capabilities compared to a modern software-enabled smartwatch; however, trust in the analog watch is not based on its performance of complex smartwatch operations, but on its ability to perform its required function of displaying time accurately. Therefore, a relevant performance (and model-optimizing) measure for an AI system might be its over-promise rate (OPR), defined as the number and variety of situations in which its level of automation, expertise, or support performance does not meet expectations, expressed as a fraction of the total number of relevant human-AI task situations in which the AI system is involved. Both a reduction in expectations and an increase in AI capability can reduce an OPR to an ideal minimum, close to zero. This conceptualization of OPR is in opposition to a marketing-based AI approach, in which proposed expectations for system performance are intentionally set high to increase the probability of research funding or product purchase. However, in the proposed area of multi-domain operations, an OPR rate based on well-calibrated expectations is far more likely to engender trust and effective overall human-AI team performance.

Research Objective 2-4: Human-AI Team Models. Predictive models of human-AI performance are needed to provide quantitative predictions of operator performance and interaction in both routine and failure conditions (Kaber, 2018). These models would do well to build on existing modeling approaches to specifically address design decisions for the human-AI interaction (Kaber, 2018; Sebok and Wickens, 2017). Computational models of human-AI team performance need to be developed to quantify expected performance outcomes along relevant metrics, and across relevant team compositions, characteristics, processes, and designs. These models would benefit from a consideration of both normal and unexpected events (outside of AI training sets), as well as issues of situation awareness, trust, and the potential for both human and AI biases.

SUMMARY

Teaming provides significant performance advantages that go beyond the aggregation of individual teammate performances. Given sufficient levels of team intelligence, including the processes, knowledge structures, and behaviors necessary to promote effective teamwork, humans can team with AI systems to achieve these benefits. Methods for promoting effective teaming between humans and AI systems need to be captured in both descriptive and computational models that can quantify the nature of human-AI team performance, its constituent components, and outcome metrics that capture team dynamics, uncertainty resolution, and the ability to meet performance expectations.

---

[1] The ratio parameter should have a maximum acceptable level much less than 1.0.

3

Human-AI Teaming Processes and Effectiveness

WHAT DOES IT MEAN FOR AI TO BE A TEAMMATE?

A team is an interdependent group of members, each with their own roles and responsibilities, that come together to address a particular goal (Salas et al., 1992). An AI system can be a member of a team if it takes on roles and responsibilities and can function interdependently. In the committee's opinion, the word *teammate* does not imply humanness; human-animal pairs make good teams. An AI team member does not necessarily need to replicate actions that humans can already do. AI is a very different sort of intelligence compared to humans, with different strengths and limitations. As discussed in Chapter 2, the human-animal team metaphor may be better suited than that of human-human teaming for this reason (see Forbus, 2016). AI ought to do what AI does best (e.g., high computational speed, expansive memory) or what humans would rather not do (e.g., work that is dull, dirty, and dangerous in the case of embodied AI) (Wojton et al., 2021).

In the committee's judgment, human-AI teaming is a step beyond human-AI interaction. The terms *team* and *teammate* express a system that is expanded from one-human-one-machine (e.g., a human-AI interaction or a human-robot interaction) to a team of more than two heterogeneous entities, each with their own roles and responsibilities (technically two members can form a team, however, the team literature tends to involve teams of three or more). Researchers can look to the human team literature, as well as to the human-animal team literature, to find novel methods to improve human-AI team effectiveness. In general, the teamwork and teammate concepts are useful for extending the science of teamwork into the field of human-centered AI.

In the committee's opinion, considering an AI system to be a teammate does not indicate that the AI system is a human, human-like, or on the same level as humans. Humans tend to anthropomorphize machines of all types (e.g., Roombas, cars, Alexa) and AI is no exception. However, in the committee's judgment, given that AI differs from humans in many ways, it is misleading to encourage anthropomorphism by designing an AI system with human-like features (Salles, Evers, and Farisco, 2020). Additionally, an AI system as a teammate does not imply loss of human control. Control structure is independent of the team concept, and the control that teammates exert over other teammates is dependent on the mission or specific task. Finally, designing an AI system to be an effective teammate does not imply that the AI system is not human-user centered. Designing an AI system to work well as a teammate increases human-centeredness, based on the results of more than three decades of teamwork literature providing extensive guidance for effective teaming (Wojton et al., 2021). Ultimately, an effective human-AI team augments human capabilities and raises performance beyond that of either entity.

In the committee's judgment, AI developers who are unfamiliar with the science of team effectiveness too often presume to know what good human-AI teaming is and what it means for AI to be a good teammate. The committee finds that the science of team effectiveness needs to be better translated to AI development. Also, research is needed on specific mechanisms for human-AI teaming that may or may not be similar to methods of human-human teaming or human-animal teaming. The remainder of this chapter explores the state-of-the-art in the science of team effectiveness, the implications for human-AI teams, and research needed to fill the gaps in effective human-AI teaming.

PROCESSES AND CHARACTERISTICS OF EFFECTIVE HUMAN-AI TEAMS

How can we achieve effective human-AI teaming by drawing on what we know about human teaming and human-animal teaming? Cuevas and colleagues (2007) developed a framework for understanding how the introduction of machine teammates can influence both individual and team cognition, implying that models of effective teaming need to be adapted to reflect the introduction of this new type of teammate.

Within the broader discussion of social units and types of tasks, McGrath (1984) describes eight types of tasks, which could be used to guide the design of appropriate human-AI teams. Task type, however, is not the only important focus of team interactions; aspects of task coordination, information flow, and role support are also vital elements (Riley et al., 2006; Salas, Bowers, and Cannon-Bowers, 1995). These tasks, including planning and creative idea generation, persuasion and conflict negotiation, and competitions and physiological performances, require different types of team structures, functional roles, and allocations of tasks over the duration of team interactions. A team may also exist in consistent form for multiple cycles of performance or may reconstitute itself with different members for each distinct task cycle. Regardless of task performance demands, it can be assumed that interdependent management of activities, goals, knowledge, roles, and task constraints are critical components of team interactions. Beginning in the 1980s, studies of military teams have emphasized team performance outcomes, processes, and effectiveness of training protocols (i.e., methods for improving outcomes and processes) (Salas, Bowers, and Cannon-Bowers, 1995; Sottilare et al., 2017). Less is known from the team literature about the types of long-term, distributed, and agile teams that will be needed to function in military multi-domain operations (MDO).

Team Heterogeneity

In the committee's judgment heterogeneity coupled with the interdependence of teammates is the main feature that distinguishes teams from groups. Teammates each have their own roles and responsibilities, which can be at the taskwork or teamwork level. For instance, one teammate may be responsible for flying the plane and another responsible for navigation; this is taskwork heterogeneity. In addition, the pilot teammate may be in command and responsible for making final decisions (i.e., teamwork heterogeneity). In the committee's opinion, this same heterogeneity is also advantageous in an AI teammate. In a good team design, the AI system will do what AI does best (e.g., tasks that require high computational speed or expansive memory) or what humans do not want to do, and humans will do what humans do best (e.g., key decision making, adaptive planning) (Nadeem, 2021). This differentiation implies that an AI system will not replicate human capabilities and limitations and will also specialize in narrow tasks, like the animal in a human-animal team. Exceptions may exist in rare cases of team training, in which synthetic teammates stand in for human counterparts (Myers et al., 2018) and potentially in social robotics, in which AI performs human care-taking roles (Lee et al., 2017). Centaur teams, in which the human and machine serve as perfect complements of each other, have the potential to operate at levels that exceed the capability of human or machine alone (Case, 2018).

It is important to note that proper team composition goes beyond simple function allocation based on a men-are-better-at/machines-are-better-at approach (Roth et al., 2019). The interdependencies are also of critical importance. Heterogeneity is an element of team *structure*, but interdependencies reflect team *process*. Johnson and colleagues (2014) have developed a method of co-active team design that puts interdependencies at the forefront. Further, responsibilities, such as the control structure of a team, may depend on context. In the committee's judgment, it is also important for long-term, distributed, and adaptive teams to have a degree of overlap in roles and responsibilities, so that teammates can back each other up or take over responsibilities when a teammate is absent. In the committee's judgment, assembling long-term, distributed, agile teams that exhibit function allocation, interdependency management, and sufficient overlap of responsibilities is a challenge and represents a research gap. In addition, because of the increasing complexity of teams, AI may be useful in the role of team assembler (see Chapter 9).

Shared Cognition

The study of internal processes of team members (i.e., mental models) to identify, refine, and improve both team performance and the relevant measures of processes and outcomes is a distinct area of research (Rouse, Cannon-Bowers, and Salas, 1992). Mental models are "mechanisms whereby humans are able to generate descriptions of system purpose and form, explanation of system functioning and observed system states, and predictions of future states" (Rouse and Morris, 1985, p. 7).

One area of team research focuses on whether teammates hold a shared mental model. A shared mental model is a consistent understanding and representation, across teammates, of how systems work (i.e., the degree of agreement of one or more mental models). A shared mental model includes models of the technology and equipment, models of taskwork, models of teamwork, and models of teammates (i.e., teammates' knowledge, skills, attitudes, and preferences) (Cannon-Bowers, Salas, and Converse, 1993). Relatedly, a team mental model is a mental model of one's teammate(s) that provides an understanding of teammates' capabilities, limitations, current goals and needs, and current and future performance (Cannon-Bowers, Salas, and Converse, 1993). The similarity of team mental models and task mental models among team members, as well as their accuracy, directly contributes to effective team processes, which significantly affect overall team performance (DeChurch and Mesmer-Magnus, 2010; Mathieu et al., 2000). Shared mental models within teams also contribute to the development of shared situation awareness (Cooke, Kiekel, and Helm, 2001; Endsley and Jones, 2001; Endsley, 2020b) (see Chapter 4). In addition, it should be noted that knowledge in teams can be emergent, with dynamic experience (Grand et al., 2016).

Thus, on a heterogeneous team, one should expect knowledge diversity (Cooke et al., 2013). Effective teammates need to have goals that are aligned; however, the true meaning of goal alignment is unclear. It is possible, especially in multi-team systems like those found in MDO, that goals are tied to tasks, roles, and responsibilities, and so may also diverge (Zaccaro, Marks, and DeChurch, 2012). Effective teammates understand the team's overarching goal and have individual goals that may be disparate but do not conflict with those of their fellow teammates.

Knowledge specialization is expected within many MDO teams due to high levels of heterogeneity. A teammate's knowledge of the task or team is generally tied to his or her roles and responsibilities. Thus, on a heterogeneous team, one should expect knowledge diversity (Cooke et al., 2013). Knowledge sharing is required when team members each hold unique information that is critical for the task and team (i.e., unique situation awareness requirements) (Endsley and Jones, 2001). Transactive memory systems represent another form of shared cognition (Brandon and Hollingshead, 2004). Transactive memory systems stipulate that knowledge of the task and team is distributed among interdependent team members, which increases the need for coordination and communication. See Chapter 4 for a discussion of team processes, mechanisms, and devices used for information sharing in teams.

Alignment of all types of information, including goals, is a form of coordination (Caldwell, Palmer, and Cuevas, 2008). In complex, long-term, distributed, agile teams, increasing complexity may result in an increased need for dynamic goal alignment, as well as teamwork and taskwork model alignment. MDO teams can be considered complex, long-term distributed teams that must be agile in their deployment and problem-solving abilities. In the committee's opinion, research is needed on mechanisms of goal- and mental-model alignment in human-AI teams, and the potential role of AI in facilitating this alignment. The alignment of goals and mental models is one of many communication and coordination challenges covered in the next section (see Chapter 4).

Communication and Coordination

Communication and coordination are essential for teamwork, given teamwork's interdependent nature. Team cognition can in fact be characterized as communication and coordination processes in addition to knowledge or shared models because team cognition involves more than just knowledge (Cooke et al., 2013). Research on group communication extends back to the 1950s and includes Leavitt's 1951 work describing circle, chain, and other configurations of people communicating with each other in a group. This research not only addresses the flow of task procedures for specific circumstances, but also the stability and robustness of communication patterns in response to changes in situation, resolution of error, and updates in plan (Gorman et al., 2020).

Communication can be verbal or nonverbal and can take place through various modalities, such as voice or text. Much progress has been made toward the creation of AI that understands natural human language; however, natural language processing remains a challenge for human-AI teaming. Moreover, natural language, with all its ambiguities, may not be the language of choice for effective teaming. For instance, humans and animals team effectively by signaling and by observing behavioral cues, without natural language communication. Similarly, in military contexts and aviation, various forms of signaling and brevity code are used (Achille, Gladwell Schulze, and Schimdt-Nielsen, 1995). In addition, it may be important to identify various communication modalities (e.g., visual, auditory, tactile) with the goal of balancing the load on each. Communication also needs to take place implicitly when direct communication is not possible. Research is needed on the language of effective human-AI teams, especially for those that are long term, distributed, and agile.

Communicating in a common language is just one requirement for effective teamwork. Communication also needs to be accurate and directed to the right team member at the right time or, in other words, coordinated. Effective teamwork requires "orchestrating the sequence and timing of interdependent actions" (Marks, Mathieu, and Zaccaro, 2001, p. 363). Recognizing "the right team member" and "the right time" can be subtle and may only be apparent with significant experience (Demir et al., 2018). In a study of three-agent remotely piloted aircraft control, a synthetic teammate succeeded in communicating with its human teammates in restricted natural language, but failed at coordination (Demir, McNeese, and Cooke, 2016; McNeese et al., 2018). Specifically, the synthetic teammate did not anticipate the information needs of human teammates (Entin and Serfaty, 1999), who consequently had to request necessary information, which delayed target processing. Interestingly, the human teammates entrained on the behavior of the synthetic teammate, and coordination ultimately broke down across the team. The level of coordination and teamwork needed for high-performing teams (e.g., players on a basketball team) requires that the AI system has a very deep model of its human teammates, including day-to-day variations in their status. This is likely an optimistic goal (Rasmussen, 1983).

On the other hand, the same study found that a synthetic teammate could model good coordination behavior and subtly coach the team's coordination. This coordination coaching was also effective at improving team process in mock code-blue resuscitation exercises (Hinski, 2017). Imbuing AI with coordination capabilities along with communication capabilities is essential for effective teaming. The need for effective coordination behaviors is even greater in long-term, distributed, agile teams, as Caldwell (2005) found for space-operations teams that had distributed expertise. In the committee's judgment AI could also play a role in coordination coaching—guiding a team's effective coordination.

Social Intelligence

Human teammates can make use of social intelligence for effective teaming. They can understand the beliefs, desires, and intentions of fellow teammates by developing a theory of mind (i.e., by observing their teammates' behaviors and ascribing mental states to them) (Premack and Woodruff, 1978; Rabinowitz et al., 2018; Wimmer and Perner, 1983). Humans can rely on theory of mind to make sense of teammate behavior and to assist with teamwork as needed. Theory of mind is also important in understanding deception. It is less clear how important theory of mind is in effective teaming. Animals are not thought of as having a theory of mind, but rather a theory of behavior (Schünemann et al., 2021). That is, animals understand the behavior of their human partners in context and can draw on this information for understanding human intent. There have been recent efforts directed toward imbuing AI with social intelligence (e.g., Dautenhahn, 2007), such as the Defense Advanced Research Project Agency's ASIST program, for example, though this may resemble a theory of behavior more than a full theory of mind (Sandberg, 2021). Further, there is considerable overlap between theory of mind and team mental models. In the committee's opinion, there is a gap in the knowledge base in terms of understanding the limitations of teaming with AI systems that possesses a theory of behavior and not a theory of mind.

Other Features of Effective Teams

Interpersonal trust and trust in the team as a whole are important in human teams and human-animal teams. Literature pertaining to trust in machine teammates is covered in depth in Chapter 7. In addition, teams do not begin as effective teams the moment they come together; instead, teams need to train together on individual and team skills. The same is true for human-animal teams. This is covered in depth in Chapter 9.

KEY CHALLENGES AND RESEARCH GAPS

The committee finds seven key gaps in the human-AI teamwork research base.

- It is not clear whether the models of human teaming or human-animal teaming, and the methods of making these teams more effective, are appropriate for human-AI teams.
- The teamwork literature has traditionally focused on teams that come together for short durations (i.e., hours, not days or weeks), are most often co-located, and are rigid in their structures. Less is known from the team literature about the types of long-term, distributed, and agile teams that will be needed to function in military MDO.
- Very little is known about how to assemble long-term, distributed, and agile teams in terms of function allocation, management of interdependencies, and assuring sufficient redundancy.
- There is limited knowledge of mechanisms of goal alignment for long-term, distributed, and agile teams with high complexity.
- Little work has been done to develop a human-AI language to replace natural language.
- It is not clear how AI can learn to coordinate across complex teams, as this is also a difficulty for human teams.
- There is a need to understand the limitations of teaming with AI systems that possess a theory of behavior and not a theory of mind.

RESEARCH NEEDS

The committee recommends addressing two major research objectives for the development of effective teamwork processes for human-AI teams.

Research Objective 3-1: Human-AI Teamwork Skills in Multi-Domain Operations. Research is needed on improving team effectiveness in long-term, distributed, and agile human-AI teams, in the areas of team assembly, goal alignment, communication, coordination, social intelligence, and a new human-AI language. Note that these areas also pose challenges for all-human teams, especially in complex environments. In human-AI team contexts, the ability of AI systems to exhibit important teamwork skills needs to be addressed, including: (1) providing support, which includes the ability of the AI system to proactively provide relevant, operation-related information, as well as to confirm and improve the confidence in other team members' understandings and task selection; and (2) answering questions within the context of other team members' expertise domains and operational constraints. Assessments of human-AI team performance need to include assessments of AI contributions in the areas of "provide support" and "answer questions," not only in interactions with not only other human team members, but also non-human team members such as dogs, sea mammals, or other AI systems in the same or different modalities (e.g., air, ground, space, water).

Research Objective 3-2: Support for Human-AI Teaming in Multi-Domain Operations. Based on some success in situations in which AI guided coordination of the team, the possibility for AI to serve multi-domain systems by acting as a coordinator, orchestrator, or human resource manager would be useful to explore (Demir et al., 2018; Hinski, 2017). AI may be well-suited to manage human teams or human-AI teams by serving as team assembler, swapping team members in and out as needed. AI may also help to manage goal alignment and alert the team in cases of conflicting goals. AI might also serve as a communication and coordination hub, clarifying miscommunication, prioritizing messages, and connecting team members. Research is needed on this type of managerial role for AI.

SUMMARY

Designing an AI system to work well as a teammate is a means of increasing human-centeredness that draws on more than three decades of teamwork literature that provides extensive guidance on effective teaming. An effective human-AI team ultimately augments human capabilities and raises performance beyond that of the component entities. Another consideration is for AI to be used to aid teaming in multi-domain systems by acting as a coordinator, orchestrator, or human resource manager (Demir et al., 2018).

4

Situation Awareness in Human-AI Teams

Situation awareness (SA) is defined as "the perception of the elements in the environment within a volume of time and space [level 1 SA], the comprehension of their meaning [level 2 SA], and the projection of their status in the near future [level 3 SA]" (Endsley, 1988, p. 97). SA is critical to effective performance. For example, in a recent meta-analysis, Endsley (2021a) found 47 studies in a variety of domains in which SA was shown to be predictive of performance, including military operations (Cummings and Guerlain, 2007; Salmon et al., 2009; Stanners and French, 2005) and military aviation (Endsley, 1990; Sulistyawati, Wickens, and Chui, 2011). It is widely recognized that human SA of AI systems (including current and projected performance, status, and the information known by the system) is critical for effective human interaction with and oversight of AI systems (Boardman and Butcher, 2019; USAF, 2015).

Over the past 30 years, extensive research on human-automation interaction has generated a large database on the importance of the display interface, the automation-interaction paradigm, the mental model, and trust for developing high levels of SA in demanding and dynamic environments (Endsley, 2017). Each of these components will be important for the successful performance of human-AI teams in the future.

SITUATION AWARENESS IN MULTI-DOMAIN OPERATIONS

Based on extensive empirical research on SA, cognitive models of SA have been established (Adams, Tenney, and Pew, 1995; Endsley, 1995a, 1995b, 2015; Wickens, 2008, 2015), and user-centered design principles have improved system design to allow for high levels of SA, including in the design of automation and AI (Amershi et al., 2019; Endsley and Jones, 2012; McDermott et al., 2018). In the committee's opinion, these principles are foundational for the design of effective system interfaces for human operators in multi-domain operations (MDO) and also for human interactions with the automation and AI that could be used in new systems developed for MDO.

In the committee's judgment, MDO poses significant challenges to SA due to the high volumes of information involved and the need to integrate data across multiple stove-piped systems. The high data load affects not only the SA of individuals, but also the formation of accurate SA across the team of human operators, who may come from very different operational backgrounds and specializations and may be performing different operational roles. Team SA is defined as "the degree to which every team member has the SA required for his or her responsibilities" (Endsley, 1995b, p. 39). This means that it is not sufficient for some members of the team to have information if the team member who needs it does not know it. This also means that people involved in MDO will have very different SA needs, in terms of information inputs and the transformations of information necessary to generate the appropriate comprehension and projections required by their roles (Bolstad et al., 2002). Related to team SA, shared SA is "the degree to which team members possess the same SA on shared SA requirements" (Endsley and Jones, 2001, p. 48). Systematic methods for determining the specific SA requirements at each level of SA (perception, comprehension, and projection) for any given operational role have been established and used extensively in many domains, including military aviation (Endsley, 1993) and command and control (Bolstad et al., 2002). Overall team SA has been shown to be predictive of team performance in a number of settings (Cooke, Kiekel, and Helm, 2001; Crozier et al., 2015; Gardner, Kosemund, and Martinez, 2017; Parush, Hazan, and Shtekelmacher, 2017; Prince et al., 2007).

Shared SA has also been shown to predict team performance (Bonney, Davis-Sramek, and Cadotte, 2016; Cooke, Kiekel, and Helm, 2001; Coolen, Draaisma, and Loeffen, 2019; Rosenman et al., 2018). As a key advantage, while it can be quite difficult to objectively measure concepts such as shared mental models, there is a well-developed research base on objective measures of SA that have been applied to assess team and shared SA (Endsley, 2021b). That is, for the subset of information common across shared goals, a consistent picture is required to support effective, coordinated actions.

It is critical that information displays for MDO be tailored to the individual SA requirements of each role, to reduce overload (Bolstad and Endsley, 1999, 2000). In addition, to support team coordination and interaction, the displays need to explicitly support team SA by providing a window into the relevant SA of other team members (Endsley, 2008). For example, displays that allow one MDO position to quickly see not only what another position is looking at, but also how information is translated into specific comprehension and projections for other roles, can be useful. This might include understanding the impact of weather on flight patterns or operational delays for an air operations role, and the impact of weather on troop positions and supply vehicles for an army role. While a given individual may not want to see information relevant to other roles constantly, effective shared displays can be designed to provide the ability to turn filters on and off to show such information. Such displays are very useful for supporting integrated operations in which the performance and actions of one teammate effect those of other interrelated operations across the joint battlespace. System displays that support the rapid transformation of information, in terms of physical vantage points, terminology, and mission perspectives of other team members, are needed (Endsley and Jones, 2012).

In many cases, MDO teams may form rapidly and uniquely, in an ad hoc manner, for short-term tasks and missions. Ad hoc teams create many challenges for SA that can negatively affect team cohesion, trust, and effectiveness. These challenges stem from the fact that team members (1) are often not co-located and are heterogeneous with respect to knowledge bases, terminology, training, and information needs; (2) participate during different shifts and along different timelines, joining and leaving the team at different times, and often have multiple responsibilities, such that they require frequent and efficient updating; (3) may have goals that are not well defined, including unclear hierarchies and lines of communications; (4) may have different security clearances; and (5) frequently have not worked with the team enough to form a good understanding of the capabilities and perspectives of their teammates, and thus lack good team mental models (Strater et al., 2008). In the committee's judgment, these SA challenges necessitate that information displays for MDO explicitly support both individual SA and SA of other team members, so that people can rapidly understand the implications of new information for both their own plans and actions as well as for activities supporting the mission of the entire team. Methods for supporting this goal have been developed and applied to army command and control operations under the Future Combat Systems/Brigade Combat Team program that would apply to MDO (Endsley and Jones, 2012; Endsley et al., 2008).

Another significant challenge in future operations will be the actions of adversaries to attack the information network through cyber attacks or manipulation of information flows. These attacks may be obvious, such as denial of service or shutdown of trusted sensors and assets, or more subtle, such as an attack on the integrity of data flowing into the system (Stein, 1996). Such information attacks can have a significant negative impact on the accuracy of human SA and decision making (Endsley, 2018a; Paul and Matthews, 2016), or could lead to difficult-to-detect AI biases, such as data poisoning.

Key Challenges and Research Gaps

The committee finds three key gaps in the research around SA in MDO.

- Work is needed to establish displays and information systems for managing overload and providing team and shared SA across joint and distributed MDO.
- Methods to support information integration, prioritization, and routing across MDO need to be investigated.
- Methodologies for detecting and overcoming adversarial attacks on SA need to be developed.

Research Needs

The committee recommends addressing two major research objectives to improve SA in multi-domain operations.

Research Objective 4-1: Team Situation Awareness in Multi-Domain Operations. Methodologies for supporting individual and team situation awareness (SA) in command and control operations need to be extended to multi-domain operations (MDO) (Endsley and Jones, 2012). Research is needed to determine effective methods for managing information overload in MDO and for supporting SA across joint operations, to include high levels of situation understanding and projection of current and potential courses of action. Interface designs to support the unique needs of ad hoc teams in MDO are needed. Methods for using AI to support information integration, prioritization, and routing across the joint battle space are needed, as are methods for improving information visualization to support SA. Human-AI teaming methodologies are needed to achieve high levels of SA when operating on-the-loop, allowing effective oversight of AI operations that occur at fast frames or contain high volumes of data that cannot be managed manually. In on-the-loop situations, there is no expectation that people will be able to monitor or intervene in operations prior to automation errors occurring; however, it may be possible to take actions to turn off the automation or change automation behaviors in an outer control loop.

Research Objective 4-2: Resilience of Situation Awareness to Information Attack. Methodologies are needed to improve the ability of humans to detect and deflect adversarial attacks on information integrity, accuracy, and confidence, which can affect the situation awareness of both humans and AI. These methods need to take human decision biases and potential AI biases into account (see Chapter 8).

SHARED SA IN HUMAN-AI TEAMS

With the move toward the expectation that AI will function as a teammate as opposed to simply a tool, a new emphasis on the importance of creating effective team SA and shared SA within the human-AI team arises (Shively et al., 2017; USAF, 2015). As AI becomes more capable as a teammate it will, in many cases, be expected to collaborate actively to support task achievement (including anticipating human needs and providing back-up when needed), ensure goal alignment, and share status on functional assignments and task progress. These expectations create new requirements for the development of shared SA between humans and AI systems (USAF, 2015). Both humans and AI systems will need to develop internal SA of the world, themselves, and others, which will need dynamic updating within the context of more static and general mental models (Figure 4-1).

The situational models required for the development of shared SA between humans and AI systems include the following:

- *Situation*: Just as the humans involved in MDO command and control need high levels of SA to support their decision making, AI will need to form and maintain an accurate situational model of the world for its own decision making (Burdick and Shively, 2000; Endsley, English, and Sundararajan, 1997; Jones et al., 2011; Kokar and Endsley, 2012; SAE International, 2013; Salerno, Hinman, and Boulware, 2005; USAF, 2015; Zacharias et al., 1996).

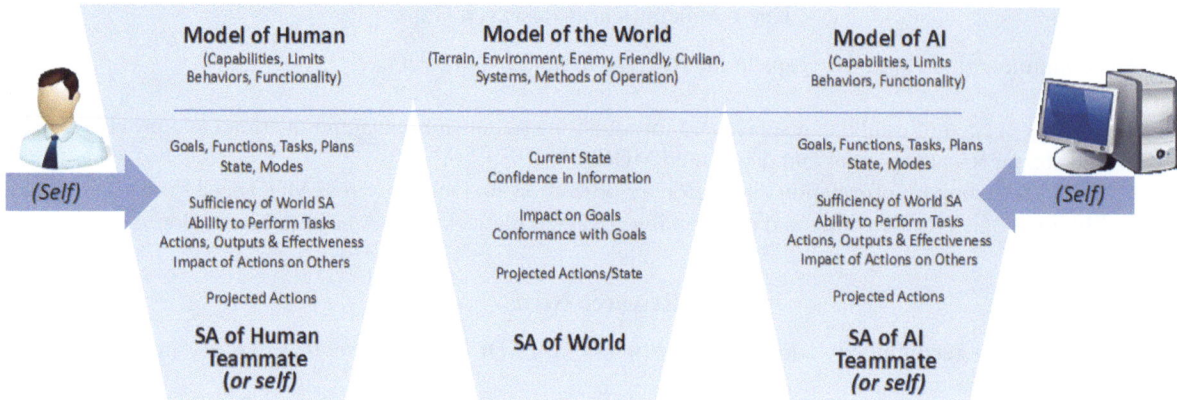

FIGURE 4-1 Mental models and situation models.

- *Task environment*: As future human-AI teaming is envisioned to involve dynamic function allocation, in which responsibility for tasks may shift between human and AI teammates dynamically over time based on current capabilities and needs (see Chapter 6), an up-to-date model of the work to be performed, including current goals, functional assignments, plans, task status, and the states and modes of human and automation involved in the work, is needed (Endsley, 2017; USAF, 2015). Whereas this type of information may have been more static in the past (and therefore part of a relatively stable mental model), systems in which roles and responsibilities may shift dynamically between human and AI teammates necessitate active maintenance of this information as a part of SA.
- *Teammate awareness*: Just as humans need to accurately understand the reliability of AI for a given situation, AI may also need to maintain a model of the state of its human teammates to perform its tasks (Barnes and Van Dyne, 2009; Carroll et al., 2019; Chakraborti et al., 2017a).
- *Self-awareness:* People need to maintain meta-awareness of their own capabilities for performing their assigned tasks. For example, awareness of the effects of fatigue, excessive workload, or insufficient training could trigger team members to shift tasks to optimize team performance (Dierdorff, Fisher, and Rubin, 2019; Dorneich et al., 2017; NRC, 1993). Similarly, AI may need to formulate a model of its own performance and limitations (i.e., AI self-awareness) (Chella et al., 2020; Lewis et al., 2011; Reggia, 2013), to alert humans to step in when needed or to assign accurate confidence levels to its outputs.[1]

In addition to the development of an accurate understanding of the situation, tasks, and teammates by both the humans and the AI system, it is important that these situation models be aligned to facilitate smooth team functioning. That is, to facilitate team performance, teammate dyads need to maintain consistent shared SA on the situational goals and responsibilities that are in common with those of each teammate (Endsley, 1995b), along with maintaining shared SA on the state of the task environment (Endsley and Jones, 2001; USAF, 2015). Similarly, to create effective teamwork, models of self and teammate may need to be aligned. Shared SA has also been referred to as "common ground" (Klein, Feltovich, and Woods, 2005), a term borrowed from verbal discourse literature (Clark and Schaefer, 1989); however, some researchers have found common ground methodologies difficult to apply in practice and lacking in measures (Koschmann and LeBaron, 2003). The shared SA literature contributes well-developed measures and models that can be applied in the context of human-AI teams (Endsley, 2021b).

The committee finds that research to date has developed models of human-human team SA that may be leveraged to understand the factors underlying effective human-AI team SA, which include a focus on (1) team SA requirements, including methodologies for determining both individual and shared SA needs; (2) team devices,

---

[1] AI self-awareness in this sense means only its ability to track its own performance and capabilities and does not imply any form of consciousness.

such as shared displays, shared environments, and communications; (3) team mechanisms, including shared mental models; and (4) team processes (Endsley, 2021b; Endsley and Jones, 2001). Other models have focused on team processes involved in establishing team SA (Gorman, Cooke, and Winner, 2006) (see Chapter 3).

The opportunities for SA mismatches within human-AI teams are significant. People and AI systems have very different sensors and input sources for gathering information and will likely have quite different mental models for interpreting that information. Thus, in the committee's judgment, significant emphasis is needed on the development of effective displays for aligning SA in human-AI teams (see Chapter 5), and on the creation of effective communications and team processes (see Chapter 3). Further, the development of human-AI interaction methods that reduce workload while maintaining engagement is important (see Chapter 6), as well as the creation of training and other processes for building team mental models (see Chapter 9). Establishing appropriate levels of trust within the human-AI team also has a direct effect on how people allocate their attention, and directly affects SA (see Chapter 7).

Key Challenges and Research Gaps

The committee finds five key research gaps that exist for SA in human-AI teams. These gaps exist in

- Methods for improving human SA of AI systems;
- Methods for improving shared SA of relevant information between human and AI teammates, across diverse types of teams, tasks, and timescales;
- The ability of an AI system's awareness of the human teammate to improve coordination and collaboration, and best methods for implementation;
- The effectiveness of an AI system's self-awareness for improving human-AI coordination; and
- The development of AI situation models to support robust decision making and human-AI coordination.

Research Needs

The committee recommends addressing five outstanding research objectives for developing effective SA and shared SA in human-AI teams.

Research Objective 4-3: Human Situation Awareness of AI Systems. Methods for improving human situation awareness of AI systems are needed. This research would be well served to consider AI systems developed for distinct types of applications (e.g., imagery analysis, course-of-action recommendations, etc.), learning-enabled systems versus static AI systems, and operations at various timescales. It would be advantageous for research on situation awareness to include a consideration of AI status, assignments, goals, task status, underlying data validity, effective communication of system confidence levels, ability to perform tasking, and projected actions.

Research Objective 4-4: Shared Situation Awareness in Human-AI Teams. Research to determine the amount of shared situation awareness (SA) needed when working with AI systems needs to consider various aspects of SA (e.g., SA of the environment, broader system and context, teammates' tasks, teammates' performance or state, etc.), and the effects of various types of tasks and concepts of operation on SA needs (e.g., flexible function allocation versus rigid functional assignments). It would also be beneficial for this research to consider the challenges of differing timescales of operation for humans and AI systems that may occur in various settings (e.g., cyber operations or imagery analysis), and the effects of team composition (e.g., multiple humans or multiple AI systems). Methods for improving shared SA between human and AI teammates need to be identified. Furthermore, it would be advantageous to study the evolution of beliefs about how much and what type of SA and shared SA is needed, as these beliefs will govern information-seeking behaviors in operational environments.

Research Objective 4-5: AI Awareness of Human Teammates. Does an AI system's awareness of the state of the human operator improve its performance? What factors of human state, processes, or performance can be leveraged? How can an AI system's awareness of the human teammate be best utilized to improve coordination and collaborative behaviors for a human-AI team? If used, what methods are best for helping the human to understand any changes that occur in AI system performance or actions, and for maintaining two-way communication regarding state assessments? Tradeoffs need to be considered as to whether to support adaptation to the individual, the role, or the notion of any human collaborator, as well as whether to support co-adaptation of human to AI system and vice versa (Gallina, Bellotto, and Di Luca, 2015).

Research Objective 4-6: AI Self-Awareness. Can AI self-awareness be employed to improve human-AI coordination? Can an AI system develop a self-awareness of its own limitations that can be actively employed to improve hand-offs to human teammates in certain environments and tasks? What types of AI self-awareness are needed?

Research Objective 4-7: AI Situation and Task Models. To perform effectively in complex situations, AI systems need to form situation models that account for a variety of contextual information, so that these systems can appropriately understand the current situation and project future situations for decision making. Although current machine learning-based AI generally performs only simple subsets of tasks (e.g., categorization of images or datasets), more complex and capable AI systems will need combined situation models across multiple objects, environmental features, and states to create more robust situation understanding. These approaches to AI will require causal models to support situation projections, and will need to incorporate methods for handling uncertainty, prioritizing information, dealing with missing data, and switching goals dynamically. Further methods are needed to create AI models of the dynamic task environment that can work with humans to align or deconflict goals and to synchronize situation models, decisions, function allocations, task prioritizations, and plans, to achieve appropriate, coordinated actions.

SUMMARY

A considerable amount of research has been conducted on supporting human SA in complex systems, including military operations. This research is directly applicable to MDO, and detailed design guidance on improving SA using automated systems and AI has been established. In addition, models and methods for supporting team and shared SA in human-human teams have been developed, which can be applied to human-AI teams. More research is needed to better understand the role of shared SA in human-AI teams for complex MDO settings, and to develop and validate effective methods for supporting shared SA.

5

AI Transparency and Explainability

The need for AI systems that are sufficiently transparent in their operations to support effective human interaction and oversight is widely recognized (Chen and Barnes, 2015; Endsley, 2017; Shively et al., 2017; USAF, 2015). Considerable attention has been paid to the idea of transparency of AI systems. Meanings associated with the term *transparency* include issues of organizational transparency, process transparency, data transparency, algorithmic (logic) transparency, and decision transparency (Ananny and Crawford, 2016; Felzmann et al., 2020). These issues are relevant to traditional forms of automation and will continue to be important with future AI systems as well. Here, the focus is on the system transparency required by the human charged with overseeing and interacting with an AI system to achieve operational objectives. This transparency is defined as "the understandability and predictability of the system" (Endsley, Bolte, and Jones, 2003, p. 146), including the AI system's "abilities to afford an operator's comprehension about an intelligent agent's intent, performance, future plans, and reasoning process" (Chen et al., 2014a, p. 2). It will be increasingly difficult to train people to maintain accurate mental models of how AI systems work, due to the ability of these systems to learn and change their functioning and capabilities over time (USAF, 2015). Further, since AI systems may be applied in new contexts and situations they were not initially trained for (i.e., concept drift, Widmer and Kubat, 1996), it will be extremely important for AI systems to be transparent. AI system transparency involves two interrelated components (Figure 5-1):

- *Display transparency*: Provides a real-time understanding of the actions of the AI system as a part of situation awareness (SA).
- *Explainability*: Provides information in a backward-looking manner on the logic, process, factors, or reasoning upon which the system's actions or recommendations are based.

In the committee's opinion, in the dynamic, time-constrained situations common to many military and operational environments, explanations will primarily contribute to the development of improved mental models that can improve SA in the future, and decision making will be primarily reliant on real-time display transparency. In other situations that involve sufficient time for reviewing and processing explanations, both display transparency and explainability may be directly impactful on decision making. The reliance of AI systems on machine learning indicates that the ability of humans to maintain an accurate and up-to-date mental model will be considerably strained as the AI system learns and changes in its capabilities and the types of decisions and actions it will execute in any given situation. In addition, training time may be limited. Thus, the committee believes there will be an

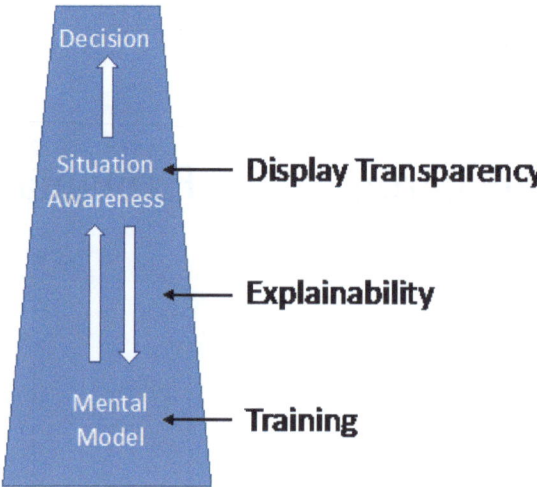

FIGURE 5-1 Effect of AI transparency and explainability on situation awareness and mental models.

increased need for both transparent AI and explainable AI, which make clear the logic or rationale being used as the AI system changes over time, to compensate for inevitable mental model deficiencies.

System functions that are important for system transparency are shown in Table 5-1. This table was generated through a literature review, in which the committee selected the key points from each reference, sorted by level of SA and type of information. Most transparency taxonomies include an understanding of the current state of the system, in terms of what is it doing and its mode (if applicable). Further, in the research, there is general agreement on the need for transparency in an AI system's purpose or goals, plans (if applicable), and its progress or performance in achieving those goals. Endsley (2019, 2020a) and Wickens (Trapsilawati et al., 2017; Wickens

TABLE 5-1 Information Needed for System Transparency

	Chen et al. (2014a, 2018)	Endsley (2017, 2020b)	Lee and See (2004)	Lyons (2013)	Sarter and Woods (1995)	Wickens et al. (2022)	U.S. Air Force (2015)
Level 1 SA System Status	Factors user is taking into account	State of knowledge				Raw data used by automation	
	Current system state	Key system states and mode transitions			Current system state	What automation is doing	Current system state and modes
	Purpose (goals)		Purpose	Goals			
	Intentions		Process	Intentional (purpose and social intent)			
	Plan of action			Tasks			
	Progress			Progress			
	Performance	Performance effectiveness	Performance	Errors			
				Environmental constraints			

TABLE 5-1 Continued

Level 2 SA Understand-ability	Reasoning	Understand-ability of actions (drivers)		Analytical - decision logic	Reasons for current behavior	How automation is doing it	Explanation of reasoning
	Trade-offs						
	Capabilities/ limits	Ability to handle current situations		Capabilities		How automaton might err	
		Confidence in assessments				Degree of uncertainty	Confidence
Level 3 SA Predictability	Planned actions	Predictability of future actions (possible and predicted)			Future behaviors		Projected actions
	Predicted consequences	Ability to handle upcoming situations					
	Predicted outcomes						
	Uncertainty						
Other	History of performance	System reliability	History				
Team and Shared SA	Teammate's roles and responsibilities, goals, projections, and reasoning	Teammate's current goals, priorities, function allocation, plans, and tasks		Team - division of labor			Teammate's current goals, function allocation, plans, and tasks
		Relative capabilities of human and autonomy		Human state - workload, performance, stress			Relative capabilities of human and autonomy
	Contributions to shared tasks	Impact of tasks on others					Impact of tasks on others
		Projected strategies, actions, and plans					Projected strategies, actions, and plans

SOURCE: Committee generated. Data compiled from the sources at the top of each column.

et al., 2022) also highlight the value of conveying the aspects of the situation (i.e., raw data) that the system is including in its assessments, to allow human teammates to better understand system limits or biases. Lyons (2013) further discusses information about environmental constraints that may affect system performance.

In addition to system status information, the behavior and recommendations of the system need to be understandable to the human teammate, to the degree that the system has an impact on human decision making. This understandability generally includes the availability of information about the system's reasons, logic, or factors driving its behavior, as well as an understanding of the system's capabilities and limitations, its ability to handle the current situation, and how it might err. Further, the amount of confidence or uncertainty underlying system assessments is relevant. Confidence in the AI system outputs (or its inverse, uncertainty) is a significant part of SA. Endsley and Jones (2012) provide a model showing that this occurs at several levels relevant to human decision making: (1) level 1 SA—data uncertainty based on the presence of missing data, reliability or credibility of the sensors or sources of data, incongruent or conflicting data, the timeliness of data, and ambiguous or noisy data; (2) level 2 SA—comprehension uncertainty based on system algorithms for integrating and classifying or categorizing the data; (3) level 3 SA—projection uncertainty, which includes projections of future events based on the current situation and models of system dynamics and future likelihoods; and (4) decision uncertainty, which is the likelihood that a selected course of action will result in desired outcomes. The amount of confidence a person has in an AI system's outputs has both direct and independent links to the likelihood of acting on that information (Endsley, 2020b) and is an important SA need that should be supported by system transparency.

The predictability of an AI system is also important for transparency. Predictability includes planned actions or behaviors, predicted outcomes or consequences associated with planned actions, the ability of the system to perform in upcoming situations, and uncertainty associated with future projections. Some research has indicated that knowledge of an AI system's history (Chen et al., 2014a; Lee and See, 2004) or general task reliability (Endsley, 2020b) should also be transparent. Finally, in moving toward consideration of a human-AI team, there will be an increased need for transparency related to team tasks (e.g., current goals, distribution of functions, plans, and the tasks of each teammate or shared tasks, which can change dynamically over time), as well as transparency regarding the relative states of the human and AI system for performing tasks, and the impact of ongoing tasks on the states of other team members (Chen et al., 2018; Lyons, 2013; USAF, 2015).

DISPLAY TRANSPARENCY

The goal of display transparency is "enabling the operator to maintain proper SA of the system in its tasking environment without becoming overloaded" (Mercado et al., 2016, p. 402). Display transparency has been shown to be valuable for:

- Improving oversight of automation and performance (Bagheri and Jamieson, 2004; Bass, Baumgart, and Shepley, 2013; Bean, Rice, and Keller, 2011; Beck, Dzindolet, and Pierce, 2007; Dzindolet et al., 2002; Mercado et al., 2016; Oduor and Wiebe, 2008; Selkowitz, Lakhmani, and Chen, 2017; Seppelt and Lee, 2007; Stowers et al., 2017);
- Improving SA (Boyce et al., 2015; Chen et al., 2014b; Schmitt et al., 2018; Selkowitz, Lakhmani, and Chen, 2017); and
- Improving the calibration of trust (Dadashi, Stedmon, and Pridmore, 2013; Gao and Lee, 2006; Hoff and Bashir, 2015; Lee and See, 2004; Mercado et al., 2016; Panganiban, Matthews, and Long, 2020; Selkowitz, Lakhmani, and Chen, 2017; Seong and Bisantz, 2008; Stowers et al., 2017; Wang, Jamieson, and Hollands, 2009).

In reviewing 15 studies of automation transparency, Wickens et al. (2022) found significant support for the benefits of system transparency for addressing the negative effects of out-of-the-loop performance. Mercado et al. (2016) showed[1] that performance increased along with increasing levels of transparency (i.e., from SA transparency level 1 alone; level 1 and level 2; to all 3 levels), as did subjective levels of trust. Misuse and disuse of automation also decreased at higher levels of transparency. Selkowitz and colleagues (2016, 2017) similarly found improved SA, performance, and trust with the addition of prediction (SA transparency level 3) information. The

---

[1] "The performance data indicated that participants' correct rejection accuracy increased in relation to transparency level, whereas correct Intelligent Agent (IA) usage increased only from Level 1 to Level 1+2. The addition of reasoning information in Level 1+2 increased correct IA use by 11% and correct rejection rate by 12%. The addition of uncertainty information (Level 1+2+3 compared with Level 1+2) improved correct IA use rate by a small amount (2%) and correct rejection rate by 14%" (p. 411).

committee found that the types of information included in various transparency studies vary widely, however, and more knowledge is needed regarding which information is the most valuable to provide in real time. Further, more research may be needed to define additional system display characteristics important for human-AI teaming. For example, Panganiban, Matthews, and Long (2020) showed that displaying autonomous system intent (benevolence) improved trust and team collaboration.

A review of research on trust showed that providing system reliability information helps to calibrate reliance on automation (Schaefer et al., 2016). Stowers et al. (2017), for example, found that adding information on system uncertainty to the other levels of transparency improved performance; Kunze et al. (2019) showed that adding this information improved trust and the performance of human take-over from the system. However, not all research has found a corresponding improvement in trust with the provision of uncertainty information (Chen and Barnes, 2015; Selkowitz, Lakhmani, and Chen, 2017; Stowers et al., 2017). Selcon (1990) showed that, for AI systems presenting the uncertainty or confidence associated with various recommendations, decision time increased when confidence levels were high. Endsley and Kiris (1994) found that decision time was significantly affected by a variety of different methods of conveying AI system confidence levels. Further research is needed on how to best determine and present AI system reliability or confidence information.

Although some research reports an increase in workload associated with increased transparency of uncertainty information (Kunze et al., 2019), other research reports that perceived workload does not increase with increased transparency (Chen et al., 2014a; Mercado et al., 2016; Selkowitz, Lakhmani, and Chen, 2017; Selkowitz et al., 2016; Stowers et al., 2017). Additional research showed that the type of transparency information provided could interact with certain operator personality types to affect the benefit of improved transparency, with too much information sometimes having a negative effect (Chen et al., 2018; Wright et al., 2016).

Key Challenges and Research Gaps

Although the benefits of transparency are apparent, the committee finds that, to discover how to best support transparency for AI systems in multi-domain operations (MDO), more research is needed in the following four areas:

- The value of various types of transparency information across task types, contexts, temporal demands, and user types;
- Best methods for providing system transparency to system operators for different types of transparency information;
- Appropriate times for providing AI system transparency information for different classes of operations and temporal demands; and
- Additional transparency requirements and methodologies for AI systems used in military MDO.

Research Needs

The committee recommends that four major research needs be addressed, to develop the levels of display transparency required for effective human-AI teams.

Research Objective 5-1: Transparency Information Requirements. Further research is needed to determine the value of specific types of transparency information for supporting situation awareness, trust, and performance in the context of human-AI interactions. Current research demonstrates the value of improved system transparency; however, there is significant variability in the types of information considered. It would be helpful for research to focus on determining which aspects of AI knowledge and performance need to be made transparent for various types of tasks and human-AI teaming arrangements. Factors such as situation types, context, temporal demands, and user types would benefit from consideration.

Research Objective 5-2: Transparency Display Methods. Research is needed to determine the best methods for providing system transparency to humans for the types of transparency information identified in Table 5-1, to improve performance, SA, and trust calibration without creating overload. Although integrated, simple, graphical displays are generally recommended, more research is needed to determine how best to present transparency information for AI systems performing realistic military tasks in multi-domain operations. Methods for supporting real-time understandability and predictability of AI systems and effective communication of confidence or uncertainty need particular emphasis. Methods for supporting human understanding of when the AI system is brittle (i.e., at or near the limits of its performance envelope) and unable to perform effectively deserve particular attention, particularly in cases when the AI system does not have sufficient self-awareness to recognize these limits. It would be advantageous to develop design guidelines for supporting transparent interfaces for AI systems.

Research Objective 5-3: Transparency Temporality. Some have argued that the introduction of AI systems that learn will create the need for increased emphasis on real-time display transparency. These arguments postulate that, when these systems are used, it is much more likely for mental models to be outdated or insufficient, and operators will be increasingly unable to accurately understand and project future AI actions and capabilities (Endsley, 2020a; USAF, 2015). Others believe that, in time-constrained and demanding military environments, human attention will be too overloaded to review and evaluate the performance of an AI system, and thus transparency requirements will need to be met either a priori (e.g., during training, planning, pre-mission briefings) or a posteriori (e.g., during debriefing, after-action reviews) (Miller, 2021). The degree to which the presentation of various aspects of AI transparency are best supported in real time, in post-hoc reviews, or in prior planning and practice activities needs to be determined for specific classes of operations and temporal demands. Further, research is needed on whether transparency information of various types would best be provided continuously, sequentially, or on-demand (Sanders et al., 2014; Vered et al., 2020).

Research Objective 5-4: Transparency of Machine Learning-Based AI in Multi-Domain Operations. Given that machine learning-based AI can change its capabilities, logic, and strategies in dynamic and perhaps unpredictable ways, and that learning systems can be opaque both in their reasoning processes and the effect of training inputs, research is needed to determine additional transparency requirements and methodologies for AI systems. The value of the transparency of the human teammate to the AI system for facilitating joint human-AI performance also needs to be determined. In addition, the effect of AI system transparency on trust and performance in distributed military operations, which include the potential for the military hierarchy and changing rules of engagement to effect decision making, needs to be explored. The effects of group dynamics, distributed responsibility, and locus of decision making in the context of human-AI interaction remain largely unexplored and would benefit from further research.

AI EXPLAINABILITY

In keeping with the definitions above, explanations are information about the rationale underlying an explanation-giver's actions or decisions, generally provided after[2] a decision or action is taken and intended to improve the questioner's understanding (or mental model) of the reasoning processes of the explanation-giver.[3] As such, extensive explanations generally cannot be provided or absorbed in moments of high workload characteristic of much human-automation collaboration but must usually be relegated to periods during which more capacity is available (e.g., provided for a recommended course of action, before a decision is to be made) or after the action is taken (e.g., in an after-action review). AI explainability is, then, the ability to provide satisfactory, accurate, and efficient explanations of the results (e.g., recommendations, decisions, and/or actions) of an AI system.

---

[2] An exception occurs when explanations are provided in anticipation of a receiver's questions—that is, when the explanation-giver anticipates the receiver's interest in and lack of understanding of the explanation-giver's rationale. Providing explanations, especially anticipatory explanations, is also a politeness strategy that can be used to signal power differentials, social distance, and imposition (Brown and Levinson, 1987). These explanations are still "after" the making of a decision but may be provided concurrently with, or even before, the presentation of that decision or action.

[3] An exception occurs when explanations are requested to interrogate or check up on reasoning processes of the explanation-giver—as a teacher will do to a student.

Explanations provided by automated systems, while varying widely in style, presentation, content, and context, have been shown to improve trust (Wang, Pynadath, and Hill, 2016), including in emergency situations (Nayyar et al., 2020). The embodiment of the explanation-giver and various social strategies (e.g., promises to repair errors) interact with such explanations to affect the resulting trust (Wang et al., 2018). Explanations perform this trust-related function at the risk of human over-reliance on the automation (Bussone, Stumpf, and O'Sullivan, 2015) even when those explanations do not provide meaningful new information to the receiver (Eiband et al., 2019; Nourani et al., 2019), (see discussion of trust in Chapter 7).

There are multiple mechanisms by which explanations affect trust and SA. Lee and See's (2004) three-tiered model of trust formation and calibration provides a framework for thinking about these mechanisms. In their model, calibration of *affective trust* relies on emotional reaction—in essence, things that make a person feel good, safe, and rewarded will tend to be trusted more. This illustrates the importance of social aspects of explanation: explanations can reinforce or undermine factors including power dynamics, friendship, and perceived confidence and expertise, by providing information about the persona of the explanation-giver and his or her relationship to the receiver. Calibration of *analogic trust* occurs by reference to known patterns of behavior or reasoning—for example, behaving and talking "like a pilot" is a mechanism by which pilot-level trust can be awarded, independently of the content of the explanation itself. An explanation that uses terms, language, formats, and concepts appropriate to the given domain will lend credibility, while unfamiliar (e.g., intensely mathematical) data presentations may decrease analogic trust. Finally, *analytic trust* calibration stems from understanding the underlying reasoning by which the conclusion is derived. Explanations that reveal aspects of this reasoning will improve the receiver's understanding of the explanation-giver and his or her mental model, but such explanations are both time-consuming and may place unrealistic demands on human understanding, especially when the AI system's reasoning is beyond the comprehension of the typical user.

Explanation has been a holy grail for AI systems for almost as long as AI has been a concept. Early AI systems such as MYCIN[4] (Buchanan and Shortliffe, 1984) used the rule structures of expert systems to provide explanations as, essentially, a trace of its chain of reasoning. These rule structures proved helpful at improving both trust and human insight into the system's reasoning, but were unsatisfactory because, as Miller argued (2018), such explanations were based on a comparatively limited and myopic view of what constitutes a good explanation for humans. In the extreme viewpoint, AI explanations have tended toward what Chakraborti and colleagues (2017b) call soliloquies—long disquisitions representing the entire thought process by which the AI system arrived at its conclusions. At best, these explanations provide more information than the human receiver is interested in obtaining and, at worst, they present information based on reasoning models that the human does not understand.

More challenging still, recent improvements in AI systems (particularly those based on deep learning), have largely stemmed from the use of black-box computational techniques (Guidotti et al., 2018), which are inherently difficult for humans to understand and explain, and similarly difficult for machines to inspect and explain—akin to understanding and explaining how to ride a bike (Kuang, 2017). Improvement in AI performance through black-box systems, combined with the increasingly apparent lack of human trust (or ability to successfully intervene) in such systems, has generated attempts to provide interpretability to such learning systems (Carvalho, Pereira, and Cardoso, 2019; Molnar, 2020) and/or to understand the trade-off between black-box and more transparent and understandable white-box approaches, which provide interpretable models that include influencing variables and explanations for predictions (Rudin, 2019).

Key Challenges and Research Gaps

The committee finds five key challenges that remain in the area of explainability in human-AI teams.

- There is a need for multi-factor models to explain dimensions of decisions involving trust and reliance, based on predictions of the trust-related impact of explanations across differing contexts.

---

[4] One of several well-known programs that embodies some intelligence and provides data on the extent to which intelligent behavior can be programmed.

- Effective mechanisms to adapt explanations to receivers' needs, prior knowledge and assumptions, and cognitive and emotional states are needed.
- Human-centered approaches for providing improved explainability of AI systems are needed, including an understanding of the factors influencing human comprehension quality and speed when such systems are used.
- The effects of anthropomorphism and message features of AI explanation on effective, calibrated trust are not well understood.
- The benefits of the human's explanations of his or her goals, intentions, or behaviors for informing and guiding an AI teammate's future behaviors have not yet been established.

Research Needs

In addition to ongoing core improvements in the algorithmic mechanisms required to characterize and present explanatory information about AI reasoning, the committee recommends that five research objectives be addressed to improve AI explainability.

Research Objective 5-5: Explainability and Trust. The offering of an explanation can have significant impacts on trust in the explanation-giver, either positive or negative, via multiple channels, as described above. Yet substantial work remains around the impact of explanations on trust, across multiple contexts. For example, how does explanation interact with the sociocultural forces within an organization to affect trust (e.g., Ho et al., 2017)? When is the offering of an explanation worthwhile in terms of enhanced trust or comprehension versus the time and attention needed to understand the explanation? How does temporality (i.e., when an explanation is offered and how long before, after, or during a decision or action the explanation is offered) contribute to the effect of an explanation on trust? It is apparent from the research cited above that explanations can sometimes affect trust in undesirable ways (e.g., by enhancing trust when it is not deserved or earned), so how can it be ensured that explanations are employed effectively? New research would be useful for the provision of improved, multi-factor models to describe the effects of various dimensions of explanation on trust and reliance decisions.

Research Objective 5-6: Adaptive (and Adaptable) Explainability. Writers from Aristotle (in his *Rhetoric*[5]) to Stephen Toulmin (1958) to Chakraborti (2017b) have pointed out that effective explanations must be adapted to the needs, beliefs, and interests of the receiver. The uses of explanation in the formation of mental models and trust reviewed above suggest some ways that explanations could be adapted. Mechanisms to adapt explanations to receivers' needs, prior knowledge and assumptions, and cognitive and emotional states need to be developed, evaluated, and their implications understood. A core question is whether (or more likely, when) automated, *adaptive* modification of an explanation to a receiver's perceived needs is more effective than user-initiated, *adaptable* modification. Since human-human explanations are frequently interactive—with both parties navigating toward a mutually satisfactory explanation—AI systems likely need to use similar techniques if they are to prove satisfactory and efficient for human receivers. This may require that AI systems maintain a model of the human receiver, in which case efficient techniques for incorporating such a model will need to be refined as well. Concurrently, techniques to allow a receiver to rapidly hone in on the portion of the AI system's reasoning that is most salient or relevant to that receiver need to be developed and validated.

Other ways of adapting the presentation of explanations are also important. Explanation content needs to be adapted to the time and the modalities available for presentation. The interactivity necessary for the adaptive or adaptable explanations described above implies a degree of verbal flexibility in information presentation that will require further advances in natural language use and understanding by AI systems. Some users are known to prefer and/or benefit from either visual or verbal presentation of content (Childers, Houston, and Heckler, 1985). Persuasion effects of various forms of presentation and content are worth considering (e.g., the framing effect described by Tversky and Kahneman (1987), whereby positive presentations of material are more likely to be

---

[5] More information at: http://classics.mit.edu/Aristotle/rhetoric.1.i.html.

accepted than negative ones), though they may raise ethical considerations. Finally, in military applications, the problem of classified information and need-to-know also needs to be considered when adapting explanations. Sometimes, the explanation for a decision may not be fully sharable with the receiver due to the need to obscure aspects of the rationale. The impacts of such necessary information withholding by an AI system on human users are not currently known and would benefit from more research.

Research Objective 5-7: Explainability of Learned Information and Change. Perhaps the biggest comparatively new challenge in explanability for AI systems is prompted by the rise of deep-learning approaches that may operate in ways that are neither amenable to explanation nor readily comprehensible by humans. Explaining the functioning of such systems on a deep, causal level may not be possible. The field of explainable AI (Arrieta et al., 2020) is largely focused on pursuing answers to this question. Even though some progress is being made (particularly, as described by Hohman et al. (2019) in the use of visual analytics to convey the significance of features contributing to a learned decision system), this problem may ultimately be one of determining when the use of deep learning and unexplainable black-box AI is warranted and when it is not, while improving the performance of explainable AI approaches as much as possible (Arrieta et al., 2020; Lipton, 2017; Rudin, 2019). Although work in the field of explainable AI has exploded recently across a number of disciplines, including medicine, financial investment, and the military, much of this work is centered in computer science. Human-centered disciplines such as human factors would do well to provide inputs to such work, including improved visualizations and definitions of the parameters (e.g., training, skillsets, and individual cognitive traits) that limit or influence human comprehension quality and the speed of such systems.

Change awareness is a related topic that pertains to change explanations (Rensink, O'Regan, and Clark, 1997; Smallman and St. John, 2003). Learning systems afford new AI automation with a remarkable flexibility and the ability to change in response to changing environments, performance, and enemy capabilities and behaviors. Even more traditional AI and automation systems can be updated, often remotely, with little notification to the human operator. But this raises the problem of human awareness and ability to predict (and trust) what may well be ever-changing machine behavior. Research would benefit from an exploration of ways to rapidly convey how and when AI behavior and underlying reasoning has changed, perhaps using prior understanding as a benchmark. Techniques for reasoning about model drift may be useful here (Sreedharan, Chakraborti, and Kambhampati, 2021).

Research Objective 5-8: Machine Personae and Explanations. The offering of an explanation, especially by an autonomous and intelligent system, is likely to promote an anthropomorphism response in the receiver (Hayes and Miller, 2010; Moon and Nass, 1996; Wynne and Lyons, 2018), precisely because it accesses human-human social protocols (Brown and Levinson, 1987). This anthropomorphism response can happen regardless of whether it was intended by the designer. Furthermore, the more responsive and reactive an explanation-giver is (particularly if it is embodied in a personified "I", a voice, or a human-like form), the stronger the anthropomorphism response is likely to be. This response can be positive or negative, depending on context, and can impact trust and reliance decisions (Nourani et al., 2019; Wang et al., 2018). It is also likely that an anthropomorphism response can serve to rapidly convey otherwise-difficult concepts, such as expertise, confidence, and aggressiveness, as well as the source and provenance of actions or recommendations—again, regardless of whether these attributions are specifically intended by the designers. Research is needed to establish the magnitude of such effects and to develop methods to either encourage or discourage such anthropomorphism to support effective, calibrated trust.

Research Objective 5-9: Machine Benefits from Human Explanations. An understudied approach that may improve human-AI teaming is the ability for humans to offer explanations of their own goals, intentions, or behaviors to inform and guide an AI teammate's future behaviors. If such explanations could be provided in natural language or a human-AI language (see Chapter 3), they would be comparatively easy and natural for humans to offer, with the acknowledged limitations of human inspectability and willingness to articulate accurate rationales. These explanations could offer another, potentially superior channel for human tasking and interacting with AI teammates[6] and

---

[6]"Slider bar" input channels for adjusting AI algorithmic weights are currently fairly ubiquitous.

would augment and complete the interaction cycle begun in Research Objective 5-6. Such an approach has roots in programming by example (e.g., Lieberman, 2001) but could allow more interactive, language-centered declarations of intent. The theoretical functions of a teammate imply that these approaches will be useful in at least some circumstances, but whether such approaches are feasible or widely useful still remains to be determined.

SUMMARY

System transparency and explainability are key mechanisms for improving SA, trust, and performance in human-AI teams. Methods for supporting transparency and explainability in future human-AI teams need to consider the appropriate types of information, methods for displaying that information, and timeliness of information presentation, particularly as these factors relate to dynamically changing AI systems. Methods for tailoring and adapting transparency and explainability information would benefit from further exploration, as would the advantages of bi-directional explanation in human-AI teams.

6

Human-AI Team Interaction

The interaction paradigms used to combine the human and AI system can have a significant effect on the joint performance of the team. These paradigms include level of automation (LOA) (i.e., the amount of control or authority granted to the AI system for a given task or function), when that control is given, the granularity of control needed, and how authority is distributed between the human and AI system (see Chapter 2). These interaction characteristics of the human-AI team are dynamic—the level of automation of the AI system can, in principle, change over time for any function of the system (Figure 6-1).

LEVEL OF AUTOMATION

The LOA, also called the degree of automation, is defined in terms of the ways portions of any given task can be allocated between the human and the automation or AI system (Endsley and Kaber, 1999; Kaber, 2018; Parasuraman, Sheridan, and Wickens, 2000; Sheridan and Verplank, 1978). Research on LOAs has primarily focused on reducing the risks associated with out-of-the-loop (OOTL) performance problems brought on by low situation awareness (SA) of the humans who monitor automation (Endsley and Kiris, 1995). OOTL performance problems can occur when humans have low SA while working with automation, due to (1) problems with monitoring, vigilance, and trust; (2) poor information feedback and low transparency of automated systems; and (3) lowered human engagement under higher LOAs (Endsley, 2017; Endsley and Kiris, 1995; Wickens, 2018). In addition, research has focused on understanding the effects of automation decisions on workload (Evans and Fendley, 2017; Harris et al., 1995; Kaber and Endsley, 2004), and understanding LOA effects on complacency and trust (Parasuraman and Manzey, 2010).

Some authors have criticized LOA taxonomies as not scientifically grounded or useful, focused on fixed function allocation, and as treating humans and automation as functionally substitutable (Bradshaw et al., 2013; Defense Science Board, 2012; Dekker and Woods, 2002). These claims are refuted by Kaber (2018) and Endsley (2018b), however, who make the case that LOA taxonomies (1) formalize the meaning of "semi-autonomous," showing the various ways control can be shared across the team for a given function; (2) provide a systematic means of determining the effects of automation on human SA, workload, and performance, linked to cognitive theory; (3) can and do change dynamically over time and are not necessarily fixed or static; and (4) are central to decisions around implementation of automation that must be addressed in system design.

Considerable work has been done describing the effects of LOA on the human workload, SA, and performance of human users, showing that the aspect of task performance being automated can impact human performance.

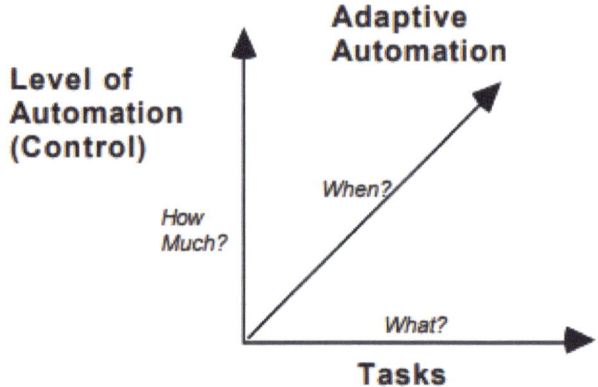

FIGURE 6-1 Automation design considerations.
SOURCE: Endsley, 1996, (p. 6). Reprinted with permission from Taylor and Francis Group, LLC.

In this research, the roles and responsibilities of the automation were varied systematically according to the LOA taxonomy, and the automation performed a variety of simulated tasks in which it was interdependent with the human for achieving overall common goals; thus, this research met the conditions for investigating human-automation team performance. The stages of task performance that were variously assigned as the responsibility of the human or automation included SA, decision making, and action implementation, as detailed in Table 6-1 (Endsley, 2017, 2018b). The results of these studies showed that the effects of automation depend strongly on how it is applied and integrated with human tasks (see Onnasch et al. (2014) and Endsley (2017) for a detailed review of these findings).

Several general findings from this body of work may be relevant to human-AI teaming, including

- *Ironies of automation*: The more advanced the automation, the more crucial the contribution of the human, the less likely the human is to have the manual skills necessary to do the work, and the more likely that workload will be high and advanced cognitive skills will be needed when humans take over task performance (Bainbridge, 1983).
- *Lumberjack effect*: "More automation yields better human-system performance when all is well but induces increased dependence, which may produce more problematic performance when things fail" (Onnasch et al., 2014, p. 477). Although increased levels of automation may improve workload under normal conditions, the tendency for lower SA increases the likelihood of failed manual recovery.
- *Automation conundrum*: "The more automation is added to a system, and the more reliable and robust that automation is, the less likely that human operators overseeing the automation will be aware of critical information and able to take over manual control when needed. More automation refers to automation use for more functions, longer durations, higher levels of automation, and automation that encompasses longer task sequences" (Endsley, 2017, p. 8).
- *Multitasking effect*: As the purpose of automation is often to allow people to perform other tasks, automation both enables and encourages the redirection of human attention, making it more likely that people will be disengaged from oversight over automation or understanding of automation when competing tasks are present (Kaber and Endsley, 2004; Moray and Inagaki, 2000; Parasuraman and Manzey, 2010; Parasuraman, Molloy, and Singh, 1993).

The committee notes that a number of major recommendations have come from this research. AI efforts directed at improving human SA and understanding of events, particularly integrations from large, heterogeneous datasets, will be most useful and least likely to suffer from negative OOTL effects. AI efforts for improving decision making may be useful if combined with information presentations that allow people to easily understand the basis

TABLE 6-1 Summary of Research on Effects of LOA on Human SA, Workload, and Performance

Taxonomy	Effect of Autonomy Applied to Stage of Task Performance				
	Situation Awareness		**Decision**		**Action**
Kaber and Endsley (1997)	Monitoring Information		Option Generation	Action Selection	Implementation
Parasuraman, Sheridan, and Wickens (2000)	Information Filtering	Information Integration	Action Selection		Action Implementation
General Findings	Significant benefit to SA, workload, and performance from systems that present needed information (Level 1 SA) Significant benefit to SA, workload, and performance from systems that integrate information needed for comprehension (Level 2 SA) and projection (Level 3 SA) Better SA and little OOTL problem compared to decision automation		Significant benefits when system is correct Decreases performance when system is incorrect due to decision biasing Slower performance due to need to compare recommendations to system information and to other options Lowers SA and increases OOTL performance problems		Significant benefits to performance for routine, repetitive manual labor if reliable Manual workload may be lower overall Increases in cognitive workload at peak times Increases in workload for systems with high false alarm rates and low reliability
Task-specific Findings	Information cueing systems create good performance when correct but poor performance when incorrect, similar to decision-biasing effects. Information filtering systems can limit Level 3 SA (projection), negatively impacting performance		Automation of selection between alternatives less of a problem for performance than automation that generates options that affect engagement Decision support based on critiquing systems or what-if reasoning and contingency planning do not create decision biasing problem due to higher engagement		Lower SA and significant OOTL problems for automation that employs advanced queuing of tasks Lower SA and significant OOTL problems for automation of continuous-control tasks

NOTE: SA – situation awareness; OOTL – out of the loop.
SOURCE: Endsley, 2017, (p. 13). Reprinted with permission from Sage Publications.

for those recommendations, although this may be subject to the challenges of decision biasing (see Chapter 8). AI efforts that focus on completing an entire function, from data gathering and integration to conducting actions, will put people the most OOTL and make them the most likely to suffer from the consequences of being wrong (i.e., the lumberjack effect). AI that executes tasks to human specifications will reduce some human workload but may either demand additional monitoring to ensure reliable performance or may produce OOTL effects when not performing reliably. Although intermediate LOAs were shown to provide improved SA compared to fully automated systems, this effect is generally insufficient for overcoming OOTL deficiencies.

AI that takes over all aspects of a function for any length of time (high LOAs) significantly increases the likelihood of low SA for the human, and new methods for rapidly regaining SA in the face of AI deficiencies are needed. This is particularly the case for unexpected or "black swan" events (Wickens, 2009). In some cases, it may be necessary for an AI system to take over action execution due to time limitations (e.g., cybersecurity). In these situations, it will be particularly important to focus on improving the transparency of the AI system for humans involved in on-the-loop operations.

Key Challenges and Research Gaps

Although the effects of LOA on human workload, SA, and performance have been addressed by existing research (Endsley, 2018b), the committee finds three primary research gaps in the following areas:

- Methods for supporting collaboration between humans and AI on shared functions;
- Methods for maintaining or regaining SA during on-the-loop operations when working with AI at high LOAs; and
- Methods for managing multiple AI systems, each of which may be operating at a different LOA.

Research Needs

The committee recommends addressing three major research objectives for improving human-AI interaction across LOAs.

Research Objective 6-1: Human-AI Team Task Sharing. Research is needed to determine improved methods for supporting collaboration between humans and AI systems in shared functions, at intermediate levels of automation. It would be beneficial for this research to focus on a more detailed understanding of the ways that people and AI systems can share tasks (Miller, 2018), and to explore various methods for combining humans and AI systems, to improve cognitive performance and resilience to errors and unforeseen conditions (Cummings et al., 2011; Smith, 2017, 2018).

Research Objective 6-2: On-the-Loop Control. Methods are needed for maintaining or regaining situation awareness when working with AI systems at high levels of automation. It is expected that human situation awareness will be low and attention will be directed elsewhere during normal operations, but high situation awareness and attention will be needed to deal with off-nominal and unusual events. People are most likely to miss events that are rare, unexpected, not salient, and outside of foveal vision (Wickens, 2009). Although improved automation transparency has been called for (Endsley, 2017; Wickens, 2018), greater transparency will only help once human attention is directed to the AI system. Given that human monitoring of AI systems will be poor and attention to competing tasks likely, methods are needed for supporting the detection of unusual events and situations the AI system is not trained to handle, and for rapidly building human understanding of the situation and the actions of the AI system (Endsley, 2017).

Research Objective 6-3: Multiple-Level-of-Automation Systems. Given that future multi-domain operations may involve multiple AI systems potentially operating at different levels of automation, research is needed to determine the effects of multiple systems on operator performance, to develop effective methods for managing multiple AI systems (Lee, 2018). It would be advantageous for this research to consider the potential for interdependencies among multiple AI systems and the resulting emergent behaviors, as well as to consider the cognitive overhead needed for tracking and managing multiple AI systems.

AI DYNAMICS AND TEMPORALITY

Another body of research has examined the impact of interjecting periods of manual performance into automated tasks, to improve human engagement and retain skills through adaptive automation (AA) (Rouse, 1988). AA can be triggered based on set time periods, the occurrence of critical events, drops in human performance, physiological measures, or human models (Scerbo, 1996). This temporal mixing of human and automated control has been demonstrated to reduce workload (de Visser and Parasuraman, 2011; Hilburn, 2017; Hilburn et al., 1997; Kaber and Endsley, 2004; Kaber and Riley, 1999), improve operator engagement during periods of manual control (Bailey et al., 2003; Prinzel et al., 2003), improve human-system performance (Parasuraman, Molloy, and Singh, 1993; Wilson and Russell, 2007), and improve skill retention (Volz et al., 2016).

As an example, the USAF has implemented AA in fighter aircraft via the Automatic Ground Collision Avoidance System, which takes over flight control when imminent terrain collision is detected. This system has been credited for saving multiple lives, but it may increase the risk of complacency (Lyons et al., 2017).

While much research has focused on the AA paradigm alone, the committee recommends that both AA and LOA be considered in conjunction. Examining the two together, Kaber and Endsley (2004) found that, while LOA primarily affects human SA, the amount of time spent in automated versus manual control primarily affects workload and associated propensity for risk taking. It is important to consider that different LOAs can be in effect at different periods of time, which constitutes a major design decision (Feigh and Pritchett, 2014; Kaber and Endsley, 2004). Most tasks can theoretically be performed manually or at varying LOAs at various times or under different conditions. Whereas decisions about LOAs are often part of system design, the flexible-autonomy approach stipulates that LOAs can shift over time, either at human discretion or based on criteria built into the automation (USAF, 2015). When flexible autonomy is employed, methods for achieving effective transitions between humans and automation are needed.

In the committee's judgment, the ways that automation levels change over time is also in need of further research. Oppermann (1994) and Miller et al. (2005) differentiate between *adaptive* automation, in which the system assigns the automation level, and *adaptable* automation, in which the human operator assigns the automation level. Adaptable automation, which keeps the human in the decision loop in terms of the appropriate LOA, is believed to be advantageous because it allows the human to anticipate and prepare for changes in LOA (van Dongen and van Maanen, 2005). Adaptable automation can avoid some of the pitfalls of AA and can result in higher levels of trust, SA, and user acceptance (Parasuraman and Wickens, 2008). As a downside, in certain circumstances operators may become too busy to make LOA changes themselves (Kaber and Riley, 1999), and adaptable automation can involve a higher manual workload (Kirlik, 1993).

In her review of the adaptable and adaptive approaches to flexible automation, Calhoun (2021) reported that studies comparing these two approaches have generally found that adaptable automation is beneficial in terms of improved workload, task performance, and subjective preference; however, she noted that the research base is limited. Miller et al. (2005) recommend that a mix of both adaptable and adaptive approaches to flexible automation may be warranted, with considerations of workload, competency, and automation predictability serving as critical mediators. In the committee's judgment, more research is needed on the relative costs and benefits of human- versus automation-based changes in LOA over time.

Key Challenges and Research Gaps

The committee finds two main research gaps that exist with respect to flexible automation, in the areas of:

- Best methods for supporting dynamic transitions between LOAs over time to maintain optimal human-AI team performance, with a consideration of both adaptable and adaptive automation approaches; and
- Requirements and methods for supporting SA, collaboration, and other teaming behaviors generated by dynamic functional assignments across the human-AI team.

Research Needs

The committee recommends addressing two major research objectives for improving human-AI teaming using a flexible automation approach.

Research Objective 6-4: Flexible Autonomy Transition Support. Research is needed to determine the best methods for supporting dynamic transitions in levels of automation over time to maintain optimal human-AI team performance, including when such transitions should occur, who should activate them, and how they should occur (USAF, 2015). It would be useful for this research to identify the task factors or contexts important for making temporal transition decisions in multi-domain operations, and mechanisms needed for those transitions. Methods for managing workload spikes and avoiding untimely interruptions need to be addressed (Feigh and Pritchett, 2014).

Research Objective 6-5: Support for Flexible Autonomy. Research is needed to determine the new requirements generated by dynamic functional assignments across the human-AI team, including new situation-awareness needs, collaboration requirements, and other necessary teaming behaviors. Shared situation-awareness needs for supporting temporal shifts in functional assignments across the human-AI team need to be determined, and research on how best to provide the necessary information for making such shifts is also needed.

GRANULARITY OF CONTROL

A third major factor relevant to human-AI interaction is the control granularity, which is the degree of specificity of control input required to interact with the AI system (USAF, 2015). Granularity of control (GOC) can be manual or programmable, with programmable GOC necessitating the programming of task specifications and parameters. GOC can also involve Playbook control, in which operators choose from a "Playbook" of adaptable, preset behaviors (Miller, 2000; Miller and Parasuraman, 2007); or it can involve goal-based control, in which only high-level goals must be provided to the AI system (USAF, 2015).

Programmable control, common for many automation systems, involves significant workload because the human must set up and control the automation under different conditions at various times. Systems with lower GOC, such as Playbook approaches, may reduce the amount of work needed to interact with the AI system.

Plays and Playbook-style delegation architectures have been studied and shown to have promise for military applications (Miller and Parasuraman, 2007). AI will likely operate at much lower levels of granularity, avoiding this problem. Plays, in this tradition, are templates of behavior known to be effective for accomplishing specific goals. Within a play, a method is a kind of task decomposition that is constrained yet offers flexibility, either for the supervisor to further restrict or specify during delegation, or for the subordinate to select during execution. Playbook delegation has been shown to be effective in reducing workload (Fern and Shively, 2009), even in unpredictable (Parasuraman et al., 2005) or non-optimal play environments—those that do not conform to the conditions for which the plays were designed (Miller et al., 2011). Playbooks have been found to be easy for users to understand while allowing for a wide range of autonomous behavior. Recent work has shown that play-based architectures are effective in multiple-actor, multiple-unmanned-aerial-vehicle control (Behymer et al., 2017; Draper et al., 2017). Potential benefits of play-based approaches include a vocabulary that allows shared expectations for human-human or human-automation communication about task performance, and streamlined communication about behaviors and outcomes, through a framework or contract against which performance can be reported and evaluated (Miller, 2014). More advanced AI, particularly based on deep-learning approaches, has not yet been integrated with play-based approaches.

Key Challenges and Research Gaps

The committee finds two major research gaps related to GOC, in the following areas:

- Effects of Playbook control on SA and OOTL; and
- Applicability of Playbook control to new applications relevant to multi-domain operations.

Research Needs

The committee recommends addressing two major research objectives related to the use of GOC as a method for integrating human-AI teams.

Research Objective 6-6: Granularity of Control (GOC) and AI Transparency. Although systems with low GOC, such those using Playbook control or goal-based control, promise to lower workload, the transparency of these systems and their effects on operator situation awareness need to be further researched. Because systems with low GOC involve increased queuing of tasks, situation awareness may decrease and the human may be less likely to detect the need for interventions in non-normal conditions (Endsley, 2017). Methods for improving situation awareness within low-GOC systems are needed.

Research Objective 6-7: Playbook Extensions for Human-AI Teaming. It would be useful for the utility of plays and Playbooks for human-AI teaming to be studied on several novel fronts, including (1) the utility of a play-based framework in communication and mental model formation before and after mission execution activities (e.g., training, debriefing, change awareness); (2) the utility of plays (and hierarchical task frameworks) in organizing, constraining, and framing change awareness of learning results against prior, functional baselines; and (3) the utility of communication based on play (and hierarchical task decomposition) frameworks for intent-centered communications between human and AI team members and how such communications need to be constructed.

OTHER HUMAN-AI TEAM INTERACTION ISSUES

The committee finds that a number of additional human-AI interaction issues remain largely unexplored and need further research. There is a paucity of design and engineering methods to support a fine-grained analysis of the interactions between human and machine agents that are necessary for optimal joint performance (Roth and Pritchett, 2018; Roth et al., 2019; Smith, 2018). Roth and colleagues (2019) argue that methods are needed to support (1) "analyzing operational demands and work requirements" (i.e., context of use); (2) "exploring alternative distribution of work" across human and AI agents; (3) "examining interdependencies" among human and AI agents required for effective "performance under both routine and off-nominal (unexpected) conditions"; and (4) "exploring the trade-space of alternative" human-AI team options (p. 200).

Several promising efforts have begun to address these needs. Matt Johnson and colleagues (Johnson, Bradshaw, and Feltovich, 2017; Johnson, Vignati, and Duran, 2020) have developed detailed representations and modeling techniques for analyzing alternative methods of distributing work across humans and AI systems, and they described the implications of these techniques for detailed human-AI interaction, including a consideration of how different human and machine agents could support each other. Several promising approaches exist. For example, Elix and Naikar (2021) are developing methods to analyze how work can be shared and/or shifted fluidly between agents, and IJtsma et al. (2019) are developing computational methods for "determining the allocation of work and interaction modes for human-robot teams" (p. 221). Calhoun (2021) and Roth and colleagues (Roth et al., 2017, 2018) are developing frameworks to inform detailed human-machine teaming interaction design. McDermott et al. (2017, 2018) have produced human-machine teaming systems engineering guidance to inform military system acquisition.

Key Challenges and Research Gaps

The committee finds three key research gaps in the area of human-AI team interaction, including

- Prediction of emergent behaviors in human-AI team interaction;
- Effects of human-AI team interaction design on skill retention, training requirements, job satisfaction, and resilience; and
- Predictive models of human-AI team performance in both routine and failure conditions.

Research Needs

The committee recommends addressing two research objectives for improving human-AI interaction.

Research Objective 6-8: Human-AI Team Emergent Behaviors. People often change their behaviors in unpredictable ways in response to automation (Woods and Hollnagel, 2006). Research is needed to better predict how human behaviors will change with the introduction of AI systems, and the potential interactions of human behaviors with AI system behavioral changes, as one influences the other. It would be beneficial for this research to explore how various forms of interaction will influence cognitive performance (Smith, 2018).

Research Objective 6-9: Human-AI Team Interaction Design. Research is needed to better understand the effects of interaction design decisions on skill retention, training requirements, job satisfaction, and overall human-AI team resilience (Roth et al., 2019). In addition, methods for managing the inherent tradeoffs in human-AI team design are needed (Hoffman and Woods, 2011; Roth et al., 2019).

SUMMARY

There are a number of factors associated with combining humans and AI systems into teams, and the ways tasks are temporally and functionally distributed between team members, that have a significant effect on the performance of the human-AI team. The LOA and the ways that LOA assignments can change over time present a key design decision for human-AI teams. Research is needed to better support flexible automation, to support low-workload GOC approaches such as Playbook control, and to explore additional features of human-AI interaction in team settings. Models of human-AI interaction need to be developed to predict the outcomes of design decisions in routine and failure conditions, as well as potential emergent behaviors.

7

Trusting AI Teammates

Trust can be defined as "the attitude that an agent will help achieve an individual's goals in a situation characterized by uncertainty and vulnerability" (Lee and See, 2004, p. 2). Trust can mediate the degree to which people rely on each other or on a technology such as AI. Studies of trust in technology (e.g., automation, computers, robots, and AI) have emerged in many work domains, including automotive, retail, healthcare, education, military, and cybersecurity (Chiou and Lee, 2021; Siau and Wang, 2018). Although myriad studies have investigated the antecedents of human trust in technology, such as personality types and characteristics of the technology, many studies concerned with system performance focus on trust defined or operationalized as reliance on or compliance with another agent (Kaplan et al., 2021).

Although this work remains useful, the committee notes two critical issues that impede future progress in understanding the role that trust plays in human-AI teaming. These issues are (1) the lack of research on understanding how organizational and social factors surrounding AI-enabled systems—including how goals are adapted, negotiated, or aligned—inform the *inter*dependent process of trusting; and (2) the strict definition of trust that limits its study to factors affecting reliance or compliance behaviors in the context of risk, rather than as a process that develops across multiple interactions and decision situations and affects broader sociotechnical and societal outcomes, such as cooperation (Coovert, Miller, and Bennett, 2017; Lee and Moray, 1994; Riley, 1994). One of the myriad factors affecting the organizational and social contexts of a team, albeit a novel one, will be the presence of one or more AI team members, and thus, trust in a team will include and be impacted by the perceived and projected decisions, actions, and impacts that the AI team member will have.

TRUST FRAMEWORKS PAST AND PRESENT

An early integration of the trust literature (Lee and See, 2004) showed that trust is one of many factors that affect reliance and compliance behaviors with automation. This framework of trust shows that self-confidence and other attitudes combine with trust to guide intention; and multiple factors, including workload and task demands, combine with intention to guide a person's action. Fishbein and Azjen's (Ajzen and Fishbein, 1980; Fishbein and Ajzen, 1975) theory of reasoned action provides a framework that links belief, attitude, intention, and behavior in a model that has been broadly applied, including to computer system acceptance (Davis, Bagozzi, and Warshaw, 1989). More recent reviews of trust in automation present evidence that, although there are similarities between people's social responses to technology and to other people (Nass and Moon, 2000), trust in technology may differ from trust in other people (Madhavan and Wiegmann, 2007). Others advance a deeper description of trust development, in terms of a framework containing three layers of trust: dispositional, situational, and learned (Hoff and Bashir, 2015). Three categories of factors have been found to influence trust: human, technology, and environmental (Hancock et al., 2011; Kaplan et al., 2021). In the committee's judgment, consistent outcomes of these analyses since 2004 include (1) trust involves analytic and affective processes; (2) trust affects decisions to rely on or comply with technology; and (3) trust is influenced by the qualities of a person, the technology, and the environment.

Another consistent finding from Lee and See (2004) through Kaplan et al. (2021) and the broader trust literature is that trust influences and is influenced by other humans who might use the automation. This idea has led to concepts like distributed dynamic team trust (Huang et al., 2021), which stems from research showing that trust in technology affects both active users and passive users (i.e., people whose interactions may be mediated or interrupted by technology) (Montague, Xu, and Chiou, 2014). Domeyer et al. (2019) reported that trust can reflect differently among incidental or indirect users (i.e., people who are not the direct customers or beneficiaries of that specific technology) when AI is deployed in systems that are more open. In the committee's judgment, trust depends on social interactions such as reputation and the formal or informal communication that contributes to that reputation, such as gossip. The committee believes this social dimension of trust, distinct from the cognitive dimensions of trust, may become more prominent in human-AI teaming situations in which an AI system is capable of more autonomy in specific roles, or when human-AI teams are completing certain tasks or operations (Chiou and Lee, 2021; Sheridan, 2019).

Figure 7-1 provides a model of relational trust that illustrates interactions between two agents. This model does not address distributed trust involving groups of three or more (Huang et al., 2021), or how distrust might spread through reputation within a network of agents (Riegelsberger, Sasse, and McCarthy, 2005). Chiou and Lee (2021) portray in Figure 7-1 that a trusting, highly capable automation depends on social decision situations that are embedded in a goal environment. Trust evolves from repeated interactions between a human agent (A_H) and an automated agent (A_A) and the outcomes of those interactions over time. Fading in this figure depicts future situations. The focus on dyadic exchanges highlights the structural influences of trust through interactions that are

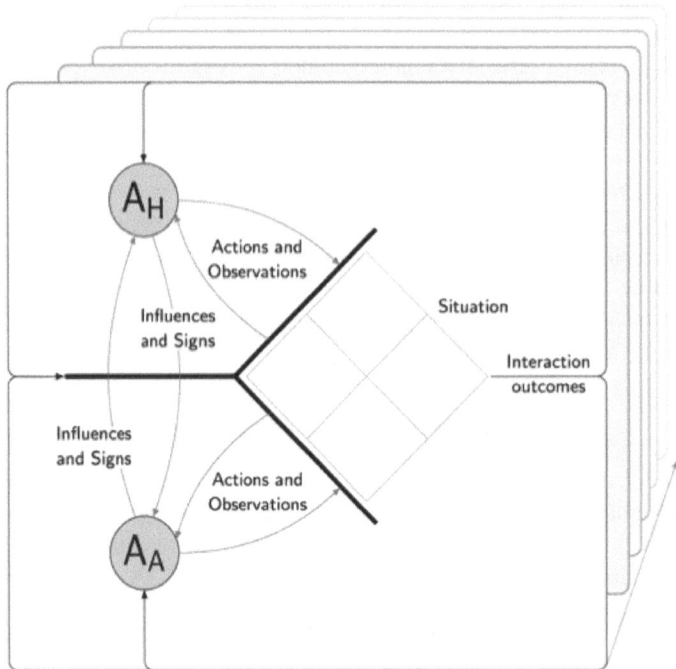

FIGURE 7-1 Goal environment.
SOURCE: Chiou and Lee, 2021, (p. 8). Reprinted with permission from Sage Publications.

not usually explicit in studies on trust between more than two interacting agents. Although this model has limitations, it uses the dyad as a simple unit of analysis to explore the relationships between inter-agent coordination and cooperation (Williams, 2010).

TRUSTING AI IN COMPLEX WORK ENVIRONMENTS

Most team, AI, and automation trust literature assumes a shared goal. In the committee's opinion, goals may become misaligned to various degrees in fast-changing, adversarial environments. Although squadron leaders have some judgment-based decision authority for on-the-ground decisions, for example, broader strategic goals could come into conflict with the goals of other units, as new information emerges. When we consider human-AI teaming in multi-domain operations (MDO) environments, there is an even more pervasive demand for rapid information gathering, processing, filtering, and communicating, to support strategic decision making between agencies in decision contexts that are also rapidly changing. Although organizational process controls may address this— through appropriate, interdependent performance measures that foster cooperation within and across agencies, for example— trust is likely to be central to smoothing these complex interactions. For the success of human-AI teams, the committee believes it is crucial to understand how the organizational and social contexts of those teams affect the evolution of trust at the interactive, front-line level of decision making (e.g., within the context of the conflicting goals of preserving the safety of civilians versus mission accomplishment). This understanding can also partly inform how trust between teams evolves (e.g., the scenario in Gao, Lee, and Zhang, 2006). Trust in other teams is complicated by the need to understand the capacity of the other team's AI system and the influence of that system on the team. Team situations require the integration of an individual with the team's goals, and, in the extreme, being a "team player" may mean a willingness to set aside individual goals and cooperate on shared, team goals.

The committee finds that any assumption of shared goals in teaming merits examination, as exemplified by AI team members such as HAL 9000 in Stanley Kubrick and Arthur C. Clarke's novel and film *2001: A Space Odyssey*, and Murderbot from Martha Well's 2017 novella *All Systems Red*. In military contexts, the dilemma of whether people should be sacrificed to achieve broader strategic goals seems central to trusting AI team members. The challenge emphasized in this report is less about the moral philosophy or ethics behind decisions, and more about how local goals will need to be adapted, negotiated, or aligned to achieve global use of human-AI teams in complex and dynamic task environments. In such environments, AI systems may be distrusted not because they perform poorly, but because they act on a broader information array that conflicts with the narrower information array available to the human, resulting in misaligned goals. In addition, the effects of concept drift, in which current situations are different from the situations the AI has been trained for (Widmer and Kubat, 1996), can negatively affect goal alignment and trust. In teaming, the process of adapting, negotiating, and aligning goals with actions depends on trust. Until recently, guidance on how to specify those increasingly complex contexts has been sparse.

In the committee's judgment, understanding the context in which AI systems will be implemented within MDO, whether in the office, on the ground, in the air, or at sea, is critical to specifying the goal environment. For example, recent work on standardizing evaluation criteria for trusting AI systems (Blasch, Sung, and Nguyen, 2020), focused heavily on criteria that identify the AI system's information credibility. This focus would be less appropriate for evaluating the trustworthiness of AI systems involved in cybersecurity access control, scheduling and logistics, or resource management domains, among many other areas with differing task demands within their respective goal environments. Even in the comparatively restricted realm of plays and Playbooks, agents must be delegated some authority to behave within the constraints of the play if there is to be workload savings for the team (Miller and Parasuraman, 2007) and truly autonomous and independent agents can, presumably, always choose to violate their orders if trust or willingness to sacrifice is lacking.

KEY CHALLENGES AND RESEARCH GAPS

The committee finds two key challenges that need to be addressed for improving the understanding of trust in an AI teammate, particularly in the MDO context.

- Trust research, testing, and evaluation environments need to be reframed. This can be accomplished by specifying the social structure of team decisions in trust research, and by moving toward directable and directive interactions, not just transparent and explainable interactions.
- Trust measures and statistical models need to be reframed. This can be accomplished by moving from technology reliance to team coordination and cooperation, delineating distrust from trust, considering dynamical models of trust evolution, and thinking about trust as a process that emerges from interacting dyads as well as from multi-echelon networked agents.

RESEARCH NEEDS

The committee recommends addressing six major research objectives for improving trust in human-AI teams.

Research Objective 7-1: Effect of Situations and Goals on Trust. To establish baseline models of trust across studies of interacting agents in various operational task contexts, situation structures could be used to study how the goal environment affects trust decisions. Situation structures (different from the task situation defined in Chapter 4) refer to a formalism in social decision making based on interdependence theory (Kelley and Thibaut, 1978) and are commonly represented as a 2 x 2 decision matrix. "[A] situation structure specifies the choices available to each actor in a dyad, the outcomes of their choices, and how those outcomes depend on the choices of the other agent" (Chiou and Lee, 2021, p. 9). Situation structures are useful in determining the relative advantages of trust for cooperation or coordination in an environment. Situation structures can be used as an organizing framework for designing evaluation environments (e.g., testbeds) for trust research in human-AI teaming (Chiou and Lee, 2021). Trust calibration, which is to align

> a person's trust with the automation's capabilities—is often described as a prerequisite for superior human–AI performance (Lee and See, 2004). However, conflicting results show that trust calibration alone is not sufficient for superior performance (McGuirl and Sarter, 2006; Merritt et al., 2015; Zhang et al., 2020). The situation structures show that when the performance profile of the person and the automation are highly correlated, trust calibration does not matter. (Zhang et al., 2020) (Chiou and Lee, 2021, p. 10)

Furthermore, situation structures can be used to show "when it might be appropriate for humans to rely on AI, even when AI performs worse on a task than humans would, "because relying on the automation enables [humans] to shift attention to a more important activity" (Chiou and Lee, 2021, p. 11). Situation structures encourage an analysis that considers reliance on AI in a broader sociotechnical context. Although formally representing situations as decision matrices can be one way for researchers and developers to quickly identify trust-relevant contextual similarities across empirical studies and to evaluate the generalizability of those studies, identifying these common structures can also help explain the variable and seemingly contradictory findings in the trust literature, and can help define the contexts within which we can begin to find consistent results. As such, field studies that leverage mixed methods, including anthropological studies with rich qualitative datasets, are also necessary to help identify the many situations that might exist within a task environment. Other computational approaches (e.g., agent-based modeling and hidden Markov modeling) that capture interaction patterns and investigate outcomes of interactions (Cummings, Li, and Zhu, 2022; Juvina, Lebiere, and Gonzalez, 2015) can also benefit from these formal representations of situations. Beyond identifying the situation structure, identifying strategies for negotiating these situations is a closely related issue. Such strategies could help the AI teammate maintain cooperation in a situation in which competition is likely (Chiou and Lee, 2021).

Research Objective 7-2: Effects of Directability on Trust. Concepts like transparency and explainability would benefit from being accompanied by concepts like directability, to better support dynamic, trusting relationships in complex task environments. Directability is "one's ability to influence the behavior of others and complementarily be influenced by others" (Johnson and Bradshaw, 2021, p. 390). Designing for AI system transparency and explainability remains important for communicating purpose, process, and performance information about an AI teammate (see Chapter 5). Such information, when communicated effectively, can facilitate smoother human-AI team integration by engendering, repairing, and sustaining trusting relationships. However, in the committee's judgment, studies that focus exclusively on how design techniques can improve human or human-AI performance tend to miss the relational aspects of these constructs that are foundational for trust. These relational aspects include the idea that transparency can mean different things to different stakeholders within and between organizations or organizational units (Ananny and Crawford, 2016), and that anthropomorphism can enable a sense of efficacy with and understanding of AI, yet its effects are highly variable and sometimes inappropriate (Epley, Waytz, and Cacioppo, 2007). To be deemed an explanation according to human social interactions, explanations must be presented relative to the explainer's beliefs about the receiver's beliefs (Miller, 2019). Furthermore, transparency and explanations may not always be necessary or possible, depending on the teaming arrangement (e.g., in human-animal teams that do not share mental models or communication modalities).

In the committee's opinion, responsivity may be a more useful concept for teaming with AI. AI responsivity refers to "the degree to which the automation effectively adapts to the person and situation" and "captures the notion that [AI] could affect trust development through its responses to common ground variables" (Chiou and Lee, 2021, p. 6). Common ground, which is a concept related to shared mental models (see Chapter 3) and shared situation awareness (see Chapter 4), refers to "the mutual knowledge, beliefs, and assumptions that support [the type of] interdependent actions" (Klein et al., 2005, p. 146; Chiou and Lee, 2021, p. 6) required in teamwork, not just task work.

Therefore, beyond thinking about transparency and explainability (or related concepts like legibility, observability, and explicability) in a more relational way, AI responsivity requires making information on the purpose, process, and performance of the AI system directable and observable (i.e., transparent). To what extent does sharing transparency information, versus behaving in a transparent manner, affect in-the-moment decisions (Takayama, 2009)? Further, AI responsivity may provide the AI system with the ability to observe and direct its human counterparts (Johnson and Bradshaw, 2021). This means going beyond simply presenting information that "privilege[s] seeing over understanding" (Ananny and Crawford, 2016, p. 8), and advances from the notion that AI reliability *alone* affects trust, if trusting relationships are to be sustained over time and across contexts. In the committee's judgment, this seems critical for the coordination and timing of AI contributions, balancing workload, and sharing tasks according to expertise, as effective teams often do. Perhaps more important is understanding whether the dynamic interaction can help to align goals for cooperation. Team situations require that people align their goals and cooperate. Although this requirement is often assumed during the formation of a team, in complex work environments with fast-paced, changing conditions, goal alignment and cooperation may additionally require setting aside individual goals (or initial goals) to align quickly to the updated goals that are in the best interests of the team. Analyzing the situation structure can identify the degree to which individual goals must be adjusted to align with team goals.

Research Objective 7-3: Cooperation as a Measure of Trust. In teaming structures, behavioral measures of cooperation would be useful to employ, to understand when trust matters beyond reliance and compliance in function allocation structures. Team science literature provides a useful framework for understanding human-AI teaming (i.e., interactions with increasingly capable automation) because teams in general tend be comprised of members with high levels of autonomy, meaning team members do not have complete control over other team members (NRC, 2015). Therefore, an assumption of teaming is that it is not deterministic (i.e., not akin to choreographing a collection of autonomous agents), but that coordination emerges from the team's interactions (Cooke et al., 2013) with trust playing a central role (i.e., in teamwork). In the function allocation approach outlined in early conceptualizations of human-automation systems (Fitts, 1951; Sheridan and Verplank, 1978), which remains prevalent in modern applications of AI with well-defined roles narrowly scoped to a particular task, reliance and compliance may make sense as primary behavioral outcomes of interest when it comes to human trust. However, coordination to achieve a specific goal in laboratory studies of teaming needs to be distinguished from coordination in more complex environments, in the field or in simulated settings, that involve uncertainty and changing goals. These environments often demand a dynamic process of trust that is central to coordination.

Whereas "coordination is about the timing or arrangement of joint decisions" (Chiou and Lee, 2021, p. 10), or dependency management (Malone and Crowston, 1994), cooperation is about negotiating and aligning individual goals when they differ from the joint goal, and it is best identified in team members willing to give up individual benefit to achieve greater benefits for the team. "Negotiating goals to cooperate—by way of trust—has different outcomes compared to coordination. Importantly, situation structures indicate which decisions require negotiation" (Chiou and Lee, 2021, p. 10). Although "trust plays a role in both coordination and cooperation situations, for coordination, the benefits of trust" (Chiou and Lee, 2021, p. 10) tend to be more interpersonal (similar to how perceived collegiality accumulates as social capital to facilitate positive downstream outcomes in a relationship) whereas, in cooperation situations, "trust directly affects the immediate decision outcome" (Chiou and Lee, 2021, p. 10). Strain test situations are one example in which decisions to cooperate can emerge from interactions. If a team member cooperates, or meaningfully helps a teammate in the moment, even though it incurs some cost to the team member (e.g., time, other resources), then that team member is said to have "passed" the strain test, and such actions are known to bolster trust in a relationship (Simpson, 2007). Behavioral outcome measures of trust that do not interfere with work performance and dynamics should be considered.

Research Objective 7-4: Investigations of Distrust. In teaming environments that are highly interactive, more granular measures may be needed to consider distrust separately from trust, rather than as opposing ends of the same linear scale. Studies on highly reliable (but not perfect) automation that fails have shown a resulting bimodal distribution in trust, which is not well explained by individual differences, such as predisposition to trust. Furthermore, there is a theoretical argument (Harrison McKnight and Chervany, 2001), and more recent empirical evidence (Dimoka, 2010; Schroeder, Chiou, and Craig, 2021; Seckler et al., 2015) that distrust is a separate, albeit related, construct from trust, and that there is merit in viewing trust and distrust as separate, simultaneously operating concepts. Yet, many studies that focused on trust in technology do not measure distrust separately from trust, possibly because influential instruments developed to measure trust have suggested that trust and distrust could be treated as part of the same continuum (Jian, Bisantz, and Drury, 2000). One working hypothesis from this committee is that active suspicion of a teammate is a different mode from looking for reasons to trust, and that distrust and trust may be more about switching between modes. For example, a system may be mistrusted due to its performance capabilities or due to a suspicion that it has been hacked. Therefore, as a dynamical system, human-AI teaming may involve not only calibrating trust or developing trust with one another (i.e., seeking out reasons to trust), but may also involve detecting adversarial behavior that leads to distrust.

Research Objective 7-5: Dynamic Models of Trust Evolution. Dynamic models of trust evolution within specified goal environments are needed, which go beyond eliciting and categorizing the factors that could affect trust in an AI teammate. For example, research has shown that trust can be lost after a system failure and may take time to recover, and that automation failures have a greater effect on trust than automation successes (de Visser, Pak, and Shaw, 2018; Lee and Moray, 1992; Lewicki and Brinsfield, 2017; Reichenbach, Onnasch, and Manzey, 2010; Yang, Schemanske, and Searle, 2021). As an analog for team outcomes, Gottman, Swanson, and Swanson (2002) show how marriage outcomes can be described and predicted through dynamical systems analysis and differential equations, an approach that is not about understanding individual differences, spousal traits, or environmental factors, but about the dynamics of partner communication. Such models are needed to understand how trust evolves and affects performance outcomes in various human-AI team contexts. These contexts can be specified through situation structures after identifying and understanding the goal environment of the human-AI team, shown in Figure 7-1, which envelops the task environment.

The citations in the previous paragraph, focused on eliciting and categorizing factors that could possibly affect trust in an AI teammate, may be useful for understanding the state-of-the-art in research (e.g., Kaplan et al., 2021), but may also do little to advance our understanding of trust dynamics, such as how trust evolves in real-world, interactive contexts. Furthermore, factor analyses that rely on a layperson's concept of the word "trust" may dilute, or worse, lead astray from, the rigorous, theoretical concept of trust as something influenced by the purpose, process, and performance information of a partner in work contexts (Lee and See, 2004; Long et al., 2020; McCroskey and Young, 1979). Dynamic models of trust help make better use of the behavioral responses that are associated with trust and that are often the primary outcomes of interest with respect to understanding trust. Such dynamic trust models, and their use of contemporary datasets, can help to capture the granularity of how interactions in one context might influence subsequent interactions in another context.

Research Objective 7-6: Trust Evolution in Multi-Echelon Networks. Trust between multi-echelon networked agents has unique properties that cannot be captured by studying dyadic trust alone. Proposed frameworks of trust in self-organizing, agent-based automation and AI-enabled teammates have raised issues including the concept of trust transitivity among multi-agent teams (Huang et al., 2021; Lee, 2001). Also, a recent meta-analysis identified reputation as an impactful AI-related antecedent of trust (Kaplan et al., 2021). Though studies of dyads remain critical for understanding the dynamics of trust through interactions, effects on critical team concepts like coordination, cooperation, or competition, and human decision making with technology, dyads are limited for understanding the spread of trust in multi-echelon networked agents and the effects of trust on broader outcomes like organizational performance (Moreland, 2010; Williams, 2010). Understanding coalition building across teams and how peripheral stakeholders within the human-AI team's goal environment form various situation structures requires further study involving larger units of analysis, including teams of three to eight, teams of teams, and networks.

SUMMARY

The development of increasingly capable AI-enabled teammates, and the flattening of organizational structures from hierarchies to MDO, mosaic-like structures, suggest that a reframing of trust is needed to advance our understanding, design, and implementation of human-AI teams. Although a good deal of research has focused on promoting human reliance on automation by calibrating trust, this approach does not address the relational aspects of teaming and system-level outcomes, such as cooperation. The proposed research objectives outline a path forward for understanding how organizational and social factors surrounding AI systems inform the interdependent process of trust in teams. These objectives go beyond the pervasive focus on calibrating trust solely for appropriate reliance and compliance.

8

Identification and Mitigation of Bias in Human-AI Teams

HUMAN BIASES

Decision bias, in the current context, is a preference toward certain information or options that is considered to be "irrational." Bias is created through systematic error introduced by selecting or encouraging one outcome or answer over others. In decision sciences, the concept of bias is related to the concept of rationality, the principle of maximization in agreement with subjective expected utility theory (Einhorn and Hogarth, 1981). The value of subjective expected utility theory as a principle of human decision making has been criticized from its inception. Notably, early critique by Simon (1955, 1957) described humans as approximately rational (i.e., boundedly rational) rather than rational. A substantial body of research on human heuristics and biases followed, which has gained significant popularity over the past several decades (Kahneman, Slovic, and Tversky, 1982; Tversky and Kahneman, 1974). This research has resulted in increased understanding of several well-known human decision biases, including anchoring, confirmation bias, framing effects, and availability. Since then, the list of human biases has grown. Most commonly, these biases describe gaps in human decision making compared to rational decisions, rather than explaining how humans actually make decisions (Gonzalez, 2017; Klein, 1993; Lipshitz, 1987). It is often assumed that the introduction of AI will reduce or eliminate human decision bias, however, this has not yet been shown to be the case in complex real-world settings. While there are important evolutionary reasons for many of these human biases, most notably their ability to reduce cognitive load and allow rapid decision making, these same benefits are not necessarily applicable to AI systems that do not suffer from the same significant attention or processing limitations as humans.

AI BIASES

AI also suffers from biases, which occur when a computer algorithm makes prejudiced decisions based on limited training data (West, Whittaker, and Crawford, 2019). AI bias can also result from certain features of the algorithm. The most common form of AI bias results when the data used to train an AI algorithm carries systematic deviations from a norm (e.g., fairness), which can result from inherent frequencies of examples in AI training sets or a lack of representativeness of the data. For example, algorithms that carry flaws based on the data they are trained on can lead to serious discrimination in the selection of job candidates, or in police actions based on race (Daugherty and Wilson, 2018). In the committee's judgment, these biases may often be hidden.

Humans can introduce multiple sources of subjectivity and bias into the design of human-AI teams (Cummings and Li, 2021b), which include (1) bias from inappropriate data curation; (2) bias in the design of one or more algorithms; and (3) bias in the interpretation of the resulting algorithms. Regarding data curation, it is well established that bias can be inadvertently introduced into an AI system due to underlying data sample selection bias (Gianfrancesco et al., 2018; Samimi, Mohammadian, and Kawamura, 2010). However, there is substantially less research on how the actual curation of the dataset affects outcome, and it is still not well understood how problems in data labeling affect algorithm brittleness. For example, inherent subjectivity in emotion labeling can make any resulting models suspect (Cowie et al., 2011).

Errors made in actual data labeling, either by humans or machine-based labeling systems, are even more problematic. One study, looking at 10 commonly used computer vision, natural language, and audio datasets, found a 3.4 percent average error rate across all datasets (Northcutt, Athalye, and Mueller, 2021). Data-labeling errors affect overall classification outcomes and can be pervasive in commercial language models and computer vision systems, which can form elements of systems used by the DOD. Ongoing research seeks to identify and correct bias in machine-learning (ML) datasets (Lee, Resnick, and Barton, 2019), but significantly more work is needed in this area.

In addition to data curation, significant bias can be introduced into an AI system when the designer subjectively selects an AI algorithm and the associated parameters for an application. One recent study illustrated that there were at least 10 significant subjective decisions made by designers of ML algorithms that could impact the overall quality of the algorithms (Cummings and Li, 2021b). The committee finds that there are currently no standards or accepted practices for how such points of bias and subjectivity could or should be evaluated or mitigated.

The third major source of bias is that generating results from ML-based probabilistic models requires interpreting complex statistics, which is a known and well-documented point of weakness, even for experts (Tversky and Kahneman, 1974). Research efforts have recently attempted to make outputs more explainable (Chandler, 2020) or interpretable through sensitivity analyses like counterfactual explanations (Fernández-Loría, Provost, and Han, 2020). However, most of these efforts attempt to explain or improve interpretability for experts and developers of these algorithms, and significantly less effort is aimed at helping users of AI systems to understand the results of such systems (see Chapter 5).

Further, bias may result when the training data is not representative of the situations in which the AI system will be applied. For example, if an AI system is trained on situations found in one environment, it will be biased in its recommendations when applied to a different type of environment. An AI system trained on the military tactics of one adversary would do poorly when directed at a different adversary because it is biased toward its training data. In this sense, bias can be thought of as resulting from over-generalization of an AI system beyond what was represented in its training.

The committee finds that the importance and impact of AI bias cannot be understated, especially for users of time-pressured systems—a hallmark of military systems. Users may be completely unaware that there are potentially flawed assumptions and biases that could call into question the results presented by AI systems, and users also do not typically have a way to understand the practical confidence intervals of AI-based recommendations. This challenge is also noteworthy because it impacts certification efforts. For example, if external system evaluators (non-creators) cannot understand how systems are developing solutions and executing operations or their possible failure modes, those evaluators cannot develop appropriate confidence that the AI systems can meet the specified requirements.

Given the increased use of AI in many societal applications, including policing, legal decision making, social benefits, hiring, and others, the committee finds that the interdependencies between human and AI bias are a major concern. In particular, in multi-domain operations (MDO), the impact of AI biases may be large and significant, given the variety of new and novel situations that may be encountered.

HUMAN-AI TEAM BIAS

Although it is often assumed that humans can oversee an AI system and correct its errors, providing independent checks on the system, this has been shown to be untrue; human decision making can be directly affected by the accuracy of the AI system, creating a human-AI team bias. Kibbe and McDowell (1995) found that when image analysts were provided with recommendations from an automated target recognition system, this rarely resulted in improved performance over either the human or the automated system working alone. Similarly, Metzger and Parasuraman (2005) found that air traffic controllers performed better on their own than with an imperfect conflict-detection system. Further, when AI systems are wrong, their human partners are much more likely (30–60%) to make errors than when they receive no advice from the AI system (Layton, Smith, and McCoy, 1994; Olson and Sarter, 1999; Sarter and Schroeder, 2001). This has also been called concept drift (Widmer and Kubat, 1996). Similarly, when automation is used to cue important information in a visual scene, users are more likely to choose a cued target, even if that target is incorrect, and to miss uncued targets (Yeh and Wickens, 2001; Yeh, Wickens, and Seagull, 1999). Selcon (1990) also showed that, when the confidence levels associated with multiple options considered by an AI system are similar, human decision making is significantly slowed.

This body of research shows that people will often anchor on the recommendation of the AI system, and then gather information to agree or disagree with it. The AI system therefore provides direct input into human decision making, increasing the risk of human error when the system is wrong, akin to confirmation bias. The time taken for the human to make that assessment can, in some cases, be significant. Rather than operating in a parallel fashion with AI systems, as independent decision makers (which would increase system reliability), humans actually operate in a serial manner with AI systems, taking their inputs into account along with data gathered independently, reducing reliability and overall human-AI team performance (Endsley and Jones, 2012).

Further, the impact of AI on human performance can depend on the way an AI system's recommendations are presented. For example, Endsley and Kiris (1994) examined methods of presenting an AI system's confidence in recommendations, including digital percentages, analog bars, rankings, and categories such as high, medium, and low. They found that performance was not significantly improved by AI advice, even for novices, and decision time increased for most methods of presentation. Decision times were slightly faster when categorical presentation was used by the AI system compared to when no information was provided by the system. More recently, Friesen et al. (2021) compared alternative advisory system displays for safe-path planning in a helicopter flight route planning application. They found that, when the advisory system generated a specific flight path, pilots tended to follow it even when there were better trajectories available that would save fuel and time. In contrast, when the advisory system used constraint-based displays showing multiple path options, pilots were more likely to select an optimal route. Framing effects have also been noted (Banbury et al., 1998). While these examples show the importance of system transparency (see Chapter 5), they also demonstrate the subtleties involved in combining human and AI system decision processes. The number of decision options generated, the agent (human or AI) generating the decision options (Endsley and Kaber, 1999), the order of exchange of decisions (human first or AI first) (Layton, Smith, and McCoy, 1994), and the format or framing of decisions have all been found to have a significant effect on decision quality. These effects can be quite insidious, as they may not be apparent to either the decision maker or the system designer.

Thus, human biases present in the selection and development of AI training datasets or in the development of AI algorithms can create AI biases. AI biases can lead to human decision-making biases when the AI system is incorrect or uncertain, and decision-making biases can negatively affect human performance. The committee finds that the interactive effects of bias in the human-AI team may often be subtle, occurring below conscious awareness, but can lead to poor decision outcomes with potential ill effects, such as increased collateral damage, fratricide, or damage from adversarial attacks. Further, human-AI teams may be subject to common team-based biases, such as information pooling or group think, that could negatively affect performance. While it is logical that people need to gather information to check the output of an AI system, the lack of independence of human and AI decision processes means that people may be inadequate at performing this important cross-check function, and it demonstrates the interdependent effects that biases can create.

KEY CHALLENGES AND RESEARCH GAPS

The committee finds five key research gaps that exist with respect to the potential for both human and AI biases that can negatively affect performance. More information is needed in the following areas:

- Improved understanding of the interdependencies between human and AI biases;
- Examination of the potential for adversarial attacks on human and AI biases, and detection and mitigation of these effects;
- Determination of human-AI biases that emerge from AI learning based on small and sparse datasets;
- Development of adaptive and personalized AI models that can predict human biases and respond appropriately; and
- Preventative detection of emergent human and AI biases within the context of online, continuously evolving learning systems.

RESEARCH NEEDS

The committee recommends addressing five related research objectives to reduce bias in human-AI teams.

Research Objective 8-1: Human-AI Partnerships in Continuous-Learning Environments. AI and human biases can feed into each other. This interconnectedness of heterogeneous and autonomous AI systems with humans who continuously learn and adapt their behaviors can generate emergent behaviors that are difficult to predict and may result in catastrophic effects (Ramchurn, Stein, and Jennings, 2021). Research is needed to determine the effects of AI biases on human biases, and of human biases on AI biases, to ensure that human-AI interdependencies are understood and their outcomes ethical, appropriate, and safe. Research is also needed to determine how human-AI interdependencies will evolve with continuous interactions, so that biases can be prevented and situation awareness of teammates' biases can be determined (see Chapter 4). It would be advantageous for research to determine the appropriate regulations of and accountability for these interdependencies in human-AI partnerships.

The interdependence of biases between humans and AI systems needs to be studied in cooperative as well as adversarial settings. Open AI and explanations that help humans identify AI anomalies need to be investigated. Very little work exists to address conflicts within human-AI relationships, in particular in team settings (Lin and Kraus, 2010). For example, how much control should be given to a human to mediate the detection of AI biases when the human can also be biased?

Research Objective 8-2: Adversarial Effects on Human-AI Team Biases. In multi-domain operations, human-AI team biases can develop within adversarial situations. For example, in the context of cybersecurity teams (Buchler et al., 2018), many human biases can be identified (Cranford et al., 2021; Gutzwiller et al., 2018) in which humans have difficulty detecting the intentions of an attacker. Cyber criminals often use human biases to conduct phishing attacks and get credentials to access an organization's systems, for example (Rajivan and Gonzalez, 2018; Singh et al., 2019). Furthermore, cyber criminals may also attack via AI biases. Adversarial machine learning research has identified many weaknesses of AI algorithms that can be easily exploited by an adversary (Harding et al., 2018). New research needs to investigate potential biases in multi-domain operations and the weaknesses these biases represent for defense. Research is greatly needed for cyber defense, to prevent enemies from gaining advantage via human-AI biases, and to determine how defenders can exploit such biases for cyber defense (Gonzalez et al., 2020). Machine-learning and AI-bias research is needed to prevent attacks to AI systems that occur by taking advantage of AI biases. Multi-domain operations research would be well served to adopt an adaptive approach to overcome biases, as in recent advancements of adaptive cyber-defense methods (Gonzalez et al., 2020; Marriott et al., 2021).

Research Objective 8-3: Biases from Small Datasets and Sparse Data. In many human-AI teams, important decision making often resides with the human, while information gathering and analysis is the job of the automation (Blaha et al., 2019; Tambe, 2011; see Gonzalez et al. (2014) for a discussion of decision making in cybersecurity teams). However, automation (specifically AI and machine learning (ML)) and similar data-driven technologies can be significantly affected by the quantity and quality of the data the systems are trained on (Ramchurn, Stein, and Jennings, 2021). Appropriately representative datasets may be limited in many multi-domain operations applications.

Work on adversarial ML demonstrates a major weakness of ML algorithms: they are prone to simple visual perturbations by an adversary (Goodfellow, Shlens, and Szegedy, 2015; Papernot et al., 2016). While ML algorithms are created to shield the human from the overwhelming amount of data he or she would fail to successfully process, humans can easily overcome this security weakness of ML algorithms by visual identification (Harding et al., 2018). This creates an ironic situation in human-AI teams: the AI system that is created to strengthen security may actually weaken it. Because ML relies on data, the performance of ML systems depends on the realism and correctness of data, and how the systems are maintained. In the committee's judgment, much research exists on methods to deal with small datasets and sparse data, but the bias problem emerging from these systems has not been addressed. Research is required to address resultant human-AI biases that emerge from AI learning based on small and sparse datasets.

Research Objective 8-4: Inductive and Emerging Human Biases. A number of consistent deviations from rational behavior have been identified using laboratory experiments with simple prospects described in terms of probabilities and outcomes (Kahneman and Tversky, 1979). However, currently, the large collection of human cognitive biases cannot all be explained by one comprehensive theory and, most importantly, it is unknown how biases develop over time or how they initially emerge (Gonzalez, 2017). As a result, little is known about how to overcome human biases.

Recently, a large amount of work has been dedicated to the development of models and approaches to determine human decisions (Erev et al., 2010; Gonzalez and Dutt, 2011). These models have been extended to involve team and group work (Gonzalez et al., 2015), but it is unclear how these models would generalize to the particularities of human-AI team interdependencies. To effectively capture human-AI biases in multi-domain operations, AI algorithms must be aware of the human's preferences and constraints (Ramchum, Stein, and Jennings, 2021). Furthermore, it would be useful for such models to be able to trace human preferences and biases dynamically and to be able to customize and personalize AI responses according to the predicted levels of biases. Such an adaptive and personalized approach is being investigated in the context of cybersecurity (Cranford et al., 2020; Ferguson-Walter, Fugate, and Wang, 2020; Gonzalez et al., 2020; Gutzwiller et al., 2018). The investigation of adaptive and personalized models that can predict human biases needs to be extended to other aspects of multi-domain operations.

Research Objective 8-5: Preventative Detection and Mitigation of Human-AI Team Biases in Learning Systems. Preventative detection of emergent human and AI biases needs to be studied within the context of continuously evolving learning systems. Identification and detection of AI biases are often difficult before a system is deployed (Slack et al., 2020). Current techniques are limited to explaining biases after they have emerged rather than preventing AI biases from emerging in the first place (Gilpin et al., 2018; Ramchum, Stein, and Jennings, 2021). More research is needed to detect, prevent, and/or mitigate potential AI biases before an AI system is deployed, and research is also needed to test AI systems against attempted adversarial exploitation. Further, methods are needed to discover, measure, and test bias in human-AI teams. It is unknown how human decision biases affect data curation, how this can be evaluated, and what can be done to mitigate such biases. It is also unclear how to overcome implicit human biases, given the limited research on the emergence of such biases. Cognitive models of learning can help identify and prevent human biases (Cranford et al., 2020, 2021), but more research targeting the identification and prevention of human biases is required. It is important to build on research on anti-fragility teams to determine how individual biases influence team biases (Taleb, 2012).

SUMMARY

Humans are subject to several well-known biases that can negatively affect their decision making. AI systems, far from being perfect, are also subject to a number of biases that may be hidden from the people who interact with them, and which can negatively affect an AI system's performance and the performance of the combined human-AI team. Research is needed to better understand the interdependencies between human and AI biases, and to detect and prevent biases that impede effective performance in human-AI teams in multi-domain operations, particularly in the face of adversarial actions that may try to exploit them.

9

Training Human-AI Teams

Training has long been a hallmark of both DOD operations and teamwork. Team training is conducted in a manner that seeks to leverage knowledge, skills, and attitudinal competencies to improve general team processes (Salas et al., 2008). The reasons for team training are abundant. Team training improves performance (Salas et al., 2008), improves adaptive response (Gorman, Cooke, and Amazeen, 2010), decreases error (Wiener, Kanki, and Helmreich, 1993), and develops team cognition (Marks et al., 2002). For these reasons, team training has a long history, spanning multiple decades (Delise et al., 2010; Salas et al., 2008; Tannenbaum and Cerasoli, 2013). Throughout the years, many types of training mechanisms and modalities have been developed and implemented in multiple contexts, to unleash the full capabilities of teams. However, to date, team training has focused primarily on human-human teaming interactions because teams have traditionally consisted only of human team members, with very few exceptions (human-animal teams being one exception, see Chapter 3), but this is changing with the advent of human-AI teaming (see O'Neill et al., 2020 for a complete review).

In response to human-AI teaming, the committee finds that training needs to adapt to account for both perceptual and procedural teaming changes. Humans perceive AI teammates as fundamentally different from human teammates (Zhang et al., 2021) and work with AI teammates differently than they do human teammates (McNeese et al., 2018). Human-AI team training can benefit significantly by leveraging current and past human-human team-training standards to inform and jumpstart its own standards. However, it is essential to consider that human-human teaming is different from human-AI teaming and, for that reason, new methods, mechanisms, and modalities will need to be developed and introduced to fully leverage human-AI teaming capabilities. This chapter will review human-human team-training methods with an eye to how they can inform human-AI team training, identify key challenges, and present relevant research needs.

HUMAN-HUMAN TEAM TRAINING TO INFORM HUMAN-AI TEAM TRAINING

As noted, the concept of team training is well established, and its impacts on improved teaming are well founded. The foundational knowledge associated with team training is focused on training humans to collaborate with other human team members to effectively work toward a shared goal. Many types of team training have been proposed.

Strategies for Team Training

The strongest theme in the human-human team-training literature is the use of various training strategies. Although teams can be trained using various methods, the focus of this chapter is limited to the three main types of training found most frequently in the literature: procedural training, cross-training, and adaptive or perturbation training. These training methods have shown consistently positive results over the decades (Delise et al., 2010; Salas et al., 2008: Tannenbaum and Cerasoli, 2013).

Procedural training is a traditional methodology that focuses on repeated introduction of team members to task-related stimuli, with positive reinforcement provided in a standardized or procedural manner (Gorman, Cooke, and Amazeen, 2010). This type of team training is often used in environments with high workloads and stressors, in which deviating from the standard work protocol can have serious adverse consequences.

Cross-training is defined as "an instructional strategy in which each team member is trained in the duties of his or her teammates" (Volpe et al., 1996, p. 87). Cross-training seeks to introduce individual team member responsibilities and tasks to other team members, so each team member has a shared understanding of all aspects of team-related taskwork. In general, cross-training has a net positive effect on team effectiveness, especially in terms of shared understanding and interaction dynamics (Marks et al., 2002).

Adaptive or perturbation training is based on the idea of purposefully perturbing or manipulating a team-related task, which then requires adaptation at the team level, either through communication or coordination. Perturbation training has been shown to be effective and, in some cases, even more effective than cross-training when the two are directly compared (Gorman, Cooke, and Amazeen, 2010). Perturbation training within teams allows more flexibility and on-demand coordination, which may increase team resiliency. Additionally, perturbation training has been utilized in human-robot teaming, leading to the development of computational models that allow for joint strategies in coordination (Ramakrishnan, Zhang, and Shah, 2017).

It is important to note that there is no universally accepted team-training method, as context and team personnel can influence team-training effectiveness. Thus, to develop human-AI team training, the committee finds that it will be necessary to experiment with many types of team training, to ascertain their effectiveness within this new paradigm. Furthermore, research may find that many team-training strategies are not well aligned with the logistics of human-AI teams.

Are training strategies that are effective for human-human teaming adequate and appropriate for human-AI teaming tasks and environments? This question remains to be answered, and research is needed to translate team-training methods and validate their utilization in this new paradigm.

The Use of Simulation

Simulations are at the heart of most team-training initiatives because training becomes more effective when it is grounded within a meaningful context (Marlow et al., 2017). Teams are inherently linked to the context they operate within; context dictates the tasks teams work on, their environment, and the tools they utilize. Thus, for teams to train realistically, simulation environments that represent real-world operations are needed. For this reason, simulation-based team training (SBTT) is viewed as integral to effective team training. SBTT is an instructional technique used for skill development by leveraging real-world environments, and it is most often utilized and cited within the healthcare community (Owen et al., 2006; Weaver et al., 2010). Simulations and simulation task environments (STEs) are used in all types of contexts and are oriented for both the physical and digital worlds (Gray, 2002). Many STEs are digital representations of the real-world environment, lowering the cost of training while still promoting significant acquisition of domain and task-relevant knowledge. Another advantage of SBTT is that trainees can experience events that would rarely occur in the real world.

The committee finds that, as human-AI teaming advances, digital STEs will be critical to training both human and autonomous team members in meaningful environments. The representation of the autonomous agent (i.e., either physical (robot) or digital (synthetic)) will dictate the type of SBTT and/or the STE. In the committee's judgment, the standardized environment of many STEs (1) will help humans to train with autonomous team members;

(2) can help autonomy to train with human team members, if properly designed; and (3) can help autonomy to train itself within the environment. In many cases, synthetic environments are the main environments in which AI teammates will be deployed.

Training Content: Taskwork and Teamwork

Teaming is generally composed of two interrelated foci: *teamwork*- and *taskwork*-related understandings and actions. The teamwork component generally focuses on understanding how team members should work together to accomplish shared goals, whereas taskwork focuses on team task-specific knowledge (Mohammed, Ferzandi, and Hamilton, 2010). Both aspects of teaming are interdependent and overlap, but it is essential to focus on specific aspects of teaming when implementing team training. To train a team generically, without a focus on specific components, will not translate into meaningful performance outcomes. Instead, in the committee's judgment team training is best when it directly targets teamwork or taskwork, or a combination of the two. At a fundamental level, teams need to be trained to understand (1) their teammates; (2) teamwork-related processes; and (3) the team task.

Training human-AI teams on both teamwork and taskwork is a challenge, specifically training for the aspects of teamwork. Autonomous team members simply do not understand teamwork-related concepts, making training them for such concepts exceptionally difficult. In the committee's judgment, first, fundamental teaming concepts need to be embedded into the AI system so that a foundation of teamwork knowledge can be established and built upon for the future. Until AI advances to the point of understanding basic teaming concepts, the focus will need to be on training taskwork team-related initiatives.

KEY CHALLENGES AND RESEARCH GAPS

The committee finds 10 key research gaps related to training human-AI teams that need to be addressed.

- Human-AI teams require the need for multi-focused levels of training—humans teaming with humans, humans teaming with autonomous agents, and autonomous agents teaming with autonomous agents. However, within each of these foci, the team still needs to train together at the team level. Research is needed on these various levels of teaming.
- In human-AI teaming, the human currently needs to train on and understand (1) his or her role; (2) the AI teammate; (3) how to interact with the AI teammate; and (4) how to interact with human teammates. Assimilating these aspects for training purposes, in a way that does not overwhelm the human operator, is challenging and needs further investigation.
- Team training is difficult when the autonomous agent cannot fully understand natural language or deploy effective natural language processing, and more research is needed in this area.
- Team training of teamwork-related components is difficult when the autonomous agent does not understand basic teaming concepts, so more work is needed in this area.
- There is a current gap in understanding the impact that training has on human-AI trust in the team setting.
- To allow for resilient teamwork in the case of AI system failure, team training needs to be conducted with both accurate and inaccurate AI. Perturbation training for human-AI teaming may be indicated.
- Simulation environments need to be built to allow for team-level human-AI training.
- The concept of the autonomous teammate as a team trainer for purposes such as coordination coaching (e.g., McNeese et al., 2018) needs to be explored.
- Training will need to be constantly reassessed for potential updating, due to the autonomous teammate's ability to train and update its skills and capabilities continually; work is needed in this area.
- There is a gap in understanding when to train human-AI teams to a diversity of experiences (perturbation/adaption) versus when to train to standardization (procedural).

RESEARCH NEEDS

The committee recommends addressing six major research objectives for improving human-AI team training.

Research Objective 9-1: Developing Human-Centered Human-AI Team-Training Content. There is a great deal of knowledge about, and resources for, training human-human teams, but none explicitly devoted to human-AI teams. Authentic training content materials and mechanisms need to be developed for human-AI teams. The human-AI teaming paradigm includes many potentially different foci, ranging from individual team responsibilities to understanding and interacting with both human and AI team members. This multi-level focus presents a challenge in terms of knowing not only *what* to focus and train on but also *how* to train on each of these areas. Directed research is needed to outline areas of focus and the content to be highlighted in training methods. For example, does a human team member need to be trained on what an AI system is and what it can do? If so, what training content is needed to impart that information? Similarly, given the issues related to training human-AI teams on teamwork-related content, how should this aspect of training best be approached?

Research Objective 9-2: Testing and Validating Traditional Team-Training Methods to Inform New Methods. As previously noted, there is a long and rich history of team-training strategies that have been successful in the human-human context. Strategies such as procedural training, cross-training, and adaptive/perturbation training all need to be adapted and translated for the human-AI teaming environment. Then, each strategy needs to be empirically validated to understand (1) if it is feasible for the human-AI team paradigm; and (2) the impact of these strategies on overall human-AI teaming performance and related teamwork outcomes, such as team cognition, shared situation awareness, and communication and coordination. Through this understanding, existing training strategies can be explicitly adapted, or new strategies can be developed for human-AI teaming.

Research Objective 9-3: Training to Calibrate Human Expectations of Autonomous Teammates. Recent work by Zhang and colleagues (2021) investigating humans' perceptions relating to human-AI teaming highlighted that, in many cases, humans have unrealistic expectations and requirements regarding autonomous teammates. Specifically, humans often indicate that they want autonomous teammates to be as good or better than human teammates. This requirement is problematic because autonomous teammates currently have inherently limited capabilities that prevent them from doing many basic teamwork-related behaviors. Thus, there seems to be a perceptual misalignment between what humans expect from AI teammates and what AI teammates can do. Specific content is needed to set adequate expectations of autonomous teammates, related to Research Objective 9-1. In other words, it would be best if training materials do not only focus on teaming procedures, but also focus on the expectations and capabilities of the autonomous system.

Research Objective 9-4: Designing Platforms for Human-AI Team Training. Human-AI teaming needs research platforms in which to develop and test teamwork procedures, especially platforms that allow for the testing of team-training strategies and methods. The explicit design of simulated task environments that allow humans and AI systems to work together is necessary. Rather than starting from the ground up, researchers could use existing videogame platforms that inherently contain both teaming and AI capabilities.

Research Objective 9-5: Adaptive Training Materials Based on Differing Team Compositions and Sizes. There is no standard composition or size of human-AI teams, and training materials need to reflect that. A human-AI team may consist of 2–10 human or autonomous entities with differing ratios, for example. McNeese and colleagues (2021b) examined various human-AI teaming compositions and found performance differences between teams with differing ratios of humans and AI teammates. Thus, it is critical that training materials be developed for various types of human-AI teams.

Research Objective 9-6: Training That Works Toward Trust in Human-AI Teaming. As outlined in Chapter 7, trust is central to effective human-AI interactions and both human-human teaming (Salas, Sims, and Burke,

2005) and human-AI teaming (McNeese et al., 2021a). Thus, team-training materials need to specifically account for the explicit development of team-level human-AI trust and calibration of that trust. It would be beneficial for training to focus not only on the human's trust in the AI teammate, but also on the human's trust in other human teammates. More work is needed to develop and test training methods designed to engender trust, and it would be useful for methods such as explanations and transparency to be a key focus when developing trust-related team-training material.

SUMMARY

Training human-AI teams is different from training human-human teams. Despite some similarities, human-human teams and human-AI teams are fundamentally different. The manners and methods by which human-AI teams conduct work and do procedural teamwork are, and will continue to be, fundamentally different from those of human-human teams. The tasks and environments in which human-AI teamwork occurs will also be different. Thus, a great deal of work is needed to create training strategies and methods to support human-AI teaming. The research community would undoubtedly benefit from exploring traditional human-human team-training techniques to inform human-AI team training, but they would also be best served to remain open to creating entirely new methods based on research outcomes. Significant research is needed to develop empirically driven training initiatives for human-AI teams.

10

HSI Processes and Measures of Human-AI Team Collaboration and Performance

Human-systems integration (HSI) addresses human considerations within the system design and implementation process, with the aim of maximizing total system performance and minimizing total ownership costs (Boehm-Davis, Durso, and Lee, 2015). HSI incorporates human-centered analyses, models, and evaluations throughout the system lifecycle, starting from early operational concepts through research, design-and-development, and continuing through operations (NRC, 2007). HSI policies and procedures applicable to defense-acquisition programs have been published (DODI 5000.02T, Enclosure 7 [DOD, 2020]), and HSI standards have been adopted by the DOD (SAE International, 2019). Further the Human Factors Ergonomic Society/American National Standards Institute (HFES/ANSI) 400 standard on human readiness levels was developed, which codifies the level of maturity of a system relative to HSI activities, ranging from human readiness level 1 (lowest) to 9 (highest) (Human Factors and Ergonomics Society, 2021). In this chapter, the committee examines the state-of-the-art, gaps, and research needs associated with design and evaluation processes for human-AI teams, and discusses the need for incorporating HSI considerations into development of AI systems in addition to the specific design and training issues discussed in previous chapters.

TAKING AN HSI PERSPECTIVE IN HUMAN-AI TEAM DESIGN AND IMPLEMENTATION

The committee notes that, to date, HSI methods have had limited application to the design of human-AI teams. This is largely attributable to the fact that AI systems are currently being developed primarily in a research-and-development context and for non-military applications, in which HSI methods are not commonly applied. While HSI methods *are* applied outside of the military, AI systems are currently being developed in areas where HSI is not common practice (e.g., automobiles, consumer apps). However, lessons learned during the design of earlier AI systems make clear the importance of taking an HSI approach, to avoid developing AI systems that fail to meet user and mission requirements, resulting in lack of system adoption or extensive need for workarounds when the systems are fielded (NRC, 2007).

The need to consider the context of use throughout the design and evaluation process is an area of consensus in HSI practice (Air Force Scientific Advisory Board, 2004; Boehm-Davis, Durso, and Lee, 2015; Evenson, Muller, and Roth, 2008; NRC, 2007; SAE International, 2019). Context of use includes characteristics of the users, the activities they perform, how the work is distributed across people and machine agents, the range and complexity of situations that can arise, and the broader sociotechnical "environment in which the system will be integrated" (NRC, 2007, p. 136). Context of use is best determined via field observations and interviews with domain practitioners (e.g., cognitive task analysis methods) to understand the pragmatics of the work context in which the human-AI team will operate (Bisantz and Roth, 2008; Crandall, Klein, and Hoffman, 2006; Endsley and Jones, 2012; Vicente, 1999).

The pitfalls of failing to take the context of use into account continue to be relearned by developers of AI systems. A recent example is a deep-learning system developed for detection of diabetic retinopathy (Beede et al., 2020). While the system achieved levels of accuracy comparable to human specialists when tested under controlled conditions, it proved unusable when implemented in actual clinics in Thailand. Beede and colleagues (2020) identified multiple socioenvironmental factors preventing the system's effective performance that were only uncovered in the field. They noted that there is currently no requirement for AI systems to be evaluated in real-world contexts, nor is it a customary practice. They advocated for human-centered field research to be conducted prior to and alongside more formal technical performance evaluations.

As a positive contrast, Singer et al. (2021) examined development of successful machine learning (ML)-based clinical support systems for healthcare settings. They reported much more active engagement in the field of practice, with back-and-forth between developers and end-users shaping the ultimately successful AI systems. The committee highlights the importance of grounding AI system designs in a deep understanding of the context of use, and the need for continual engagement with users throughout the development and fielding process, to understand the impact of user engagement on practice.

Another point of emphasis in HSI is the need for analysis, design, and testing to ensure resilient performance of the human-AI team in the face of off-normal situations that may be beyond the boundary conditions of the AI system (Woods, 2015; Woods and Hollnagel, 2006). Resilience refers to the capacity of a group of people and/or automated agents to respond to change and disruption in a flexible and innovative manner, to achieve successful outcomes. Unexpected, off-normal conditions are variously referred to as black swans (Wickens, 2009) and dark debt (Woods, 2017), as well as edge, corner, or boundary cases (Allspaw, 2016). These events tend to be rare and often involve subtle, unanticipated system interactions that make them challenging to anticipate ahead of time (Woods, 2017). Allspaw (2012) argued for the need to continuously search for and identify ways to mitigate these anomalies, starting in development and continuing into operation. Neville, Rosso, and Pires (2021) are developing a framework (called Transform with Resilience during Upgrades to Socio-Technical Systems) that characterizes the sociotechnical system properties that enable human-AI teams to anticipate, adapt, and respond to situations that may be at or beyond the edge of the AI system's competency envelope. The Neville, Rosso, and Pires framework is being used to derive tools and metrics for evaluating system resilience and guiding technology transition processes. Gorman et al. (2019) have similarly developed a method of measuring the dynamics of the human and machine components of a system before, during, and after a perturbation in a simulated setting, to understand the system interdependencies and possible unintended consequences of unanticipated events. In the committee's judgment, these are promising directions, but more research is needed to develop and validate effective methods for design and evaluation of resilient human-AI teaming.

Key Challenges and Research Gaps

The committee finds three key gaps related to HSI for human-AI teams.

- Currently, the development of AI systems often does not follow HSI best practices.
- Context-of-use analyses to inform design and evaluation of AI systems are not commonly practiced.
- There is limited research and guidance to support analysis, design, and evaluation of human-AI teams to ensure resilient performance under challenging conditions at the boundaries of an AI system's capabilities.

Research Needs

The committee recommends addressing the following research objective for improved HSI practice relevant to human-AI teaming.

Research Objective 10-1: Human-AI Team Design and Testing Methods. There is a need to develop and evaluate design/engineering methods for effective human-AI teaming. There is a need to develop and test methods for analysis, design, and evaluation of human-AI team performance under conditions that are at or beyond the competence boundary of the AI system(s).

REQUIREMENTS FOR RESEARCH IN HUMAN-AI TEAM DEVELOPMENT

The development of high-quality system requirements includes specifying high-level goals and functions for a desired system, and typically includes assigning responsibilities to various agents (human or computer-based) to complete these goals (MITRE, 2014). Ideally, requirements should be understandable, succinct, unambiguous, comprehensive, and complete (Turk, 2006). When a cognitive systems engineering approach is used to augment the development of requirements, such requirements will address information needs that explicitly consider human decisions and cognitive work, for individuals, human-human teams, and possibly human-AI teams (Elm et al., 2008).

The committee finds that the rise of AI has introduced new problems currently not addressed by either traditional or cognitive systems-engineering approaches. Although there is a substantial body of literature addressing how requirements should and could be developed for military systems, the bulk of this work assumes that the underlying decision-support systems rely upon deterministic algorithms that perform the same way for every use. Thus, in earlier research, while the underlying algorithms may not always exhibit high performance, they exhibit *consistent* performance (Turban and Frenzel, 1992), and so it is relatively straightforward to determine whether information requirements are met and under what conditions.

In the committee's opinion, the increasing use of connectionist or ML-based AI in safety-critical systems, like those in military settings, has brought into sharp contrast the inability of traditional systems-engineering and cognitive systems-engineering approaches to address how development of requirements needs to adapt. A major current limitation of ML-based AI systems is that their use could affect cognitive work and role allocation, and may create the need for new functionalities due to use of systems that reason in ways that are unknown to their designers (Knight, 2017).

Another major problem with ML-based AI is its inability to cope with uncertainty. AI powered by neural networks can work well in very narrow applications, but the algorithms of an autonomous system can struggle to make sense of data that is even slightly different in presentation from the data on which it was originally trained (Cummings, 2021). Such brittleness means humans may need to adjust their cognitive work and unexpectedly take on new functions due to limitations in the underlying AI. In addition, much recent work has revealed how vulnerable ML-based AI systems are to adversarial attacks (Eykholt et al., 2017; Su, Vargas, and Sakurai, 2019). So, in addition to managing AI systems that are inherently brittle, humans may also be burdened with monitoring such systems for signs of potential adversarial attacks.

Key Challenges and Research Gaps

The committee finds that an improved ability to determine requirements for human-AI teams, particular those that involve ML-based AI, is needed.

Research Needs

The committee recommends addressing the following research objective for improved HSI requirements relevant to human-AI teaming.

Research Objective 10-2: Human-AI Team Requirements. A number of requirements for AI system development will likely change in the presence of machine learning-based AI. Research is needed to address several overarching issues. When and where should machine learning-based AI be used as opposed to symbolic in systems that support human work? What new functions and tasks are likely to be introduced as a result of incorporating brittle AI into human-AI teams? What is the influence of time pressure on decision making for systems that leverage different kinds of AI? How could or should acceptable levels of uncertainty be characterized in the requirements process, especially as these levels of uncertainty relate to human decision making? How can competency boundaries of both humans and AI systems be mapped so that degraded and potentially dangerous phases of operational systems can be avoided?

RESEARCH TEAM COMPETENCIES

To address the gap in understanding how AI systems could and should influence requirements and the design of systems that support human work, particularly in settings that are high in uncertainty, the committee finds that a new approach is needed for the formation of research teams to tackle such problems. There is a research gap that misses interconnections between fields of focus, partially because scientists and researchers often work in "silos" but also due to a lack of formal interdisciplinary programs that train people to be proficient in more than one field. To address these issues, the committee believes that research teams looking at basic and applied problems in human-AI team development will need to be multi-disciplinary to address the myriad of problems that overlap separate fields.

The exact makeup of any specific research team will depend on the nature of the research question(s), as Figure 10-1 illustrates for human-AI team development. The committee finds that there are four clusters of desired research competencies: (1) computer science; (2) human factors engineering; (3) sociotechnical science; and (4) systems engineering.

In the committee's opinion, these competencies represent the broad areas needed to support numerous human-AI team research scenarios. Computer science is at the core because any system that incorporates any kind of AI will necessarily have computer scientists (or related disciplines) as the creators of the underlying technology. The importance of computer scientists teaming with other researchers, like those in human factors, systems engineering, and sociotechnical aspects, cannot be overstated. Such multi-disciplinary teams promote an understanding of the broader impacts of the technology and help to make it functional and successful in real-world applications (Dignum, 2019). Table 10-1 illustrates representative topics within each of the research thrusts that the committee finds may be needed to support human-AI teaming research projects; it is likely that even a single project would benefit from collaboration between individuals in multiple blocks of the table.

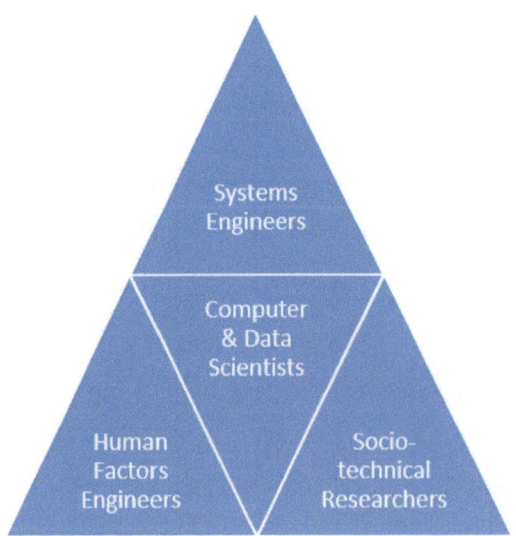

FIGURE 10-1 Research team competencies human-AI teaming.

TABLE 10-1 Representative Multi-Disciplinary Team Competency Topics

Computer and Data Science	Systems Engineering	Human Factors Engineering	Sociotechnical Research
Machine/Deep Learning	Requirements Engineering	Cognition	Ethics
Artificial Intelligence	Test and Evaluation	Human Performance	Philosophy
Computer Vision	Safety Engineering	Experimental Psychology	Law
Natural Language Processing	Risk Modeling	Human Computer/Robot Interaction	Policy and Regulation

Key Challenges and Research Gaps

The committee finds that, to develop AI systems with competent human-AI teaming, a new approach to the formation of research teams is needed, which incorporates competencies and approaches from multiple disciplines.

Research Needs

The committee recommends addressing the following research objective for improved human-AI team development.

Research Objective 10-3: Human-AI Team Development Teams. New multidisciplinary teams and approaches to the development of human-AI teams need to be created. A systems perspective is needed to create successful human-AI teams that will be effective in future multidisciplinary operations, and this will require synergistic work across multiple disciplines that cannot be achieved through a siloed approach. Exploration and evaluation of mechanisms for achieving successful team collaboration in human-AI development teams are needed.

HSI CONSIDERATIONS FOR HUMAN-AI TEAMS

Biased or brittle AI creates a significant challenge for certification efforts. Understanding these biases and limitations is critical for framing the developmental, operational, and support requirements any program must address (MITRE, 2014). Within the DOD, HSI is divided into a number of domains: manpower, personnel, training, human factors engineering, safety and occupational health, force protection and survivability. These encompass a number of important developmental objectives and requirements that have traditionally been called *ilities*.

Relevant to AI systems, three overarching ilities are paramount (Simpkiss, 2009):

- *Usability*: "[Usability] means 'cradle-to-grave' including operations, support, sustainment, training, and disposal. This includes survivability" (Simpkiss, 2009, p. 4).
- *Operational suitability*: "Includes utility, lethality, operability, interoperability, dependability, survivability" (Simpkiss, 2009, p. 4).
- *Sustainability*: Includes supportability, serviceability, reliability, availability, maintainability, accessibility, dependability, interoperability, interchangeability, and survivability.

Other important ilities include functionality, reliability, supportability, and flexibility among others (de Weck et al., 2011). In addition to these important considerations, there are also new ilities to consider for human-AI teams. Table 10-2 outlines both how traditional ilities will need to be adapted for human-AI teams and new ilities that need to be considered. In addition to traditional usability concerns that are well-known to the HSI community, there will need to be added focus on making the limits of AI transparent to users. As noted previously, though there has been a recent increase in research on explainability and interpretability for AI (see Chapter 5), a large part of this research focuses on explainability and interpretability for the *developers* of AI, with far less focus on the *users* of AI in practical settings. This is of particular concern to the USAF because time pressure is an attribute of many operational environments and, given the propensity for biased decision making in such settings (Cummings, 2004), in the committee's judgment it is especially important that AI systems be truly usable and transparent.

TABLE 10-2 HSI Considerations for Human-AI Teams: Traditional and New Ilities

Ility	Needs
Traditional	
Usability	• AI operational limitations and competency boundaries need to be made transparent to users. • In appropriate settings, users need the ability to conduct sensitivity analyses to explore a decision space, as well as the limitations. • Routine feedback about usability needs to be elicited from users, including post-software updates.
Operational Suitability	• A process for tracking and documenting issues with concept drift as well as operator disuse, misuse, or abuse of AI would be useful. • A process needs to be implemented that maps any operational dependencies created in the implementation of AI systems, to determine which downstream processes could be negatively affected if an AI system is degraded or fails.
Sustainability	• A process for identifying changes in operations or environmental conditions that affect model outcomes would be useful, including when retraining should occur for ML-based AI systems. • An incident repository needs to be created and routinely analyzed for all AI systems, in which users and supervisors can document erroneous, unusual, and unexpected system behaviors. • A process for tracking software changes and possible unintended impacts on either operations or human activity would be useful.
New	
Auditability	• Data and resulting models need to be periodically audited to uncover issues with suitability and sustainability, as well as possible issues with bias. • Automated tools will be needed to support humans conducting auditing tasks.
Passive Vulnerability	• Adversarial machine-learning vulnerabilities need to be identified and mitigated.

In the operational suitability category, the biggest need is to address the notion of concept drift, also known as model drift. Concept drift occurs when the relationship between input and output data changes over time (Widmer and Kubat, 1996), making the predictions of such systems irrelevant at best, and potentially dangerous at worst. In the DOD, an embedded AI system that relies on an older training set of data as it attempts to analyze images to find targets in a new and different region will likely experience concept drift. Thus, concept drift is a possible source of dynamic uncertainty that needs to be considered when determining whether an analysis in one setting may adapt well to a different setting. The committee finds that the DOD does not currently have a system in place to ensure the periodical evaluation of AI systems to ensure drift has not occurred or to inform the human operator of the level of applicability of an AI system to current problem sets (see Chapter 8).

The notion of concept drift also affects the sustainability category, given that the best way to prevent such drift is to ensure the underlying data are adequately represented in any AI model. The USAF clearly recognizes that sustainability, reliability, serviceability, and maintainability are key considerations (Simpkiss, 2009), but it is not clear that the USAF has mapped out the workforce changes needed to adequately address these concerns for AI systems. In the committee's judgment, as there are for aircraft, there will need to be an AI maintenance workforce whose jobs entail database curation, continual model accuracy and applicability assessment, model retraining thresholds, and coordination with testing personnel. In the committee's judgment, the USAF should create an AI maintenance workforce, which, if done correctly, could be the model for both other military branches and commercial entities.

In addition to the changes needed in terms of the more traditional ilities, the committee finds that there is also a need to explicitly consider auditability, which is the need to document and assess the data and models used in developing an AI system, to reveal possible biases and concept drift. Although there have been recent efforts in developing processes to better contextualize the appropriateness of datasets (Gebru et al., 2018) and model performance with a given dataset (Mitchell et al., 2019), there are no known organized efforts for military applications. In the committee's opinion, military AI systems could require a level of auditability that far exceeds commercial systems, due to their use on the battlefield. Auditability could fall under the purview of an AI maintenance workforce, as mentioned above.

The last new ility category that will likely need to be expressly considered by the USAF for AI systems is that of passive vulnerability. There is increasing evidence that ML-based AI systems trained on large datasets can be especially vulnerable to forms of passive hacking, in which the environment is modified in small ways to leverage vulnerabilities in the underlying deep-learning algorithms. For example, adversarial ML techniques can deceive face recognition algorithms using relatively benign glasses (Sharif et al., 2016), and recently a Tesla was tricked into going 85 mph versus 35 mph using a small amount of tape on a sign (O'Neill, 2020). Such scenarios, though predominantly occurring in the civilian domain, have clear relevance for military operations, and occur not only in computer vision applications of AI but also in natural language processing (Morris et al., 2020). Such results indicate that, to combat this new source of vulnerability, the USAF will need to continue to develop new cybersecurity capabilities that will require reskilling of the workforce and advanced training.

Key Challenges and Research Gaps

The committee finds that the requirements for the development of trained workforces and methods for detecting problems and testing AI systems need to be determined.

Research Needs

The committee recommends addressing the following two research objectives to develop an understanding of workforce needs to support future human-AI teams.

Research Objective 10-4: AI System Lifecycle Testing and Auditability. The required workforce skillsets, tools, methodologies, and policies for AI maintenance teams need to be determined. There is also a need to find methods for AI system life-cycle testing and auditing to determine the validity and suitability of the AI system for current use conditions. Determining the enabling processes, technologies, and systems that need to be incorporated into fielded AI systems to support the work of AI maintenance teams is necessary.

Research Objective 10-5: AI Cyber Vulnerabilities. The necessary workforce skillsets, tools, methodologies, and policies need to be determined for detecting and ameliorating AI cyber vulnerabilities and for detecting and responding to cyber attacks on human-AI teams.

TESTING, EVALUATION, VERIFICATION, AND VALIDATION OF HUMAN-AI TEAMS

Because of the nascent nature of embedded AI in safety-critical systems, testing, evaluation, validation, and verification (TEVV) has been recognized as a potential Achilles' heel for the DOD (Flournoy, Haines, and Chefitz, 2020; Topcu et al., 2020). A recent report highlighted the significant organizational issues surrounding TEVV for defense systems and spelled out the policies and actions that the DOD is advised to implement in the near- and far-term to address current inadequacies (Flournoy, Haines, and Chefitz, 2020). While this effort outlined the many high-level issues associated with AI TEVV, this section will detail more nuanced areas of TEVV inquiry with a focus on needed areas of research. These issues are also relevant to the training of human-AI teams (see Chapter 9), however, the committee emphasizes that training can never be a substitute for proper design and testing of the AI system.

In the committee's opinion, the primary reason that TEVV for human-AI teams needs significant attention is the problem with how such systems cope with known and unknown uncertainty. There are three primary sources of uncertainty in any human-AI team, as illustrated in Figure 10-2. As is familiar to the HSI community, human behavior for actors both within and external to a system can be widely variable and can carry significant uncertainty. For the military, the environment is also a major contributor to operational uncertainty, often referred to as the fog of war. What is new in human-AI teams is the need to account for the variability, (i.e., blind spots) in the embedded AI, and how those blind spots could lead to problems in human performance during the operation of human-AI teams (Cummings, 2019).

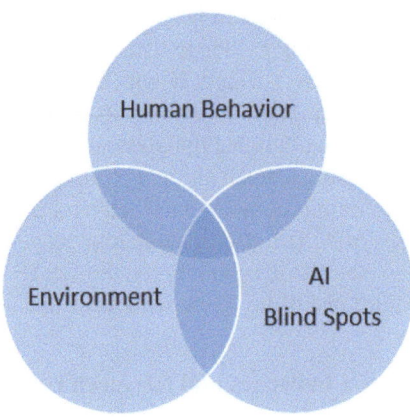

FIGURE 10-2 Sources of uncertainty in human-AI teams.

Previous technological interventions (e.g., radar, decision-support tools, etc.) were meant to reduce uncertainty but, with the insertion of AI (particularly ML-based AI), there is now a third axis of uncertainty to be considered: that of AI blind spots. As discussed previously, AI can be brittle and fail in unexpected ways. One recent example is the interpretation of the moon as a stoplight by a Tesla vehicle (Levin, 2021). Although such a mistake seems relatively benign, there have also been several high-profile incidents in which a Tesla crashed broadside into a tractor trailer or hit a barrier head on, killing the drivers; so the combination of significant AI blind spots and human inattention can be deadly (NTSB, 2020).

It is generally recognized that significantly more work is needed in the area of assured autonomy, in which autonomy reliably performs within known and expected limits (Topcu et al., 2020). Assured autonomy requires significant advances in AI testing. In the committee's judgment, to reach acceptable assurance levels, the DOD needs to adapt its testing practices to address the AI blind-spot issues, but there has been little tangible progress. The DOD's current approach to testing generally includes developmental tests at the earlier stages of a technology's development, followed by operational testing as system development matures. The committee finds that, although this approach is reasonable for deterministic systems, it will not be sustainable for systems with embedded AI. The constant updating of software code that is a necessary byproduct of modern software-development methods is a major reason that the DOD needs to adopt new testing practices. Seemingly small changes in software can sometimes lead to unexpected outcomes. Without principled testing, particularly for software that can have a derivative effect on human performance, the stage will be set for potential latent system failures. Moreover, because software is typically updated continuously throughout the lifecycle of a system, it will also be necessary to adapt testing to catch the emergence of a problem in a system with embedded AI. It is not ideal to rely on system users to discover issues during actual operations, and it is particularly problematic in safety-critical operations such as multi-domain operations (MDO). There is a need for user testing prior to issuing each software update, particularly in cases when the update will impact how the user interacts with the system (e.g., changes the information displayed or the behavior of the system).

In addition, users of the system will inevitably discover issues during actual operations, regardless of the testing or development approaches. The question is not whether these surprises will occur, because generally they will. The committee's goal is to improve DOD testing practices to reduce the occurrence of surprises, by incorporating tests prior to the introduction of any software change. These tests could probe for potential effects of software changes on the ways people must interact with the system. Considerations include assessing (1) how easy it will be for humans (especially users) to anticipate and detect unexpected behavior; and (2) how easy it will be for humans (especially DevOps personnel) to make quick adjustments to the code to mitigate, block, or otherwise make moot the results of the unexpected behavior.

In addition, the committee finds that the DOD's current staged approach to testing does not explicitly account for the need to test AI blind spots, as illustrated in Figure 10-2 and discussed previously. There is a dearth of research and knowledge around how the subjective choices of AI designers could lead to AI blind spots, poor human-AI interaction, and, ultimately, system failure (Cummings and Li, 2021a). As a result of the new sources of uncertainty that require rethinking TEVV, particularly in terms of human work, new testbeds will be needed that allow for not only investigation of such uncertainties, but also use by the various research areas outlined in Figure 10-2.

Key Challenges and Research Gaps

The committee finds that methods, processes, and systems for testing, evaluation, verification, and validation of AI systems across their lifespans are needed, particularly with respect to AI blind spots and edge cases, as well as managing the potential for drift over time.

Research Needs

The committee recommends addressing the following research objective to improve testing and verification of human-AI teams.

Research Objective 10-6: Testing of Evolving AI Systems. Effective methods need to be determined for testing AI systems to determine AI blind spots (i.e., conditions for which the system is not robust). How could or should test cases be developed so that edge and corner cases are identified, particularly where humans could be affected by brittle AI? How can humans certify machine learning-based and probabilistic AI systems in real-world scenarios? Certification includes not just understanding technical capabilities but also understanding how to determine trust for systems that may not always behave in a repeatable fashion. The National Science Foundation recently published an in-depth study on assured autonomy, so there is a potential important collaboration between this organization and the AFRL (Topcu et al., 2020). Given that changes in both software and environmental conditions occur almost continually (due to the potential for concept drift) in AI systems, how to identify, measure, and mitigate concept drift is still very much an open research question. Living labs involving disaster management may form suitable surrogates for research on multi-domain operations human-AI teams.

HUMAN AI-TEAM RESEARCH TESTBEDS

To address the numerous complexities inherent in human-AI research, the committee finds that there needs to be substantially improved testbed availability, above and beyond what the USAF currently has. One of the core issues at the heart of human-AI experimentation is the role of simulation versus real-world testing (Davis and Marcus, 2016). As seen in Figure 10-3, simulation is generally thought to be the appropriate testbed for basic research, while a shift toward real-world testing (or approximations of such) is needed for more applied research. While these principles are also valid for human-AI research, there is a clear need to consider the role of uncertainty, as previously outlined.

Because uncertainty is a potential "unknown unknown" that can come from the design of AI systems, the environment, humans, and the interplay of these factors (Figure 10-2), the committee believes that much greater emphasis is needed on studying this effect in human-AI research. To that end, Figure 10-3 illustrates that, while some human-AI testing can occur in simulations, testbeds that cannot incorporate elements of real-world uncertainty will necessarily miss a critical element of research.

Regardless of whether the testbeds are in simulations or with real-world elements, they need to be designed to support the multi-disciplinary efforts outlined in Figure 10-1. This means it would likely be beneficial for testbeds to support different kinds of users (e.g., researchers who code as well as researchers studying people). The committee believes that, ideally, testbeds would be modular so that, for example, different datasets, algorithms, or decision-support systems could be substituted as needed, without requiring major system overhauls. In addition, given the realistic constraints of a post-Covid-19 world, testbeds would ideally be usable both in person, for those researchers who need physical access to the testbed, and remotely.

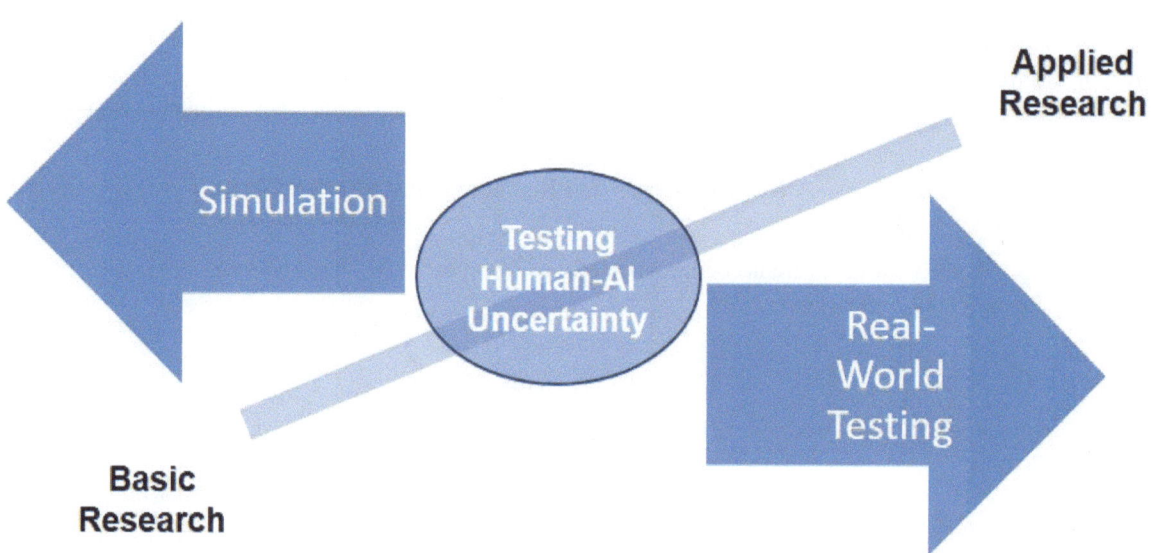

FIGURE 10-3 The relationship of human-AI testing fidelity to the nature of research questions.

Key Challenges and Research Gaps

The committee finds that testbeds for human-AI teaming are needed that can support relevant interdisciplinary research, challenging scenarios, and both pre- and post-deployment testing needs.

Research Needs

The committee recommends addressing the following research objective for developing testbeds to support human-AI teaming research-and-development activities.

Research Objective 10-7: Human-AI Team Testbeds. Given the changes that AI is bringing and will continue to bring to both the design of systems and their uses, flexible testbeds for evaluating human-AI teams are needed. It would be advantageous to use these testbeds to examine relevant research questions included throughout this report. The testbeds need to allow for multi-disciplinary interactions and inquiry and include enough real-world data to allow for investigation on the role of uncertainty as it relates to AI blind spots and drift. It would also be useful for testbeds to accommodate the need for routine post-deployment testing, including person-in-the-loop evaluations, anytime meaningful software changes (which need to be defined) are made, or whenever environmental conditions change, which could lead to latent problems.

HUMAN-AI TEAM MEASURES AND METRICS

The establishment of appropriate evaluation measures and metrics is an important element in evaluating human-AI teams (see Chapter 2). Measures typically refer to the measurement scale used for evaluation, and metrics typically refer to the threshold levels on the measurement scale that serve as reference points for evaluation judgments (Hoffman et al., 2018). Multiple types of measures are relevant for evaluating human-AI teams, including individual cognitive process measures, teamwork measures, and outcome performance measures. Although some measures are highly mature, others are just emerging and in need of further study.

Cognitive process measures such as workload and situation awareness have been extensively studied and validated in the context of human-automation interaction (e.g., Endsley and Kaber, 1999) and continue to be relevant for evaluating the cognitive impact of human-AI teaming on human team members (Chen et al., 2018; Mercado et al., 2016) (for reviews of situation awareness and workload measures, see Endsley, 2020b, 2021a; Kramer, 2020; Young et al., 2015; Zhang et al., 2020.)

Because AI systems exhibit complex behavior and, in some cases, provide explanations for their performance, new measures are being developed that are particularly applicable to human-AI teaming. One of the most prominent new measures relates to trust in the AI system. A variety of rating-scale measures of trust have been developed that vary in the number and type of items included, as well as the rating scale used (see Hoffman et al., 2018 for a review of representative measures of trust).

There is growing interest in measuring people's mental models of AI systems to assess their understanding of those systems. There have been a variety of approaches developed to assess mental models of AI systems, including think-aloud protocols, question answering/structured interviews, self-explanation tasks, and prediction tasks that ask people to predict what an AI system will do in various situations (see Hoffman et al., 2018 for a review of representative measures). With the recent emphasis on generating AI systems that are explainable, interest has also emerged in developing measures of explainability. Hoffman et al. (2018) present a questionnaire that can be used to measure people's assessment of explanation satisfaction, which is defined as the degree to which they feel they understand the AI system or process being explained. Sanneman and Shah (2020) propose a measure of explanation quality that is based on the situation awareness global assessment technique (Endsley, 1995a).

Measures of teamwork processes that have been used in all-human teams have been adapted for measuring teamwork in human-AI teams. These teamwork processes include communication, coordination, team situation assessment, team trust, and team resilience. Though scales exist for self-assessment of team process or observer-assessment of team process (Entin and Entin, 2001), there is a growing trend toward measuring teamwork in an unobtrusive manner, in real or near-real time (Cooke and Gorman, 2009; Gorman, Cooke, and Winner, 2006; Huang et al., 2020). These measures rely heavily on communication data, which is readily available from most teams. However, communication flow patterns are used more than communication content. McNeese et al. (2018) found that the communication patterns displayed by the AI system were less proactive than those of human teammates and, over time, the human-AI team's coordination suffered, as even the humans became less proactive in their communication. Physiological measures of teamwork such as neural synchrony have also been used (Stevens, Galloway, and Lamb, 2014); however, these present a challenge in terms of identifying the sensor that is the AI counterpart. Though a challenge, the prospect of collecting sensor data from an AI system that is akin to human physiological signals is, in the committee's judgment, more promising than measuring AI teamwork through survey data.

Another important set of measures for evaluating human-AI teams relates to the objective performance of the human-AI team on specific tasks. Traditionally, outcome measures have included quality of performance and completion time. It is possible that human-AI team performance may be objectively worse than the performance of the human(s) working without AI support (e.g., Layton, Smith, and McCoy, 1994; see Chapter 8 for additional discussion). It is possible that human-AI team performance may be objectively worse than the performance of the human(s) working without AI support (see Chapter 8). Figure 10-4 shows pertinent measures for evaluating human-AI teams, including overall team performance, team knowledge structures, team processes, team efficiency measures, and team sustainability considerations.

The ability of the human-AI team to perform effectively in unanticipated conditions at or beyond the boundaries of the AI system is an important concern in measuring human-AI team outcome performance. This is often measured in terms of out-of-the-loop recovery time (Endsley, 2017; Onnasch et al., 2014). There are also ongoing efforts to develop methods for measuring resilience (Hoffman and Hancock, 2017; Neville, Rosso, and Pires, 2021). More research is needed to provide practical measures and metrics that can be used to assess human-AI team resilience as part of performance-evaluation efforts.

Team Performance
- Quality
  - Decision Making
  - Performance Outcomes
- Time on Task
- Operations Under Failure or Unanticipated Conditions
  - Recovery Time
  - Recovery Quality
  - Resilience
  - Bias Propagation
  - Adaptability
- Safety

Team Sustainability
- Human
  - Job Satisfaction
  - Skill Retention
- System
  - Maintainability & Auditability
  - Vulnerability
  - Suitability

Team Knowledge
- Situation Awareness (Models)
  - Team
  - Shared
- Mental Models
  - Team
  - Shared
- Knowledge
  - Teamwork
  - Taskwork

Team Processes
- Team Situation Awareness Processes
- Team Trust
- Team Distrust
- Teamwork Quality
  - Cohesion
  - Coordination
  - Cooperation
- Communications
- Behaviors

Team Efficiency
- Training Time
- Team Organization Optimality
  - Effectiveness of Resource Utilization
  - Mutual Performance Monitoring
  - Coordination Efficiency
  - Flexibility
  - Time to Resolve Uncertainty (TRU)
- Workload
- System
  - Usability
  - Understandability
  - Predictability
  - Controllability
  - Trustworthiness
  - Responsivity
  - Reliability
  - Robustness
  - Over-Promise Rate (OPR)
  - Bias

FIGURE 10-4 Human-AI team metrics.

Key Challenges and Research Gaps

The committee finds four key gaps related to metrics for human-AI teaming.

- Although emerging measures of trust, mental models, and explanation quality are important additions for evaluation of people's understanding and level of trust in AI systems, there is a growing proliferation of alternative methods for measuring each of these constructs. The reliability and validity of these alternative methods need to be determined.
- The impact of AI systems to bias human performance, resulting in negative impacts, is an important concern. Practical methods for assessing such biases are needed.
- Although there are ongoing efforts to develop measures of the resilience of the human-AI team, these efforts remain in the early stages and more research is needed.
- In real-time measurement of human-AI teams, there is a need to understand the best source of signals from the AI agent, and to be able to interpret human-AI interaction patterns in terms of team state.

Research Needs

The committee recommends addressing the following research objective for improved metrics relevant to human-AI teaming.

Research Objective 10-8: Additional Metrics for Human-AI Teaming. There is a need for more research to establish the reliability and validity of alternative methods for measuring trust, mental models, and explanation quality. Ideally, the research community would converge on a common set of methods for measuring these parameters, to facilitate comparison of results across studies. This research also needs to develop (1) methods to measure the potential bias that AI agents can have on human decision-making processes and overall quality of performance; and (2) methods to measure human-AI team resilience in the face of unanticipated conditions that require adaptation.

AGILE SOFTWARE DEVELOPMENT AND HSI

Agile software processes first emerged more than 20 years ago, with the goal of developing quality software more rapidly, to increase responsiveness to dynamically changing user needs (Dybå and Dingsøyr, 2008). Typically, agile software-development processes occur through multiple short sprints (each on the order of weeks), with the idea of delivering usable software early, followed by the delivery of incremental improvements generated through subsequent sprints. More recently, the trend toward agile software has been extended into software-development operations (DevOps) for more seamless, continuous delivery of quality software (Allspaw and Hammond, 2009; Ebert et al., 2016). DevOps represents a new paradigm with associated tools and processes intended to tighten the loop between software development and operations. The goal is to shorten the cycle time for delivery of software and upgrades as well as enable software to be easily changed during operations (not just prior to deployment).

Agile software-development processes and DevOps have been widely embraced by industry and more recently by government and DOD operations (Sebok, Walters, and Plott, 2017). DOD Instruction 5000.02 lays out policies and procedures for implementing an adaptive acquisition framework to improve acquisition process effectiveness (DOD, 2020). It specifically calls for the use of agile software development, security operations, and lean practices to facilitate rapid and iterative delivery of software capability to the warfighter.

Adopting agile software approaches has many important benefits. Particularly, it results in more rapid delivery to users than has been possible with traditional waterfall-engineering and acquisition approaches. Equally important, the agile software approach allows the software-development process to be more responsive to changing user needs (or changing understanding of user needs). Unlike traditional approaches, requirements need not be fully defined at the start of the program but can emerge while working in collaboration with the user community. These are important attributes of effective software development that were explicitly called for in the National Research Council *Human-System Integration in the System Development Process: A New Look* report (2007) on HSI. Further, agile development approaches make auditability of the software easier.

The committee finds that, although agile approaches to software development have clear benefits, there are also significant challenges that will be particularly relevant to the development of AI systems that can work effectively as teammates with humans. There is growing recognition that the focus on delivering software quickly can incur technical debt. Technical debt refers to design or implementation choices that may be expedient in the short term but may make future changes more costly or impossible (Boodraj, 2020; Kruchten, 2016). A literature review examining causes and consequences of technical debt in agile software development found that, for architecture and design issues, "a lack of understanding of the system being built (requirements), and inadequate test coverage" were among the most cited causes of technical debt (Behutiye et al., 2017, p. 154). The committee acknowledges that technical debt can arise with any software-development approach, including waterfall methods. Our point in raising a concern with respect to technical debt in the case of agile software relates to the specific types of technical debt documented in the literature—most particularly lack of understanding of system requirements and inadequate test coverage. These are precisely the concerns that were expressed in presentations to the committee.

Similar conclusions were drawn from a review of agile development processes used for safety and mission-critical applications (Sebok, Walters, and Plott, 2017). Among the challenges identified in the use of agile methods was the limited opportunity to develop a consistent, coherent vision for the overall system. These researchers recommended including a "sprint 0" that involved more extensive analysis of the demands of the work domain and the needs of the user, as well as development of an integrated design concept to provide a larger, coherent structure to inform later sprints. They also emphasized the need for more holistic verification and validation processes of the larger system, as well as more comprehensive documentation.

These findings highlight that, if not conducted in a thoughtful manner, agile software processes may limit the ability to produce coherent, innovative software solutions that depend on a comprehensive understanding of mission and performance requirements. By emphasizing rapid sprints without the benefit of a big-picture understanding of the larger problem space, there is a real risk of missing important mission requirements or opportunities to dramatically improve performance. The potential to miss mission-critical requirements is a particular concern in MDO, in which there are myriad sources, complexity, constraints, and objectives to be satisfied, and where the evolving concept of operation can result in system deficiencies. The committee acknowledges that completely bug-free and surprise-free software is an unattainable goal, and that missing requirements and failing to anticipate all edge-cases can occur with any software-development approach, not just agile. Our point is the need to develop more effective and efficient approaches for capturing critical system requirements early in the development process. The objective is to impose some upfront, high-level analyses to reduce the chance, of missing important requirements early in the design process that may be much harder, and more expensive, to accommodate later in the design process. This is particularly important in complex systems such as MDO, in which there are many roles, each with interrelated functionality and information needs.

In recognition of these concerns, the Human Readiness Level Scale in the System Development Process (HFES/ANSI 400-2021 standard) has developed guidance for more effectively incorporating HSI approaches into the agile development process that are highly relevant to AI and MDO (Human Factors and Ergonomics Society, 2021). These include the following:

- Agile software should only be applied when "human capabilities and limitations are known and design guidelines for software system are established" (p. 28).
- While, in agile processes, user requirements are typically determined during each sprint for small portions of the system, for complex and safety-critical systems (such as military operations), "more upfront analysis of human performance requirements may be needed" (p. 28).
- "Cross-domain and cross-position information sharing requirements may need more extensive upfront analysis of user needs" (p. 28), which certainly applies to MDO command and control.
- "Graphical user interface design standards must be established and applied consistently across software iterations and design teams, enabled by human factors engineering and user experience style guides" (p. 28). This is especially important for multiple-position operations, such as in MDO command and control.
- Objective and comprehensive testing is required, involving human factors in the development teams, and considering both normal and off-normal events.

The committee recognizes that the HFES/ANSI recommendations represent an ideal that is not always completely achievable. For example, while it is important to strive for objective and comprehensive testing, we recognize that there are no known methods that guarantee complete test coverage or guarantee that all problems will be caught. Nevertheless, this report highlights areas in which more attention is needed to insure that HSI concerns are adequately addressed within an agile development process.

Key Challenges and Research Gaps

The committee finds that best-practice HSI methods are currently not incorporated into the agile development process. This can lead to a failure to systematically gather user performance requirements, develop coherent innovative solutions that support human performance, and conduct comprehensive evaluations to ensure effective performance across a range of normal and off-normal conditions.

Research Needs

The committee recommends following research objective to address the incorporation of HSI into agile software development, particularly as it relates to human-AI teaming and MDO.

Research Objective 10-9: Human-Systems Integration for Agile Software Development. There is a need to develop and validate methods for more effectively integrating human-systems integration (HSI) best practices into the agile software-development process. This may include identifying and building upon success stories in which HSI analyses have been successfully inserted into agile processes, as well as developing and testing new approaches for incorporating HSI activities into agile development processes as called for in HFES/ANSI 400. HSI standards, tools, and methodologies need to be explicitly incorporated into agile software-development processes for AI and multi-domain operations.

SUMMARY

The development of AI systems that can work effectively with humans depends on meeting a number of new requirements for successful human-AI interaction. A reliance on good HSI practices is essential, as is improving analyses, metrics, methods, and testing capabilities, to meet new challenges. A focus on testing, evaluation, verification, and validation of AI systems across their lifespans will be needed, along with AI maintenance teams that can take on relevant upkeep and certification processes. Further, HSI will need to be better integrated into agile software-development processes, to make these processes suitable for addressing the complexity and high-consequence nature of military operations. The committee believes that all these suggestions should be applied to the development of AI systems.

The committee also suggests that the AFRL put into place best practices for AI system development based on existing HSI practice guidelines and current research. These include the following:

- Adopting DOD HSI practices in development and evaluation;
- Adopting human readiness levels in evaluating and communicating the maturity of AI systems;
- Conducting human-centered, context-of-use research and evaluations, prior to and alongside more formal technical performance evaluations;
- Including a focus on systems engineering of human-AI teams within the USAF HSI program;
- Establishing an AI maintenance workforce;
- Establishing an AI TEVV capability that can address human use of AI, and that would feed into existing development and operational test efforts;
- Documenting and assessing the data and models used in developing AI systems to reveal possible biases and concept drift;
- Continuing to monitor performance of the human-AI team after implementation and throughout the lifecycle, to identify any bias or concept drift that may emerge from changes to the environment, the human, or the AI system;
- Incorporating and analyzing real-time audit logs of system performance failures throughout the lifecycle of an AI system, to identify and correct performance deficiencies; and
- Assessing the state-of-the-art in agile software-development practices in the DOD and in industry, and developing recommendations for more effective processes for incorporating agile software methods into the DOD HSI and acquisition process.

11

Conclusions

The introduction of AI into advanced command and control systems brings with it many challenges, not least of which will be the development of reliable and robust technology capable of high levels of performance within the highly complex, variable, and changing scenarios common for peacekeeping and warfare operations. Further, the challenges of cyber attacks and more subtle information attacks may offer new pathways for adversarial actions against AI systems. Nonetheless, there is a likelihood that the military may begin to adopt AI systems, at least for limited applications, in the foreseeable future.

In keeping with DOD directives and ethical considerations, as well as in attempt to ensure that AI systems operate in a manner that is safe and consistent with military objectives, there will be a need for people to direct and oversee the operations of AI systems. However, decades of research have shown that people often struggle to perform this role adequately, due to both cognitive limitations (e.g., poor vigilance in monitoring, inappropriate levels of trust) and inadequate design of the technology (e.g., inadequate transparency, system designs that create low engagement levels or bias human decision making). It is imperative that AI systems be designed to support the needs of the warfighters who will have the ultimate responsibility for successful mission execution.

As AI is developed to provide more intelligent behaviors, there will be an increased need for AI systems to function effectively as teammates with humans. Just as human-only teams have many advantages over people working alone (e.g., the ability to spread work to manage workload fluctuations, the provision of diverse skills, knowledge, and capabilities toward the completion of common goals, and the ability to compensate for deficiencies or challenges faced by individuals) human-AI teams can have similar benefits. When considering an AI system as a part of a team, rather than simply a tool capable of limited actions, the need for a framework for improving the design of AI systems to enhance the overall success of human-AI teams becomes apparent. A failure to consider the needs of the many airmen, soldiers, seamen, guardians, and marines who are responsible for successful military operations will result in AI technologies that ultimately fail to provide the necessary high levels of performance and may instead cause harm.

The design of AI systems for human-AI teams needs to incorporate several highly interrelated considerations. These include designing the AI system to support not only taskwork, but also teamwork. AI systems capable of communication, coordination, cooperation, social intelligence, and human-AI language exchange will be needed. In addition, there will be a need to support ongoing shared situation awareness (SA) between humans and AI teammates, including SA of the environment, SA of the broader system and context, SA of each other's tasks, and SA of one's own and each other's performance or state. SA includes the need to maintain a representation and alignment of changing goals, functional assignments, tasks, plans, and actions across the distributed team.

Improved methods for supporting trust assessment are needed that consider the situational factors that inform humans of when it is appropriate to rely on an AI system (allowing attention to be shifted to other tasks) and when to be less reliant or to intervene. The effects of directability, transparency, and explainability on evolving trust and cooperation need to be further explored. Issues of both distrust and trust are important, as is an understanding of how trust evolves over time, trust repair, and how trust is affected by changing goals within the team. Further, a consideration of trust and SA within multi-echelon, distributed, and ad hoc networks of teams, potentially with multiple AI systems, presents new challenges that need to be addressed.

A key means of providing the needed SA and trust to support effective human-AI teaming is the development of AI systems with high levels of transparency and explainability, without information overload. Transparent, explainable AI systems are required to support decision making, often in time-critical situations. Potential challenges, such as bias or brittleness in AI system capabilities, multiple AI systems that each work differently, and AI systems that learn and change over time, accentuate the need for high levels of real-time transparency and explainability. Humans cannot function effectively with AI systems in the absence of the ability to accurately understand and project the behavior of the AI systems.

Training of the human-AI team as a unit will also become increasingly important. Training is essential for building accurate mental models of an AI system to support SA and trust, and for forming accurate expectations regarding teamwork behaviors. While training will need to include formal instruction, it will also increasingly need to rely on simulated, structured practice scenarios in which perturbations, edge cases, and novel events can be introduced. Opportunities for training and for observing AI system transparency prior to mission events (e.g., during planning, pre-mission briefings) or after mission events (e.g., during debriefing, after-action reviews) would also benefit from exploration, as these opportunities use periods of lower workload to provide high levels of relevant context. Considerable research is needed to determine effective methods for training human-AI teams. New research can leverage current knowledge on training in all-human teams, but also needs to extend beyond human-human team research to address the unique challenges associated with establishing appropriate expectations for human-AI interaction and trust.

Central human-AI interaction design decisions, such as the distribution of responsibilities within the team (i.e., the level of automation) and the ways in which those responsibilities shift over time (i.e., flexible autonomy), have significant impacts on human workload, SA, and the overall success of the team in both routine and novel situations. Methods for supporting the smooth functioning of the team, such as Playbook or goal-based interaction, provide potential opportunities, but more research is needed to predict how design decisions affect emergent behaviors, skill retention, training requirements, job satisfaction, and overall human-AI team resilience. Research is also needed to develop predictive models of human-AI performance. AI system responsivity and directability may also provide methods for improving levels of trust, via system interaction design.

Several significant challenges exist for successful AI system development. These include detecting and preventing information attacks and the systematic bias that can undermine AI system performance and negatively affect human decision making. AI systems with robust situation models and causal models will be needed for decision making. The challenges of maintaining SA in high-speed, on-the-loop operations are significant and will require new breakthroughs in information presentation and AI system capabilities.

AI may also be beneficial in directly supporting the performance of team operations, including detecting and mitigating human biases and customizing AI system behaviors to adapt to the needs of its teammates. It would also be beneficial to explore the potential role of an AI system as a coordinator, orchestrator, or human-resource manager. Two-way communication between humans and AI systems may be important to consider, including the need to provide the AI system with explanations from humans, or to transmit information on human goals or states to the AI system.

Good human-systems integration systems and practices underpin the ability of the USAF to address these various research-and-development goals. To support the development of AI systems that work effectively as a part of human-AI teams, improved methods for setting system requirements and analysis, design, and evaluation of human-AI team performance will be needed. These requirements are particularly important for systems developed via agile software-development processes, which need detailed safeguards for effectively incorporating human-systems integration best practices. An increased emphasis on interdisciplinary research-and-development teams is needed, along with research on workforce skillsets, tools, methodologies, and policies for new AI maintenance teams, and cyber detection and response teams. Methods, processes, and systems for testing, evaluation, verification, and validation of AI systems across their lifespans are needed, particularly with respect to AI blind spots and edge cases, as well as managing the potential for software drift over time, supported by robust human-AI testbeds.

This report establishes a number of interrelated research objectives for meeting these needs. Table 11-1 provides a summary of these research objectives, aligned along near- (1–5 years), mid- (6–10 years) and far-term (11–15 years) objectives, with the most immediately accessible and foundational needs listed as near-term objectives and more advanced goals listed as mid- or far-term objectives. Because these objectives are all important for the development of AI systems that will work effectively with people in future military operations, it is not possible to fully prioritize them.

Taken together, this integrated set of research priorities will help to achieve significant advances in human-AI teaming competence. These priorities are fundamental prerequisites to the safe introduction of AI systems into critical situations such as multi-domain operations.

TABLE 11-1 Summary of Human-AI Teaming Research Objectives Aligned Along Near-, Mid-, and Far-Term Objectives

	Near-Term (1–5 years)	Mid-Term (6–10 years)	Far-Term (11–15 years)
Team Effectiveness	2-1: Human-AI Team Effectiveness Metrics		
		2-2: AI Uncertainty Resolution	
		2-3: AI Over-Promise Rate	
		2-4: Human-AI Team Models	
Team Processes	3-1: Human-AI Teamwork Skills in MDO		
		3-2: Support for Human-AI Teaming in MDO	
Situation Awareness	4-1: Team SA in MDO		
	4-2: Resilience of SA to Information Attack		
	4-3: Human SA of AI Systems		
	4-4: Shared SA in Human-AI Teams		
	4-5: AI Awareness of Human Teammate		
			4-6: AI Self-Awareness
		4-7: AI Situation and Task Models	

continued

TABLE 11-1 Continued

	Near-Term (1–5 years)	Mid-Term (6–10 years)	Far-Term (11–15 years)
Transparency and Explainability	5-1: Transparency Information Requirements		
	5-2: Transparency Display Methods		
	5-3: Transparency Temporality		
		5-4: Transparency of Machine Learning-Based AI in MDO	
	5-5: Explainability and Trust		
		5-6: Adaptive (and Adaptable) Explainability	
		5-7: Explainability of Learned Information and Change	
		5-8: Machine Personae and Explanations	
			5-9: Machine Benefits from Human Explanations
Interaction	6-1: Human-AI Team Task Sharing		
		6-2: On-the-Loop Control	
			6-3: Multiple LOA Systems
	6-4: Flexible Autonomy Transition Support		
	6-5: Support for Flexible Autonomy		
	6-6: GOC and AI Transparency		
		6-7: Playbook Extensions for Human-AI Teaming	
	6-8: Human-AI Team Emergent Behaviors		
		6-9: Human-AI Team Interaction Design	
Trust	7-1: Effects of Situations and Goals on Trust		
	7-2: Effects of Directability on Trust		
	7-3: Cooperation as a Measure of Trust		
	7-4: Investigations of Distrust		
		7-5: Dynamic Models of Trust Evolution	
			7-6: Trust Evolution in Multi-Echelon Networks

TABLE 11-1 Continued

	Near-Term (1–5 years)	Mid-Term (6–10 years)	Far-Term (11–15 years)
Human and AI Bias	8-1: Human-AI Partnership in Continuous Learning Environments		
		8-2: Adversarial Effects on Human-AI Team Biases	
		8-3: Biases from Small Datasets and Sparse Data	
	8-4: Inductive and Emerging Human Biases		
			8-5: Preventative Detection and Mitigation of Human-AI Team Biases in Learning Systems
Training	9-1: Developing Human-Centered Human-AI Team-Training Content		
	9-2: Testing and Validating Traditional Team Training Methods to Inform New Methods		
		9.3: Training to Calibrate Human Expectations of Autonomous Teammates	
	9-4: Designing Platforms for Human-AI Team Training		
		9-5: Adaptive Training Materials Based on Differing Team Compositions and Sizes	
		9-6: Training That Works Toward Trust in Human-AI Teaming	
HSI Processes, Measures, and Testing	10-1: Human-AI Team Design and Testing Methods		
		10-2: Human-AI Team Requirements	
	10-3: Human-AI Team Development Teams		
		10-4: AI System Lifecycle Testing and Auditability	
		10-5: AI Cyber Vulnerabilities	
		10-6: Testing of Evolving AI Systems	
	10-7: Human-AI Team Testbeds		
	10-8: Additional Metrics for Human-AI Teaming		
	10-9: HSI for Agile Software Development		

References

Abrahamsson, P., Salo, O., Ronkainen, J., and Warsta, J. 2017. Agile software development methods: Review and analysis. *arXiv*:1709.08439.

Achille, L.B., Gladwell Schulze, K., and Schimdt-Nielsen, A. 1995. An analysis of communication and use of military terms in Navy team training. *Military Psychology, 7*(2), 95–107. doi: 10.1207/s15327876mp0702_4.

Ackerman, E., and Stavridis, J. 2021. *2034: A Novel of the Next World War*. London: Penguin Press.

Adams, M.J., Tenney, Y.J., and Pew, R.W. 1995. Situation awareness and the cognitive management of complex systems. *Human Factors, 37*(1), 85–104.

Air Force Scientific Advisory Board. 2004. Human-System Integration in Air Force Weapon Development and Acquisition. Available: https://www.scientificadvisoryboard.af.mil/Studies/.

Ajzen, I., and Fishbein, M. 1980. *Understanding Attitudes and Predicting Social Behavior*. Englewood Cliffs, NJ: Prentice Hall.

Akhtar, N., and Mian, A. 2018. Threat of adversarial attacks on deep learning in computer vision: A survey. *IEEE Access, 6*, 14410–14430.

Alcorn, M.A., Li, Q., Gong, Z., Wang, C., Mai, L., Ku, W.-S., and Nguyen, A. 2019. Strike (With) A Pose: Neural Networks Are Easily Fooled by Strange Poses of Familiar Objects. *Proceedings of the IEEE/CVF Conference on Computer Vision and Pattern Recognition*, pp. 4845–4854.

Alliger, G.M., Beard, R., Bennett Jr., W., Colegrove, C.M., and Garrity, M. 2007. Understanding Mission Essential Competencies as a Job Analytic Method. Pp. 603–624 in *The Handbook of Work Analysis: Methods, Systems, Applications and Science of Work Measurement in Organizations* (M.A. Wilson, W. Bennett Jr., S.G. Gibson, and G.M. Alliger, eds.). New York: Routledge Taylor & Francis Group.

Allspaw, J. 2016. Human Factors and Ergonomics Practice in Web Engineering and Operations: Navigating a Critical Yet Opaque Sea of Automation in *Human Factors and Ergonomics in Practice: Improving System Performance and Human Well-Being in the Real World*. London: CRC Press. doi: 10.1201/9781315587332-26.

Allspaw, J. 2012. Fault injection in production: Making the case for resilience testing. *Queue, 10*(8), 30–35. doi: 10.1145/2346916.2353017.

Allspaw, J., and Hammond, P. 2009. 10+ deploys per day: Dev and ops cooperation at Flickr. Available: https://www.slideshare.net/jallspaw/10-deploys-per-day-dev-and-ops-cooperation-at-flickr/.

Amershi, S., Weld, D., Vorvoreanu, M., Fourney, A., Nushi, B., Collisson, P., Suh, J., Iqbal, S., Bennett, P.N., Inkpen, K., Teevan, J., Kikin-Gil, R., and Horvitz, E. 2019. Guidelines for Human-AI interaction. *Proceedings of the 2019 CHI Conference on Human Factors in Computing Systems*, Glasgow, Scotland, pp. 1–13. doi: 10.1145/3290605.3300233.

Ananny, M., and Crawford, K. 2016. Seeing without knowing: Limitations of the transparency ideal and its application to algorithmic accountability. *New Media and Society, 20*(3), 1–17. doi: 10.1177/1461444816676645.

Arrieta, A.B., Díaz-Rodríguez, N., Del Ser, J., Bennetot, A., Tabik, S., Barbado, A., Garciag, A., Gil-Lopeza, S., Molinag, D., Benjaminsh, R., Chatilaf, R., and Herrera, F. 2020. Explainable artificial intelligence (XAI): Concepts, taxonomies, opportunities and challenges toward responsible AI. *Information Fusion, 58*, 82–115.

Bagheri, N., and Jamieson, G.A. 2004. The Impact of Context-Related Reliability on Automation Failure Detection and Scanning Behaviour. *2004 IEEE International Conference on Systems, Man and Cybernetics* (IEEE Cat. No. 04CH37583), vol. 1, 212–217.

Bailey, N.R., Scerbo, M.W., Freeman, F.G., Mikulka, P.J., and Scott, L.A. 2003. A brain-based adaptive automation system and situation awareness: The role of complacency potential. *Proceedings of the Human Factors and Ergonomics Society Annual Meeting, 47*(9), 1048–1052.

Bainbridge, L. 1983. Ironies of automation. *Automatica, 19,* 775–779.

Banbury, S., Selcon, S., Endsley, M., Gorton, T., and Tatlock, K. 1998. Being certain about uncertainty: How the representation of system reliability affects pilot decision making. *Proceedings of the Human Factors and Ergonomics Society Annual Meeting, 42*(1), 36–39.

Barnes, C.M., and Van Dyne, L. 2009. I'm tired: Differential effects of physical and emotional fatigue on workload management strategies. *Human Relations, 62*(1), 59–92.

Bass, E.J., Baumgart, L.A., and Shepley, K.K. 2013. The effect of information analysis automation display content on human judgment performance in noisy environments. *Journal of Cognitive Engineering and Decision Making, 7*(1), 49–65.

Bean, N.H., Rice, S.C., and Keller, M.D. 2011. The effect of gestalt psychology on the system-wide trust strategy in automation. *Proceedings of the Human Factors and Ergonomics Society Annual Meeting, 55*(1), 1417–1421.

Beck, H.P., Dzindolet, M.T., and Pierce, L.G. 2007. Automation usage decisions: Controlling intent and appraisal errors in a target detection task. *Human Factors, 49*(3), 429–437.

Beck, K., Beedle, M., van Bennekum, A., Cockburn, A., Cunningham, W., Fowler, M., Grenning, J., Highsmith, J., Hunt, A., Jeffries, R., Kern, J., Marick, B., Martin, R., Mellor, S., Schwaber, K., Sutherland, J., and Thomas, D. 2001. *Manifesto for Agile Software Development.* Available: http://AgileManifesto.org.

Beede, E., Baylor, E., Hersch, F., Iurchenko, A., Wilcox, L., Ruamviboonsuk, P., and Vardoulakis, L. 2020. A Human-Centered Evaluation of a Deep Learning System Deployed in Clinics for the Detection of Diabetic Retinopathy. *Proceedings of the 2020 CHI Conference on Human Factors in Computing Systems*, April 25–30, Honolulu, HI, pp. 1–12.

Behutiye, W.N., Rodríguez, P., Oivo, M., and Tosun, A. 2017. Analyzing the concept of technical debt in the context of agile software development: A systematic literature review. *Information and Software Technology, 82,* 139–158.

Bennett, W., Alliger, G.M., Colegrove, C.M., Garrity, M.J., and Beard, R.M. 2017. Mission Essential Competencies: A Novel Approach to Proficiency-Based Live, Virtual, and Constructive Readiness Training and Assessment. Pp. 47–62 in *Fundamental Issues in Defense Training and Simulation*. Boca Raton, FL: CRC Press.

Behymer, K., Rothwell, C., Ruff, H., Patzek, M., Calhoun, G., Draper, M., Douglass, S., and Lange, D. 2017. *Initial Evaluation of the Intelligent Multi-UxV Planner with Adaptive Collaborative/Control Technologies (IMPACT)*. Beavercreek, OH: Infoscitex Corp.

Bhatt, U., Xiang, A., Sharma, S., Weller, A., Taly, A., Jia, Y., Ghosh, J., Puri, R., Moura, J., and Eckersley, P. 2020. Explainable Machine Learning in Deployment. *Proceedings of the 2020 Conference on Fairness, Accountability, and Transparency*, pp. 648–657.

Bhatti, S., Demir, M., Cooke, N.J., and Johnson, C.J. 2021. Assessing Communication and Trust in an AI Teammate in a Dynamic Task Environment. *2021 IEEE 2nd International Conference on Human-Machine Systems (ICHMS)*, pp. 1–6, doi: 10.1109/ICHMS53169.2021.9582626.

Bisantz, A., and Roth, E.M. 2008. Analysis of Cognitive Work. Pp. 1–43 in *Reviews of Human Factors and Ergonomics,* vol. 3 (D.A. Boehm-Davis, ed.). Santa Monica, CA: Human Factors and Ergonomics Society.

Blaha, L.M., Bos, N., Fallon, C.K., Gonzalez, C., and Gutzwiller, R.S. 2019. Opportunities and challenges for human-machine teaming in cybersecurity operations. *Proceedings of the Human Factors and Ergonomic Society Annual Meeting, 63*(1), 442–446.

Blasch, E., Sung, J., and Nguyen, T. 2020. Multisource AI Scorecard Table for System Evaluation. *AAAI FSS-20: Artificial Intelligence in Government and Public Sector,* Washington, DC.

Boardman, M., and Butcher, F. 2019. *An Exploration of Maintaining Human Control in AI Enabled Systems and the Challenges of Achieving It*. Brussels: North Atlantic Treaty Organization Science and Technology Organization.

Boehm-Davis, D.A., Durso, F.T., and Lee, J.D. 2015. *APA Handbook of Human Systems Integration*. Washington DC: American Psychological Association.

Bolstad, C.A., and Endsley, M.R. 1999. Shared mental models and shared displays: An empirical evaluation of team performance. *Proceedings of the Human Factors and Ergonomics Society Annual Meeting, 43*(3), 213–217.

Bolstad, C.A., and Endsley, M.R. 2000. The effect of task load and shared displays on team situation awareness. *14th Triennial Congress of the International Ergonomics Association* and *Proceedings of the Human Factors and Ergonomics Society Annual Meeting, 44*(1), 189–192.

Bolstad, C.A., Riley, J.M., Jones, D.G., and Endsley, M.R. 2002. Using goal directed task analysis with Army brigade officer teams. *Proceedings of the Human Factors and Ergonomics Society Annual Meeting, 46*(3), 472–476.

Bonney, L., Davis-Sramek, B., and Cadotte, E.R. 2016. "Thinking" about business markets: A cognitive assessment of market awareness. *Journal of Business Research, 69*(8), 2641–2648.

Boodraj, M. 2020. Managing technical debt in agile software development projects. Dissertation, Georgia State University. Available: https://scholarworks.gsu.edu/cis_diss/77.

Boyce, M.W., Chen, J.Y., Selkowitz, A.R., and Lakhmani, S.G. 2015. Effects of Agent Transparency on Operator Trust. *Proceedings of the Tenth Annual ACM/IEEE International Conference on Human-Robot Interaction Extended Abstracts*, Portland, Oregon, pp. 179–180.

Bradshaw, J.M., Hoffman, R.R., Woods, D.D., and Johnson, M. 2013. The seven deadly myths of autonomous systems. *IEEE Intelligent Systems, 28*(3), 54–61.

Brandon, D.P., and Hollingshead, A.B. 2004. Transactive memory systems in organizations: Matching tasks, expertise, and people. *Organization Science, 15*(6), 633–644.

Brandt, S.L., Lachter, J., Russell, R., and Shively, R.J. 2017. A Human-Autonomy Teaming Approach for a Flight-Following Task. Pp. 12–22 in Advances in Neuroergonomics and Cognitive Engineering, AHFE 2017. *Advances in Intelligent Systems and Computing*, vol. 586. Springer, Cham.

Brown, P., and Levinson, S.C. 1987. *Politeness: Some Universals in Language Usage*, vol. 4. Cambridge: Cambridge University Press.

Bryson, J.J., and Theodorou, A. 2019. How Society Can Maintain Human-Centric Artificial Intelligence. Pp. 305–323 in *Human-Centered Digitalization and Services*, vol. 19. Singapore: Springer. doi: 10.1007/978-981-13-7725-9_16.

Buchanan, B., and Shortliffe, E. 1984. *Rule-Based Expert Systems: The MYCIN Experiments of the Stanford Heuristic Programming Project*. Boston, MA: Addison-Wesley.

Buchler, N., Rajivan, P., Marusich, L.R., Lightner, L., and Gonzalez, C. 2018. Sociometrics and observational assessment of teaming and leadership in a cyber security defense competition. *Computers and Security, 73*, 114–136. doi: 10.1016/j.cose.2017.10.013.

Burdick, M.D., and Shively, R.J. 2000. Evaluation of a Computation Model of Situational Awareness. *Proceedings of the Joint IEA 14th Triennial Congress and Human Factors and Ergonomics Society 44th Annual Meeting, 44*(1), 109–112.

Burkart, N., and Huber, M.F. 2021. A survey on the explainability of supervised machine learning. *Journal of Artificial Intelligence Research, 70*, 245–317.

Burke, J.L., Murphy, R.R., Coovert, M.D., and Riddle, D.L. 2004. Moonlight in Miami: Field study of human-robot interaction in the context of an urban search and rescue disaster response training exercise. *Human–Computer Interaction, 19*(1–2), 85–116.

Burns, C.M., Bryant, D.J., and Chalmers, B.A. 2005. Boundary, purpose, and values in work-domain models: Models of naval command and control. *IEEE Transactions on Systems, Man, and Cybernetics-Part A: Systems and Humans, 35*(5), 603–616.

Bussone, A., Stumpf, S., and O'Sullivan, D. 2015. The Role of Explanations on Trust and Reliance in Clinical Decision Support Systems. *2015 International Conference on Healthcare Informatics*, pp. 160–169.

Caldwell, B. 2005. Multi-team dynamics and distributed expertise in mission operations. *Aviation, Space, and Environmental Medicine, 76*, 145–153.

Caldwell, B.S., and Onken, J.D. 2011. Modeling and Analyzing Distributed Autonomy for Spaceflight Teams. *41st International Conference on Environmental Systems*, Portland, OR. doi: 10.2514/6.2011-5135.

Caldwell, B.S., and Wang, E. 2009. Delays and user performance in human-computer-network interaction tasks. *Human Factors, 51*(6), 813–830.

Caldwell, B.S., Palmer III, R.C., and Cuevas, H.M., 2008. Information alignment and task coordination in organizations: An 'information clutch' metaphor. *Information Systems Management, 25*(1), 33–44.

Calhoun, G. 2021. Adaptable (not adaptive) automation: The forefront of human–automation teaming. *Human Factors*, 00187208211037457.

Cannon-Bowers, J.A., Salas, E., and Converse, S. 1993. Shared Mental Models in Expert Team Decision Making. Pp. 221–246 in *Current Issues in Individual and Group Decision Making* (J. Castellan Jr., ed.). Hillsdale, NJ: Lawrence Erlbaum.

Canonico, L.B., Flathmann, C., and McNeese, N. 2019. Collectively intelligent teams: Integrating team cognition, collective intelligence, and AI for future teaming. *Proceedings of the Human Factors and Ergonomics Society Annual Meeting*, 63(1), 1466–1470.

Carroll, M., Shah, R., Ho, M.K., Griffiths, T., Seshia, S., Abbeel, P., and Dragan, A. 2019. On the utility of learning about humans for human-AI coordination. *Advances in Neural Information Processing Systems, 32*, 5174–5185.

Carvalho, D.V., Pereira, E.M., and Cardoso, J.S. 2019. Machine learning interpretability: A survey on methods and metrics. *Electronics, 8*(8), 832.

Case, N. 2018. How to become a centaur. *Journal of Design and Science*. doi: 10.21428/61b2215c.

Casner, S.M., Geven, R.W., Recker, M.P., and Schooler, J.W. 2014. The retention of manual flying skills in the automated cockpit. *Human Factors, 56*(8), 1506–1516.

Chakraborti, T., Kambhampati, S., Scheutz, M., and Zhang, Y. 2017a. AI challenges in human-robot cognitive teaming. *arXiv*:1707.04775.

Chakraborti, T., Sreedharan, S., Zhang, Y., and Kambhampati, S. 2017b. Plan Explanations as Model Reconciliation: Moving Beyond Explanation as Soliloquy. Pp. 156–163 in *Proceedings of the International Joint Conference on Artificial Intelligence*, New York, NY: IEEE.

Chandler, S. 2020. How Explainable AI Is Helping Algorithms Avoid Bias. *Forbes*, February 18. Available: https://www.forbes.com/sites/simonchandler/2020/02/18/how-explainable-ai-is-helping-algorithms-avoid-bias/#4c16d79e5ed3.

Chella, A., Pipitone, A., Morin, A., and Racy, F. 2020. Developing self-awareness in robots via inner speech. *Frontiers in Robotics and AI, 7*, 16.

Chen, J.Y.C., and Barnes, M.J. 2015. Agent Transparency for Human-Agent Teaming Effectiveness. *2015 IEEE International Conference on Systems, Man, and Cybernetics*, pp. 1381–1385.

Chen, J.Y.C., Lakhmani, S.G., Stowers, K., Selkowitz, A.R., Wright, J.L., and Barnes, M. 2018. Situation awareness-based agent transparency and human-autonomy teaming effectiveness. *Theoretical Issues in Ergonomics Science, 19*(3), 259–282. doi: 10.1080/1463922X.2017.1315750.

Chen, J.Y.C., Procci, K., Boyce, M., Wright, J., Garcia, A., and Barnes, M. 2014a. *Situation Awareness-Based Agent Transparency*. Aberdeen Proving Ground, MD: Army Research Laboratory. Available: https://apps.dtic.mil/sti/pdfs/ADA600351.pdf.

Chen, T.B., Campbell, D., Gonzalez, F., and Coppin, G. 2014b. The Effect of Autonomy Transparency in Human-Robot Interactions: A Preliminary Study on Operator Cognitive Workload and Situation Awareness in Multiple Heterogeneous UAV Management. *Proceedings of the Australasian Conference on Robotics and Automation*, December 2–4, Melbourne, Australia.

Childers, T.L., Houston, M.J., and Heckler, S.E. 1985. Measurement of individual differences in visual versus verbal information processing. *Journal of Consumer Research, 12*(2), 125–134.

Chiou, E.K., and Lee, J.D. 2021. Trusting automation: Designing for responsivity and resilience. *Human Factors: The Journal of the Human Factors and Ergonomic Society,* online April 27. doi: 10.1177/00187208211009995.

Clark, H.H., and Schaefer, E.F. 1989. Contributing to discourse. *Cognitive Science, 13*, 259–294.

Cockburn, A. 2002. *Agile Software Development*. Boston, MA: Addison-Wesley.

Cook, B. 2021. The future of artificial intelligence in ISR Operations. *Air and Space Power Journal* (Summer), 41–55. Available: https://www.airuniversity.af.edu/Portals/10/ASPJ/journals/Volume-35_Special_Issue/F-Cook.pdf.

Cooke, N.J. 2018. 5 ways to help robots work together with people. *The Conversation*. Available: https://theconversation.com/5-ways-to-help-robots-work-together-with-people-101419.

Cooke, N.J., and Gorman, J.C. 2009. Interaction-based measures of cognitive systems. *Journal of Cognitive Engineering and Decision Making: Special Section on: Integrating Cognitive Engineering in the Systems Engineering Process: Opportunities, Challenges and Emerging Approaches 3*, 27–46.

Cooke, N.J., Gorman, J.C., Duran, J.L., and Taylor, A.R. 2007. Team cognition in experienced command-and-control teams. *Journal of Experimental Psychology: Applied, 13*(3), 146.

Cooke, N.J., Gorman, J.C., Myers, C.W., and Duran, J.L. 2013. Interactive team cognition. *Cognitive Science, 37*(2), 255–285.

Cooke, N.J., Kiekel, P.A., and Helm, E.E. 2001. Measuring team knowledge during skill acquisition of a complex task. *International Journal of Cognitive Ergonomics, 5*(3), 297–315.

Coolen, E., Draaisma, J., and Loeffen, J. 2019. Measuring situation awareness and team effectiveness in pediatric acute care by using the situation global assessment technique. *European Journal of Pediatrics, 178*(6), 837–850.

Coovert, M.D., Miller, E.E.P, and Bennett, W., Jr. 2017. Assessing trust and effectiveness in virtual teams: Latent growth curve and latent change score models. *Social Sciences, 6*(3), 87.

Copeland, B.J. 2021. Artificial Intelligence. Available: https://www.britannica.com/technology/artificial-intelligence.

Cowie, R., Cox, C., Martin, J.-C., Batliner, A., Heylen, D.K.J., and Karpouzis, K. 2011. Issues in Data Labelling. Pp. 213–241 in *Emotion-Oriented Systems: The Humaine Handbook* (P. Petta, C. Pelachaud, C. Roddy, eds.), Berlin, Heidelberg: Springer-Verglag.

Crandall, B., Klein, G., and Hoffman, R.R. 2006. *Working Minds: A Practitioner's Guide to Cognitive Task Analysis.* Cambridge, MA: MIT Press.

Cranford, E.A., Gonzalez, C., Aggarwal, P., Cooney, S., Tambe, M., and Lebiere, C. 2020. Toward personalized deceptive signaling for cyber defense using cognitive models. *Topics in Cognitive Science, 12*(3), 992–1011.

Cranford, E.A., Gonzalez, C., Aggarwal, P., Tambe, M., Cooney, S., and Lebiere, C. 2021. Towards a cognitive theory of cyber deception. *Cognitive Science, 45*(7), e13013.

Crozier, M.S., Ting, H.Y., Boone, D.C., O'Regan, N.B., Bandrauk, N., Furey, A., Squires, C., Hapgood, J., and Hogan, M.P. 2015. Use of human patient simulation and validation of the Team Situation Awareness Global Assessment Technique (TSAGAT): A multidisciplinary team assessment tool in trauma education. *Journal of Surgical Education, 72*(1), 156–163.

CRS (Congressional Research Service). 2020. *Defense Primer: U.S. Policy on Lethal Autonomous Weapon Systems.* Washington, DC: Congressional Research Service. Available: https://sgp.fas.org/crs/natsec/IF11150.pdf.

Cuevas, H.M., Fiore, S.M., Caldwell, B.S., and Strater, L. 2007. Augmenting team cognition in human-automation teams performing in complex operational environments. *Aviation, Space, and Environmental Medicine, 78*(5, Supp. Section II), B63–70.

Cummings, M.L. 2004. Automation Bias in Intelligent Time Critical Decision Support Systems. *AIAA 3rd Intelligent Systems Conference*, Chicago, IL.

Cummings, M.L. 2019. Lethal autonomous weapons: Meaningful human control or meaningful human certification?" *IEEE Technology & Society 38*(10), 20–26.

Cummings, M.L. 2021. Rethinking the maturity of artificial intelligence in safety-critical settings. *Artificial Intelligence Magazine, 42*(1), 6–15.

Cummings, M.L., and Guerlain, S. 2007. Developing operator capacity estimates for supervisory control of autonomous vehicles. *Human Factors, 49*(1), 1–15.

Cummings, M.L., and Li, S. 2021a. Sources of subjectivity in machine learning models. *ACM Journal of Data and Information Quality,* 13(2), 1–9.

Cummings, M.L., and Li, S. 2021b. Subjectivity in the creation of machine learning models. *Journal of Data and Information Quality,* 13(2), 1–19. doi: 10.1145/3418034.

Cummings, M.L., How, J.P., Whitten, A., and Toupet, O. 2011. The impact of human–automation collaboration in decentralized multiple unmanned vehicle control. *Proceedings of the IEEE, 100*(3), 660–671.

Cummings, M.L., Li, S., and Zhu, H. 2022. Modeling operator self-assessment in human-autonomy teaming settings. *International Journal of Human-Computer Studies, 157.* doi: 10/gngrwc.

Dadashi, N., Stedmon, A.W., and Pridmore, T.P. 2013. Semi-automated CCTV surveillance: The effects of system confidence, system accuracy and task complexity on operator vigilance, reliance and workload. *Applied Ergonomics, 44*(5), 730–738.

Daugherty, P.R., and Wilson, H.J. 2018. *Human + Machine: Reimagining Work in the Age of AI.* Cambridge, MA: Harvard Business Press.

Dautenhahn, K. 2007. A Paradigm Shift in Artificial Intelligence: Why Social Intelligence Matters in the Design and Development of Robots with Human-Like Intelligence. Pp 288–302 in *50 Years of Artificial Intelligence.* Berlin, Heidelberg: Springer-Verlag.

Davis, E., and Marcus, G. 2016. The scope and limits of simulation in automated reasoning. *Artificial Intelligence, 233,* 60–72.

Davis, F.D., Bagozzi, R.P., and Warshaw, P.R. 1989. User acceptance of computer technology: A comparison of two theoretical models. *Management Science, 35*(8), 903–1028.

de Visser, E., and Parasuraman, R. 2011. Adaptive aiding of human-robot teaming: Effects of imperfect automation on performance, trust, and workload. *Journal of Cognitive Engineering and Decision Making, 5*(2), 209–231.

de Visser, E.J., Pak, R., and Shaw, T.H. 2018. From 'automation' to 'autonomy': The importance of trust repair in human–machine interaction. *Ergonomics, 61*(10), 1409–1427.

de Weck, O.L., Roos, D., Magee, C.L, and Vest, C.M. 2011. Life-Cycle Properties of Engineering Systems: The Ilities. Pp. 65–96 in *Engineering Systems: Meeting Human Needs in a Complex Technological World.* Cambridge, MA: MIT Press.

DeChurch, L.A., and Mesmer-Magnus, J.R. 2010. The cognitive underpinnings of effective teamwork: A meta-analysis. *Journal of Applied Psychology, 95*(1), 32.

Defense Innovation Board. 2019. *AI Principles: Recommendations on the Ethical Use of Artificial Intelligence by the Department of Defense.* Washington, DC: Defense Innovation Board. Available: https://media.defense.gov/2019/Oct/31/2002204459/-1/-1/0/DIB_AI_PRINCIPLES_SUPPORTING_DOCUMENT.PDF.pdf.

Defense Science Board. 2012. *The Role of Autonomy in DoD Systems*. Washington, DC: Office of the Under Secretary of Defense for Acquisition, Technology and Logistics. Available: https://irp.fas.org/agency/dod/dsb/autonomy.pdf.

Dekker, S., and Woods, D.D. 2002. MABA-MABA or abracadabra? Progress on human-automation coordination. *Cognition, Technology and Work, 4*, 240–244.

Delise, L.A., Allen Gorman, C., Brooks, A.M., Rentsch, J.R., and Steele-Johnson, D. 2010. The effects of team training on team outcomes: A meta-analysis. *Performance Improvement Quarterly, 22*(4), 53–80.

Demir, M., Likens, A.D., Cooke, N.J., Amazeen, P.G., and McNeese, N.J. 2018. Team coordination and effectiveness in human-autonomy teaming. *IEEE Transactions on Human-Machine System*, 1–10. doi: 10.1109/THMS.2018.2877482.

Demir, M., McNeese, N.J., and Cooke, N.J. 2016. Team Communication Behaviors of the Human Automation Teaming. *2016 IEEE International Multi-Disciplinary Conference on Cognitive Methods in Situation Awareness and Decision Support*, San Diego, CA, pp. 28–34. doi: 10.1109/COGSIMA.2016.7497782.

Demir, M., McNeese, N.J., Gorman, J.C., Cooke, N.J., Myers, C.W., and Grimm, D.A. 2021. Exploration of teammate trust and interaction dynamics in human-autonomy teaming. *IEEE Transactions on Human-Machine Systems, 51*(6), 696–705.

Dignum, V. 2019. AI is multidisciplinary. *AI Matters, 5*(4), 18–21. doi: 10.1145/3375637.3375644.

Dierdorff, E.C., Fisher, D.M., and Rubin, R.S. 2019. The power of percipience: Consequences of self-awareness in teams on team-level functioning and performance. *Journal of Management, 45*(7), 2891–2919.

Dimoka, A. 2010. What does the brain tell us about trust and distrust? Evidence from a functional neuroimaging study. *MIS Quarterly, 34*(2), 373. doi: 10.2307/20721433.

DOD (Department of Defense). 2012. *DoD Directive 3000.09: Autonomy in Weapon Systems*. Washington, DC: Department of Defense.

DOD. 2020. *DOD Instruction 5000.02: Operation of the Adaptive Acquisition Framework*. Washington, DC: Department of Defense. Available: https://www.esd.whs.mil/Portals/54/Documents/DD/issuances/dodi/500002p.pdf.

Domeyer, J., Dinparastdjadid, A., Lee, J.D., Douglas, G., Alsaid, A., and Price, M. 2019. Proxemics and kinesics in automated vehicle–pedestrian communication: Representing ethnographic observations. *Journal of the Transportation Research Board, 2673*(10), 70–81.

Dorneich, M.C., Passinger, B., Hamblin, C., Keinrath, C., Vašek, J., Whitlow, S.D., and Beekhuyzen, M. 2017. Evaluation of the display of cognitive state feedback to drive adaptive task sharing. *Frontiers in Neuroscience, 11*, 144.

Draper, M., Calhoun, G., Hansen, M., Douglass, S., Spriggs, S., Patzek, M., Rowe, A., Ruff, H., Behymer, K., Howard, M., Bearden, G., and Frost, E. 2017. Intelligent Multi-Unmanned Vehicle Planner with Adaptive Collaborative/Control Technologies (IMPACT). *19th International Symposium on Aviation Psychology*, p. 226.

Driskell, T., Salas, E., and Driskell, J.E. 2018. Teams in extreme environments: Alterations in team development and teamwork. *Human Resource Management Review 28*(4), 434–449.

Dybå, T., and Dingsøyr, T. 2008. Empirical studies of agile software development: A systematic review. *Information and Software Technology, 50*(9–10), 833–859.

Dzindolet, M.T., Pierce, L., Peterson, S., Purcell, L., Beck, H., and Beck, H. 2002. The influence of feedback on automation use, misuse, and disuse. *Proceedings of the Human Factors and Ergonomics Society Annual Meeting, 46*(1), 551–555.

Ebert, C., Gallardo, G., Hernantes, J., and Serrano, N. 2016. DevOps. *IEEE Software, 33*, 94–100.

Eiband, M., Buschek, D., Kremer, A., and Hussmann, H. 2019. The Impact of Placebic Explanations on Trust in Intelligent Systems. *Extended Abstracts of the 2019 CHI Conference on Human Factors in Computing Systems*, pp. 1–6.

Einhorn, H.J., and Hogarth, R.M. 1981. Behavioral decision theory: Processes of judgment and choice. *Annual Review of Psychology, 32*(1), 53–88.

Elix, B., and Naikar, N. 2021. Designing for adaptation in workers' individual behaviors and collective structures with cognitive work analysis: Case study of the diagram of work organization possibilities. *Human Factors, 63*(2), 274–295.

Elm, W.C., Gualtieri, J.W., McKenna, B.P., Tittle, J.S., Peffer, J.E., Szymczak, S.S., and Grossman, J.B. 2008. Integrating cognitive systems engineering throughout the systems engineering process. *Journal of Cognitive Engineering and Decision Making, 2*(3), 249–273.

Endsley, M.R. 1988. Design and evaluation for situation awareness enhancement. *Proceedings of the Human Factors Society Annual Meeting, 32*(2), 97–101.

Endsley, M.R. 1990. Predictive utility of an objective measure of situation awareness. *Proceedings of the Human Factors Society Annual Meeting, 34*(1), 41–45.

Endsley, M.R. 1993. A survey of situation awareness requirements in air-to-air combat fighters. *International Journal of Aviation Psychology, 3*(2), 157–168.

Endsley, M.R. 1995a. Measurement of situation awareness in dynamic systems. *Human Factors, 37*(1), 65–84.

Endsley, M.R. 1995b. Toward a theory of situation awareness in dynamic systems. *Human Factors, 37*(1), 32–64.

REFERENCES

Endsley, M.R. 1996. Automation and Situation Awareness. Pp. 163–181 in *Automation and Human Performance: Theory and Applications* (R. Parasuraman and M. Mouloua, eds.), Mahwah, NJ: Lawrence Erlbaum.

Endsley, M.R. 2008. Situation Awareness: A Key Cognitive Factor in Effectiveness of Battle Command. Pp. 95–119 in *The Battle of Cognition: The Future of Information-Rich Warfare and the Mind of the Commander* (A. Kott, ed.), Westport, CT: Praeger.

Endsley, M.R., 2015. Situation awareness misconceptions and misunderstandings. *Journal of Cognitive Engineering and Decision Making, 9*(1), 4–32.

Endsley, M.R. 2017. From here to autonomy: Lessons learned from human-automation research. *Human Factors, 59*(1), 5–27.

Endsley, M.R. 2018a. Combating information attacks in the age of the internet: New challenges for cognitive engineering. *Human Factors, 60*(8), 1081–1094.

Endsley, M.R. 2018b. Level of automation forms a key aspect of autonomy design. *Special Issue on Advancing Models of Human-Automation Interaction, Journal of Cognitive Engineering and Decision Making, 12,* 29–34.

Endsley, M.R. 2019. Human factors and aviation safety: Testimony to the United States House of Representatives Hearing on Boeing 737-Max8 crashes. Available: https://transportation.house.gov/imo/media/doc/Endsley%20Testimony.pdf.

Endsley, M.R. 2020a. Human-Automation Interaction and the Challenge of Maintaining Situation Awareness in Future Autonomous Vehicles. Pp. 151–168 in *Automation and Human Performance: Theory and Applications,* 2nd ed. (M. Mouloua and P. Hancock, eds.). Boca Raton, FL: CRC Press.

Endsley, M.R. 2020b. The divergence of objective and subjective situation awareness: A meta-analysis. *Journal of Cognitive Engineering and Decision Making, 14*(1), 34–53.

Endsley, M.R. 2021a. A systematic review and meta-analysis of direct objective measures of situation awareness: A comparison of SAGAT and SPAM. *Human Factors, 63*(1), 124–150.

Endsley, M.R. 2021b. Situation Awareness in Teams: Models and Measures. Pp. 1–28 in *Handbook of Distributed Team Cognition: Contemporary Research Models, Methodologies, and Measures in Distributed Team Cognition* (M. McNeese, E. Salas, and M. Endsley, eds.). Boca Raton, FL: CRC Press.

Endsley, M.R., and Jones, D.G. 2012. *Designing for Situation Awareness: An Approach to Human-Centered Design,* 2nd ed. London: Taylor and Francis.

Endsley, M.R., and Jones, W.M. 2001. A Model of Inter- and Intrateam Situation Awareness: Implications for Design, Training and Measurement. Pp. 46–67 in *New Trends in Cooperative Activities: Understanding System Dynamics in Complex Environments* (M. McNeese, E. Salas, and M. Endsley, eds.). Santa Monica, CA: Human Factors and Ergonomics Society.

Endsley, M.R., and Kaber, D.B. 1999. Level of automation effects on performance, situation awareness and workload in a dynamic control task. *Ergonomics, 42,* 462–492.

Endsley, M.R., and Kiris, E.O. 1994. Information presentation for expert systems in future fighter aircraft. *International Journal of Aviation Psychology, 4*(4), 333–348.

Endsley, M.R., and Kiris, E.O. 1995. The out-of-the-loop performance problem and level of control in automation. *Human Factors, 37*(2), 381–394.

Endsley, M.R., Bolte, B., and Jones, D.G. 2003. *Designing for Situation Awareness: An Approach to Human-Centered Design.* London: Taylor and Francis.

Endsley, M.R., English, T.M., and Sundararajan, M. 1997. The modeling of expertise: The use of situation models for knowledge engineering. *International Journal of Cognitive Ergonomics, 1*(2), 119–136.

Endsley, M.R., Jones, D.G., Hannen, M., and Dunlap, K.L. 2008. *A Case Study in Systems-Of-Systems Engineering: Cognitive Engineering in the Army's Future Combat Systems.* Marietta, GA: SA Technologies.

Entin, E.E., and Serfaty, D. 1999. Adaptive team coordination. *Human Factors, 41*(2), 312–325. doi: 10.1518/001872099779591196.

Entin, E.E., and Entin, E.B. 2001. Measures for Evaluation of Team Process and Performance in Experiments and Exercises. *Proceedings of the 6th International Command and Control Research and Technology Symposium,* Washington, DC: Command and Control Research Program.

Epley, N., Waytz, A., and Cacioppo, J.T. 2007. On seeing human: A three-factor theory of anthropomorphism. *Psychological Review, 114*(4), 864–886.

Erev, I., Ert, E., Roth, A.E., Haruvy, E., Herzog, S.M., Hau, R., Hertwig, R., Stewart, T., West, R., and Lebiere, C. 2010. A choice prediction competition: Choices from experience and from description. *Journal of Behavioral Decision Making, 23*(1), 15–47.

Ernest D., and Marcus, G. 2016. The scope and limits of simulation in automated reasoning. *Artificial Intelligence, 233,* 60–72, doi: 10.1016/j.artint.2015.12.003.

Evans, D.C., and Fendley, M. 2017. A multi-measure approach for connecting cognitive workload and automation. *International Journal of Human-Computer Studies, 97,* 182–189.

Evenson, S., Muller, M., and Roth, E.M. 2008. Capturing the context of use to inform system design. *Journal of Cognitive Engineering and Decision Making, 2*(3), 181–203.

Eykholt, K., Evtimov, I., Fernandes, E., Bo, L., Rahmati, A., Xiao, C., Prakash, A., Kohno, T., and Song, D. 2017. Robust physical-world attacks on deep learning models. *arXiv:*1707.08945.

Federal Aviation Administration Human Factors Team. 1996. The Interfaces Between Flightcrews and Modern Flight Deck Systems. Available: http://www.tc.faa.gov/its/worldpac/techrpt/hffaces.pdf.

Feigh, K.M., and Pritchett, A.R. 2014. Requirements for effective function allocation: A critical review. *Journal of Cognitive Engineering and Decision Making, 8*(1), 23–32.

Felzmann, H., Fosch-Villaronga, E., Lutz, C., and Tamò-Larrieux, A. 2020. Towards transparency by design for artificial intelligence. *Science and Engineering Ethics, 26*(6), 3333–3361.

Ferguson-Walter, K., Fugate, S., and Wang, C. 2020. Introduction to the Minitrack on Cyber Deception for Defense. In *Proceedings of the 53rd Hawaii International Conference on System Sciences,* pp. 1823–1824.

Fern, L., and Shively, R.J. 2009. A Comparison of Varying Levels of Automation on the Supervisory Control of Multiple UASs. *Proceedings of AUVSI's Unmanned Systems North America 2009,* Washington, DC, pp. 10–13.

Fernández-Loría, C., Provost, F., and Han, X. 2020. Explaining data-driven decisions made by AI systems: The counterfactual approach. *arXiv:*2001.07417.

Ferrer, X., van Nuenen, T., Such, J.M., Coté, M., and Criado, N. 2021. Bias and discrimination in AI: A cross-disciplinary perspective. *IEEE Technology and Society Magazine, 40*(2), 72–80.

Fishbein, M., and Ajzen, I. 1975. *Belief, Attitude, Intention, and Behavior: An Introduction to Theory and Research.* Boston, MA: Addison-Wesley.

Fitts, P.M. 1951. *Human Engineering for an Effective Air-Navigation and Traffic-Control System.* Washington, DC: National Research Council. Available: https://apps.dtic.mil/sti/pdfs/ADB815893.pdf

Flathmann, C., Schelble, B.G., Zhang, R., and McNeese, N.J. 2021. Modeling and Guiding the Creation of Ethical Human-AI Teams. *Proceedings of the 2021 AAAI/ACM Conference on AI, Ethics, and Society,* pp. 469–479.

Flournoy, M.A., Haines, A., and Chefitz, G. 2020. Building Trust through Testing. Available: https://cset.georgetown.edu/wp-content/uploads/Building-Trust-Through-Testing.pdf.

Forbus, K.D. 2016. Software social organisms: Implications for measuring AI progress. *AI Magazine, 37*(1), 85–90.

Friesen, D., Borst, C., Pavel, M.D., Masarati, P., and Mulder, M. 2021. Design and Evaluation of a Constraint-Based Helicopter Display to Support Safe Path Planning. *Nitros Safety Workshop,* April 9–11.

Gallina, P., Bellotto, N., and Di Luca, M. 2015. Progressive Co-Adaptation in Human-Machine Interaction. *2015 12th International Conference on Informatics in Control, Automation and Robotics (ICINCO),* pp. 362–368.

Ganaie, M.Y., and Mudasir, H. 2015. A study of social intelligence & academic achievement of college students of District Srinagar, J&K, India. *Journal of American Science, 11*(3) 23–27.

Gao, J., and Lee, J.D. 2006. Effect of shared information on trust and reliance in a demand forecasting task. *Proceedings of the Human Factors and Ergonomics Society Annual Meeting, 50*(3), 215–219.

Gao, J., Lee, J.D., and Zhang, Y. 2006. A dynamic model of interaction between reliance on automation and cooperation in multi-operator multi-automation situations. *International Journal of Industrial Ergonomics, 36*(5), 511–526.

Gardner, A.K., Kosemund, M., and Martinez, J. 2017. Examining the feasibility and predictive validity of the SAGAT tool to assess situation awareness among medical trainees. *Simulation in Healthcare, 12*(1), 17–21.

Gebru, T., Morgenstern, J., Vecchione, B., Vaughan, J.W., Wallach, H., Daumé III, H., and Crawford, K. 2018. Datasheets for Datasets. *5th Workshop on Fairness, Accountability, and Transparency in Machine Learning,* Stockholm, Sweden.

Gianfrancesco, M.A., Tamang, S., Yazdany, J., and Schmajuk, G. 2018. Potential biases in machine learning algorithms using electronic health record data. *JAMA Internal Medicine, 178*(11), 1544–1547.

Gilpin, L.H., Bau, D., Yuan, B.Z., Bajwa, A., Specter, M., and Kagal, L. 2018. Explaining Explanations: An Overview of Interpretability of Machine Learning. *2018 IEEE 5th International Conference on Data Science and Advanced Analytics (DSAA),* Turin, Italy, pp. 80–89.

Gonzalez, C. 2017. Decision Making: A Cognitive Science Perspective. Pp. 249–263 in *The Oxford Handbook of Cognitive Science* (S.E.F. Chipman, ed.). Oxford University Press. doi: 10.1093/oxfordhb/9780199842193.013.6.

Gonzalez C., and Dutt, V. 2011. Instance-based learning: Integrating sampling and repeated decisions from experience. *Psychological Review, 118*(4), 523–551.

Gonzalez, C., Aggarwal, P., Cranford, E., and Lebiere, C. 2020. Design of Dynamic and Personalized Deception: A Research Framework and New Insights. *Proceedings of the 53rd Hawaii International Conference on System Sciences HICSS 2020,* January 7–10, pp. 1825–1834. doi: 10.24251/HICSS.2020.226.

REFERENCES

Gonzalez, C., Ben-Asher, N., Martin, J. and Dutt, V. 2015. A cognitive model of dynamic cooperation with varied interdependency information. *Cognitive Science, 39*, 457–495.

Gonzalez, C., Ben-Asher, N., Oltramari, A., and Lebiere, C. 2014. Cognition and Technology. Pp. 93–117 in *Cyber Defense and Situational Awareness*, vol. 62 (C. Kott, A. Wang, and R. Erbacher, eds.). Switzerland: Springer International Publishing. doi: 10.1007/978-3-319-11391-3.

Goodfellow, I.J., Shlens, J., and Szegedy, C. 2015. Explaining and harnessing adversarial examples. *arXiv:*1412.6572.

Goodwin, G.F., Blacksmith, N., and Coats, M.R. 2018. The science of teams in the military: Contributions from over 60 years of research. *American Psychologist, 73*(4), 322.

Gorman, J.C., Cooke, N.J., and Amazeen, P.G. 2010. Training adaptive teams. *Human Factors, 52*(2), 295–307.

Gorman, J.C., Cooke, N.J., and Winner, J.L. 2006. Measuring team situation awareness in decentralized command and control environments. *Ergonomics, 49*(12–13), 1312–1325.

Gorman, J.C., Demir, M., Cooke, N.J., and Grimm, D.A. 2019. Evaluating sociotechnical dynamics in a simulated remotely piloted aircraft system: A layered dynamics approach. *Ergonomics, 62*(5), 1–44. doi: 10.1080/00140139.2018.1557750.

Gorman, J.C., Grimm, D.A., Stevens, R.H., Galloway, T., Willemsen-Dunlap, A.M., and Halpin, D.J. 2020. Measuring real-time team cognition during team training. *Human Factors: The Journal of the Human Factors and Ergonomics Society, 62*(52), 825–860.

Gottman, J., Swanson, C., and Swanson, K. 2002. A general systems theory of marriage: Nonlinear difference equation modeling of marital interaction. *Personality and Social Psychology Review, 6*(4), 326–340.

Graham, J., Schneider, M., Bauer, A., Bessiere, K., and Gonzalez, C. 2004. Shared mental models in military command and control organizations: Effect of social network distance. *Proceedings of the Human Factors and Ergonomics Society Annual Meeting, 48*(3), 509–512.

Grand, J.A., Braun, M.T., Kuljanin, G., Kozlowski, S.W., and Chao, G.T. 2016. The dynamics of team cognition: A process-oriented theory of knowledge emergence in teams. *Journal of Applied Psychology, 101*(10), 1353.

Gray, W. 2002. Simulated task environments: The role of high-fidelity simulations, scaled worlds, synthetic environments, and laboratory tasks in basic and applied cognitive research. *Cognitive Science Quarterly, 2*, 205–227.

Groom, V., and Nass, C. 2007. Can robots be teammates?: Benchmarks in human–robot teams. *Interaction Studies, 8*(3), 483–500.

Groover, M. 2020. *Automation, Production Systems, and Computer-Integrated Manufacturing*, 5th ed. New York, NY: Pearson.

Guidotti, R., Monreale, A., Ruggieri, S., Turini, F., Giannotti, F., and Pedreschi, D. 2018. A survey of methods for explaining black box models. *ACM Computing Surveys (CSUR), 51*(5), 1–42.

Gunderson, E.K.E. 1973. Psychological Studies in Antarctica: A Review. *Polar Human Biology: The Proceedings of the SCAR/IUPS/IUBS Symposium on Human Biology and Medicine in the Antarctic*. London: Butterworth-Heinemann, pp. 352–361.

Gutzwiller, R., Ferguson-Walter, K., Fugate, S., and Rogers, A. 2018. "Oh, look, a butterfly!" A framework for distracting attackers to improve cyber defense. *Proceedings of the Human Factors and Ergonomics Society Annual Meeting, 62*(1), 272–276. doi: 10.1177/1541931218621063.

Hagendorff, T. 2020. The ethics of AI ethics: An evaluation of guidelines. *Minds and Machines, 30*(1), 99–120.

Hallaq, B., Somer, T., Osula, A.M., Ngo, K., and Mitchener-Nissen, T. 2017. Artificial Intelligence Within the Military Domain and Cyber Warfare. *European Conference on Cyber Warfare and Security ECCWS*, pp. 153–157.

Hancock, P.A., Billings, D.R., Schaefer, K.E., Chen, J.Y.C., de Visser, E.J., and Parasuraman, R. 2011. A meta-analysis of factors affecting trust in human-robot interaction. *Human Factors: The Journal of the Human Factors and Ergonomics Society, 53*(5), 517–527.

Hancock, P., and Verwey, W.B. 1997. Fatigue, workload and adaptive driver systems. *Accident Analysis and Prevention, 29*(4), 495–506.

Harding, S M., Rajivan, P., Bertenthal, B.I., and Gonzalez, C. 2018. Human Decisions on Targeted and Non-Targeted Adversarial Samples. *40th Annual Meeting of the Cognitive Science Society (CogSci 2018)*, July 25–28, Madison, WI.

Harris, W.C., Hancock, P.A., Arthur, E.J., and Caird, J.K. 1995. Performance, workload, and fatigue changes associated with automation. *The International Journal of Aviation Psychology, 5*(2), 169–185.

Harrison McKnight, D., and Chervany, N.L. 2001. Trust and Distrust Definitions: One Bite at a Time. Pp. 27–54 in *Trust in Cyber-societies*, vol. 2246 (R. Falcone, M. Singh, and Y.-H. Tan, eds.). Berlin Heidelberg: Springer. doi: 10.1007/3-540-45547-7_3.

Hayes, C., and Miller, C.A. 2010. *Human-Computer Etiquette*. New York: Auerbach Publications.

Hilburn, B. 2017. Dynamic Decision Aiding: The Impact of Adaptive Automation on Mental Workload. Pp. 193–200 in *Engineering Psychology and Cognitive Ergonomics* Abingdon: Routledge.

Hilburn, B., Jorna, P.G., Bryne, E.A., and Parasuraman, R. 1997. The Effect of Adaptive Air Traffic Control Decision Aiding on Controller Mental Workload. Pp. 84–91 in *Human Automation Interaction: Research and Practice* (M. Mouloua and J.M. Koonce, eds.). Mahwah, NJ: LEA.

Hill, S.C. 2021. Joint all-domain operations: The key to decision dominance and overmatch. *Breaking Defense*. Available: https://breakingdefense.com/2021/2005/joint-all-domain-operations-the-key-to-decision-dominance-and-overmatch/.

Hinski, S. 2017. Training the code team leader as a forcing function to improve overall team performance during simulated code blue events. PhD thesis, Human Systems Engineering, Arizona State University.

Ho, N., Sadler, G.G., Hoffmann, L.C., Zemlicka, K., Lyons, J., Fergueson, W., Richardson, C., Cacanindin, A., Cals, S., and Wilkins, M. 2017. A longitudinal field study of auto-GCAS acceptance and trust: First-year results and implications. *Journal of Cognitive Engineering and Decision Making, 11*(3), 239–251.

Hoff, K.A., and Bashir, M. 2015. Trust in automation: Integrating empirical evidence on factors that influence trust. *Human Factors: The Journal of the Human Factors and Ergonomic Society, 57*(3), 407–434.

Hoffman, R.R., and Hancock, P.A. 2017. Measuring resilience. *Human Factors, 59*, 564–581.

Hoffman, R.R., and Woods, D.D. 2011. Beyond Simon's slice: Five fundamental trade-offs that bound the performance of macrocognitive work systems. *IEEE Intelligent Systems, 26*(6), 67–71.

Hoffman, R.R., Mueller, S.T., Klein, G., and Litman, J. 2018. Metrics for explainable AI: Challenges and prospects. *arXiv*:1812.04608.

Hohman, F., Kahng, M., Pienta, R., and Chau, D. 2019. Visual analytics in deep learning: An interrogative survey for the next frontiers. *IEEE Transactions on Visualization and Computer Graphics, 25*(8), 2674–2693.

Howard, A., and Borenstein, J. 2018. The ugly truth about ourselves and our robot creations: The problem of bias and social inequity. *Science and Engineering Ethics, 24*(5), 1521–1536.

Huang, L., Cooke, N., Johnson, C., Lematta, G., Bhatti, S., Barnes, M., and Holder, E. 2020. *Human-Autonomy Teaming: Interaction Metrics and Models for Next Generation Combat Vehicle Concepts*. Technical Report for ARL Grant W911NF1820271.

Huang, L., Cooke, N.J., Gutzwiller, R.S., Berman, S., Chiou, E.K., Demir, M., and Zhang, W. 2021. Distributed Dynamic Team Trust in Human, Artificial Intelligence, and Robot Teaming. Pp. 301–319 in *Trust in Human-Robot Interaction*. Academic Press. doi: 10.1016/B978-0-12-819472-0.00013-7.

Human Factors and Ergonomics Society. 2021. *Human Readiness Level Scale in the System Development Process ANSI/HFES 400-2021*. Washington, DC: Human Factors and Ergonomics Society.

Hutchins, E. 1990. The Technology of Team Navigation. Pp. 191–220 in *Intellectual Teamwork: Social and Technological Foundations of Cooperative Work* (J. Galegher, R.E. Kraut, and C. Egido, eds.). Hillsdale, NJ: Lawrence Erlbaum Associates.

IJtsma, M., Ma, L.M., Pritchett, A.R., and Feigh, K.M. 2019. Computational methodology for the allocation of work and interaction in human-robot teams. *Journal of Cognitive Engineering and Decision Making, 13*(4), 221–241. doi:10.1177/1555343419869484.

Jian, J.-Y., Bisantz, A.M., and Drury, C.G. 2000. Foundations for an empirically determined scale of trust in automated systems. *International Journal of Cognitive Ergonomics, 4*(1), 53–71.

Johnson, M., and Bradshaw, J.M. 2021. The Role of Interdependence in Trust. Pp. 379–403 in *Trust in Human-Robot Interaction*. Elsevier, Inc. doi: 10.1016/B978-0-12-819472-0.00016-2.

Johnson, M., and Vera, A. 2019. No AI is an island: The case for teaming intelligence. *AI Magazine, 40*(1), 16–28.

Johnson, M., Bradshaw, J.M., and Feltovich, P.J. 2017. Tomorrow's human–machine design tools: From levels of automation to interdependencies. *Journal of Cognitive Engineering and Decision Making, 12*(1), 77–82.

Johnson, M., Bradshaw, J.M., Feltovich, P.J., Jonker, C.M., van Riemsdijk, M.B., and Sierhuis, M. 2014. Coactive design: Designing support for interdependence in joint activity. *Journal of Human Robot Interaction, 3*(1), 43–69.

Johnson, M., Vignati, M., and Duran, D. 2020. Understanding Human-Machine Teaming Through Interdependence Analysis. Pp. 209–233 in *Contemporary Research*. Boca Raton, FL: CRC Press.

Jones, R.E.T., Connors, E.S., Mossey, M.E., Hyatt, J.R., Hansen, N.J., and Endsley, M.R. 2011. Using fuzzy cognitive mapping techniques to model situation awareness for army infantry platoon leaders. *Computational Mathematical Organizational Theory, 17*(3), 272–295.

Juvina, I., Lebiere, C., and Gonzalez, C. 2015. Modeling trust dynamics in strategic interaction. *Journal of Applied Research in Memory and Cognition, 4*(3), 197–211.

Kaber, D.B. 2018. Issues in human-automation interaction modeling: Presumptive aspects of frameworks of types and levels of automation. *Special Issue on Advancing Models of Human-Automation Interaction, Journal of Cognitive Engineering and Decision Making, 12*, 7–24.

Kaber, D.B., and Endsley, M.R. 2004. The effects of level of automation and adaptive automation on human performance, situation awareness and workload in a dynamic control task. *Theoretical Issues in Ergonomic Science, 5*(2), 113–153.

Kaber, D.B., and Endsley, M.R. 1997. Level of Automation and Adaptive Automation Effects on Performance in a Dynamic Control Task. *Proceedings of the 13th Triennial Congress of the International Ergonomics Association*, pp. 202–204. Helsinki: Finnish Institute of Occupational Health.

Kaber, D.B., and Riley, J. 1999. Adaptive automation of a dynamic control task based on secondary task workload measurement. *International Journal of Cognitive Ergonomics, 3*(3), 169–187.

Kahneman, D., and Tversky, A. 1979. Intuitive prediction: Biases and corrective procedures. *Studies in Management Sciences, 12*, 313–327.

Kahneman, D., Slovic, P., and Tversky, A. 1982. *Judgment Under Uncertainty: Heuristics and Biases*. Cambridge: Cambridge University Press.

Kaplan, A.D., Kessler, T.T., Brill, J.C., and Hancock, P.A. 2021. Trust in artificial intelligence: Meta-analytic findings. *Human Factors,* online May 28. doi: 10.1177/00187208211013988.

Kelley, H.H., and Thibaut, J. 1978. *Interpersonal Relations: A Theory of Interdependence*. New York: Wiley.

Kibbe, M., and McDowell, E.D. 1995. Operator Decision Making: Information on Demand. Pp. 43–48 in *Human Factors in Aviation Operations,* vol 3 (R. Fuller, N. Johnston, and N. McDonald, eds.). Aldershot, UK: Avebury.

Kirlik, A. 1993. Modeling strategic behavior in human-automation interaction: Why an "aid" can (and should) go unused. *Human Factors, 35*(2), 221–242.

Klein, G.A. 1993. A Recognition Primed Decision (RPD) Model of Rapid Decision Making. Pp. 138–147 in *Decision Making in Action: Models and Methods* (G.A. Klein, J. Orasanu, R. Calderwood, and C.E. Zsambok, eds.). Norwood, NJ: Ablex.

Klein, G., Feltovich, P.J., and Woods, D.D. 2005. Common Ground and Coordination in Joint Activity. Pp. 139–184 in *Organizational Simulation* (W.B. Rouse and K.R. Boff, eds.). New York: John Wiley and Sons, Inc.

Knight, W. 2017. *The Dark Secret at the Heart of AI*. Cambridge, MA: MIT Technology Review.

Kokar, M.M., and Endsley, M.R. 2012. Situation awareness and cognitive modeling. *IEEE Intelligent Systems, 27*(3), 91–96.

Konaev, M., Chahal, H., Fedasiuk, R., Huang, T., and Rahkovsky, I. 2020. *US Military Investments in Autonomy and AI: Costs, Benefits, and Strategic Effects*. Washington, DC: Center for Security and Emerging Technology. doi: 10.51593/20190044.

Koschmann, T., and LeBaron, C.D. 2003. Reconsidering Common Ground: Examining Clark's Contribution Theory in the OR. *Proceedings of the Eighth European Conference on Computer-Supported Cooperative Work,* Helsinki, Finland, pp. 81–98.

Kott, A. 2008. *Battle of Cognition: The Future Information-Rich Warfare and the Mind of the Commander*. Westport, CT: Praeger Security International.

Kramer, A.F. 2020. Physiological Metrics of Mental Workload: A Review of Recent Progress. Pp. 279–328 in *Multiple-Task Performance*. London: CRC Press. doi: 10.1201/9781003069447.

Kruchten, P. 2016. Refining the definition of technical debt. Available: https://philippe.kruchten.com/2016/04/22/refining-the-definition-of-technical-debt/.

Kuang, C. 2017. Can AI be taught to explain itself? *New York Times Magazine,* November 21. Available: https://www.nytimes.com/2017/11/21/magazine/can-ai-be-taught-to-explain-itself.html.

Kunze, A., Summerskill, S.J., Marshall, R., and Filtness, A.J. 2019. Automation transparency: Implications of uncertainty communication for human-automation interaction and interfaces. *Ergonomics, 62*(3), 345–360.

Layton, C., Smith, P.J., and McCoy, C.E. 1994. Design of a cooperative problem-solving system for en-route flight planning: An empirical evaluation. *Human Factors, 36*(1), 94–119.

Leavitt, H.J. 1951. Some effects of certain communication patterns on group performance. *The Journal of Abnormal and Social Psychology, 46*(1), 38.

Lee, J.D. 2001. Emerging challenges in cognitive ergonomics: Managing swarms of self-organizing agent-based automation. *Theoretical Issues in Ergonomics Science, 2*(3), 238–250.

Lee, J.D. 2018. Perspectives on automotive automation and autonomy. *Journal of Cognitive Engineering and Decision Making, 12*(1), 53–57.

Lee, J.D., and Moray, N. 1992. Trust, control strategies and allocation of function in human-machine systems. *Ergonomics, 35*, 1243–1270. doi: 10.1080/00140139208967392.

Lee, J.D., and Moray, N. 1994. Trust, self-confidence, and operations' adaptation of automation. *International Journal of Human-Computer Studies, 40*, 153–184.

Lee, J.D., and See, K.A. 2004. Trust in automation: Designing for appropriate reliance. *Human Factors, 46*(1), 50–80.

Lee, N.T., Resnick, P., and Barton, G. 2019. Algorithmic bias detection and mitigation: Best practices and policies to reduce consumer harms. Available: https://www.brookings.edu/research/algorithmic-bias-detection-and-mitigation-best-practices-and-policies-to-reduce-consumer-harms/.

Lee, N., Kim, J., Kim, E., and Kwon, O. 2017. The influence of politeness behavior on user compliance with social robots in a healthcare service setting. *International Journal of Social Robotics, 9*, 727–743. doi: 10.1007/s12369-017-0420-0.

Levin, T. 2021. Tesla's full self-driving tech keeps getting fooled by the moon, billboards, and Burger King signs. Available: https://www.businessinsider.com/tesla-fsd-full-self-driving-traffic-light-fooled-moon-video-2021-7.

Lewicki, R.J., and Brinsfield, C. 2017. Trust repair. *Annual Review of Organizational Psychology and Organizational Behavior, 4*, 287–313.

Lewis, P.R., Chandra, A., Parsons, S., Robinson, E., Glette, K., Bahsoon, R., Torresen, J., and Yao, X. 2011. A Survey of Self-Awareness and Its Application in Computing Systems. *2011 Fifth IEEE Conference on Self-Adaptive and Self-Organizing Systems Workshops*, pp. 102–107.

Lieberman, H. 2001. *Your Wish Is My Command: Programming by Example*. San Francisco, CA: Morgan Kaufmann Publishers.

Lin, R., and Kraus, S. 2010. Can automated agents proficiently negotiate with humans? *Communications of the ACM, 53*(1), 78–88.

Lipshitz, R. 1987. *Decision Making in the Real World: Developing Descriptions and Prescriptions from Decision Maker's Retrospective Accounts*. Boston, MA: Boston University Center for Applied Sciences.

Lipton, Z.C. 2017. The doctor just won't accept that!. *arXiv:*1711.08037.

Littman, M.L., Ajunwa, I., Berger, G., Boutilier, C., Currie, M., Doshi-Velez, F., Hadfield, G., Horowitz, M.C., Isbell, C., Kitano, H., Levy, K., Lyons, T., Mitchell, M., Shah, J., Sloman, S., Vallor, S., and Walsh, T. 2021. *Gathering Strength, Gathering Storms: The One Hundred Year Study on Artificial Intelligence (AI100) 2021 Study Panel Report*. Stanford, CA: Stanford University. Available at: http://ai100.stanford.edu/2021-report.

Long, S.K., Sato, T., Millner, N., Loranger, R., Mirabelli, J., Xu, V., and Yamani, Y. 2020. Empirically and theoretically driven scales on automation trust: A multi-level confirmatory factor analysis. *Proceedings of the Human Factors and Ergonomics Society Annual Meeting, 64*(1), 1829–1832. doi: 10.1177/1071181320641440.

Lyons, J.B. 2013. Being Transparent About Transparency: A Model for Human-Robot Interaction. *2013 AAAI Spring Symposium Series*, pp. 48–53.

Lyons, J.B., Ho, N.T., Van Abel, A.L., Hoffmann, L.C., Sadler, G.G., Fergueson, W.E., Grigsby, M.W., and Wilkins, M. 2017. Comparing trust in auto-GCAS between experienced and novice air force pilots. *Ergonomics in Design, 25*(4), 4–9.

Lyons, J.B., Sycara, K., Lewis, M., and Capiola, A. 2021. Human-autonomy teaming: Definitions, debates, and directions. *Frontiers in Psychology, 12*, 589585.

Madhavan, P., and Wiegmann, D.A. 2007. Similarities and differences between human-human and human-automation trust: An integrative review. *Theoretical Issues in Ergonomics Science, 8*(4), 277–301. doi: 10/d4sv4f.

Malone, T.W. 2018. How human-computer 'superminds' are redefining the future of work. *MIT Sloan Management Review, 59*(4), 34–41.

Malone, T.W., and Crowston, K. 1994. The interdisciplinary study of coordination. *ACM Computing Surveys, 26*(1), 87–119.

Malone, T.W., and Crowston, K. 2001. The Interdisciplinary Study of Coordination. Pp. 7–50 in *Coordination Theory and Collaboration Technology* (G.M. Olson, T.W. Malone, and J.B. Smith, eds.). Mahwah, NJ: Lawrence Erlbaum Associates, Inc.

Marks, M.A., DeChurch, L.A., Mathieu, J.E., Panzer, F.J., and Alonso, A. 2005. Teamwork in multiteam systems. *Journal of Applied Psychology, 90*(5), 964.

Marks, M.A., Mathieu, J.E., and Zaccaro, S.J. 2001. A temporally based framework and taxonomy of team processes. *Academy of Management Review, 26*(3), 356–376.

Marks, M.A., Sabella, M.J., Burke, C.S., and Zaccaro, S.J. 2002. The impact of cross-training on team effectiveness. *Journal of Applied Psychology, 87*(1), 3.

Marlow, S.L., Lacerenza, C.N., Reyes, D., and Salas, E. 2017. The Science and Practice of Simulation-Based Training in Organizations. Pp. 256–277 in *The Cambridge Handbook of Workplace Training and Employee Development* (K.G. Brown, ed.). New York, NY: Cambridge University Press.

Marriott, D., Ferguson-Walter, K., Fugate, S., and Carvalho, M. 2021. Proceedings of the 1st International Workshop on Adaptive Cyber Defense. *arXiv:*2108.08476.

Mathieu, J.E., Heffner, T.S., Goodwin, G.F., Salas, E., and Cannon-Bowers, J.A. 2000. The influence of shared mental models on team process and performance. *Journal of Applied Psychology, 85*(2), 273.

McClumpha, A., and James, M. 1994. Understanding Automated Aircraft. Pp. 183–190 in *Human Performance in Automated Systems: Current Research and Trends* (M. Mouloua and R. Parasuraman, eds.). Hillsdale, NJ: Erlbaum.

McCroskey, J.C., and Young, T.J. 1979. The use and abuse of factor analysis in communication research. *Human Communication Research, 5*(4), 375–382. doi: 10.1111/j.1468-2958.1979.tb00651.x.

McDermott, P., Dominguez, C., Kasdaglis, N., Ryan, M., Trahan, I., and Nelson, A. 2018. *Human-Machine Teaming Systems Engineering Guide*. Bedford, MA: MITRE.

McDermott, P., Walker, K., Dominguez, C., Nelson, A., and Kasdaglis, N. 2017. Quenching the Thirst for Human-Machine Teaming Guidance: Helping Military Systems Acquisition Leverage Cognitive Engineering Research. *Proceedings of the 13th International Conference on Naturalistic Decision Making 2017*, Bath, UK, pp. 236–240.

McGrath, J.E. 1984. *Groups: Interaction and Performance*. Englewood Cliffs: Prentice Hall.

McGrath, J.E. 1990. Time Matters in Groups. Pp. 23–61 in *Intellectual Teamwork: Social and Technological Foundations of Cooperative Work* (J. Galegher, R.E. Kraut, and C. Egido, eds.). Mahwah, NJ: Lawrence Erlbaum Associates, Inc.

McGuirl, J.M., and Sarter, N.B. 2006. Supporting trust calibration and the effective use of decision aids by presenting dynamic system confidence information. *Human Factors: The Journal of the Human Factors and Ergonomics Society*, 48(4), 656–665.

McNeese, N.J., Demir, M., Cooke, N.J., and Myers, C. 2018. Teaming with a synthetic teammate: Insights into human-autonomy teaming. *Human Factors*, 60, 262–273. doi: 10.1177/0018720817743223.

McNeese, N.J., Demir, M., Chiou, E.K., and Cooke, N.J. 2021a. Trust and team performance in human–autonomy teaming. *International Journal of Electronic Commerce*, 25(1), 51–72.

McNeese, N., Schleble, B., Barberis Canonico, L., and Demir, M. 2021b. Who/what is my teammate? Team composition considerations in human-AI teaming. *IEEE Transactions on Human-Machine Systems*, 51(4).

Mercado, J.E., Rupp, M.A., Chen, J.Y.C., Barnes, M.J., Barber, D., and Procci, K. 2016. Intelligent agent transparency in human-agent teaming for multi-UxV management. *Human Factors*, 58, 401–415. doi: 10.1177/0018720815621206.

Merritt, S.M., Lee, D., Unnerstall, J.L., and Huber, K. 2015. Are well-calibrated users effective users? Associations between calibration of trust and performance on an automation-aided task. *Human Factors: The Journal of the Human Factors and Ergonomics Society*, 57(1), 34–47.

Metzger, U., and Parasuraman, R. 2005. Automation in future air traffic management: Effects of decision aid reliability on controller performance and mental workload. *Human Factors*, 47(1), 35–49.

Miller, C.A. 2000. From the Microsoft Paperclip to the Rotorcraft Pilot's Associate: Lessons Learned from Fielding Adaptive Automation Systems. *Human Performance, Situation Awareness and Automation: User-Centered Design for the New Millennium Conference*, Savannah, GA.

Miller, C.A. 2014. Delegation and Transparency: Coordinating Interactions so Information Exchange Is No Surprise. *International Conference on Virtual, Augmented and Mixed Reality*, pp. 191–202.

Miller, C.A. 2018. The risks of discretization: What is lost in (even good) levels-of-automation schemes. *Journal of Cognitive Engineering and Decision Making*, 12(1), 74–76.

Miller, C.A. 2021. Trust, Transparency, Explanation, and Planning: Why We Need a Lifecycle Perspective on Human-Automation Interaction. Pp. 233–257 in *Trust in Human-Robot Interaction*. Academic Press.

Miller, C.A., and Parasuraman, R. 2007. Designing for flexible interaction between humans and automation: Delegation interfaces for supervisory control. *Human Factors*, 49(1), 57–75.

Miller, C.A., Funk, H., Goldman, R., Meisner, J., and Wu, P. 2005. Implications of Adaptive vs. Adaptable UIs on Decision Making: Why "Automated Adaptiveness" Is Not Always the Right Answer. *Proceedings of the 1st International Conference on Augmented Cognition*. Las Vegas, Nevada.

Miller, C.A., Shaw, T., Emfield, A., Hamell, J., de Visser, E., Parasuraman, R., and Musliner, D. 2011. Delegating to automation: Performance, complacency and bias effects under non-optimal conditions. *Proceedings of the Human Factors and Ergonomics Society Annual Meeting*, 55(1), 95–99.

Miller, J.G., and Miller, J.L. 1991. Introduction: The nature of living systems. *Behavior Science*, 36, 157–163.

Miller, T. 2019. Explanation in artificial intelligence: Insights from the social sciences. *Artificial Intelligence*, 267, 1–38. doi: 10/gfwcxw.

Mitchell, M., Wu, S., Zaldivar, A., Barnes, P., Vasserman, L., Hutchinson, B., Spitzer, E., Raji, I.D., and Gebru, T. 2019. Model Cards for Model Reporting. *FAT* '19: Proceedings of the Conference on Fairness, Accountability, and Transparency*. Atlanta, Georgia, pp. 220–229.

MITRE. 2014. *Systems Engineering Guide*. McLean, VA: The MITRE Corporation.

Mohammed, S., Ferzandi, L., and Hamilton, K. 2010. Metaphor no more: A 15-year review of the team mental model construct. *Journal of Management*, 36(4), 876–910.

Molnar, C. 2020. Interpretable Machine Learning: A Guide for Making Black Box Models Explainable. Available: https://christophm.github.io/interpretable-ml-book/.

Montague, E., Xu, J., and Chiou, E. 2014. Shared experiences of technology and trust: An experimental study of physiological compliance between active and passive users in technology-mediated collaborative encounters. *IEEE Transactions on Human-Machine Systems*, 44(5), 614–624. doi: 10/f6hs5c.

Montréal Responsible AI Declaration Steering Committee. 2018. *The Montreal Declaration for the Responsible Development of Artificial Intelligence*. Canada: Universite de Montreal.

Moon, Y., and Nass, C. 1996. How "real" are computer personalities? Psychological responses to personality types in human-computer interaction. *Communication Research, 23*(6), 651–674.

Moore, R.A., Schermerhorn, J.H., Oonk, H.M., and Morrison, J.G. 2003. *Understanding and Improving Knowledge Transactions in Command and Control*. San Diego, CA: Pacific Science and Engineering Group Inc.

Moray, N. 1986. Monitoring Behavior and Supervisory Control. Pp. 40/41–40/51 in *Handbook of Perception and Human Performance,* vol. 2 (K.R. Boff, L. Kaufman, and J.P. Thomas, eds.). New York: John Wiley and Sons.

Moray, N., and Inagaki, T. 2000. Attention and complacency. *Theoretical Issues in Ergonomics Science, 1*(4), 354–365.

Moreland, R.L. 2010. Are dyads really groups? *Small Group Research, 41*(2), 251–267.

Morgan, B.B.J., Salas, E., and Glickman, A.S. 1993. An analysis of team evolution and maturation. *Journal of General Psychology, 120,* 277–291.

Morris, J.X., Lifland, E., Yoo, J.Y., Grigsby, J., Jin, D., and Qi, Y. 2020. TextAttack: A framework for adversarial attacks, data augmentation, and adversarial training in NLP. *arXiv:2005.05909*.

Murphy, R.R. 2021. Role of Autonomy in DoD Systems and HADR. *Human-AI Teaming Through Warfighter-Centered Designs Workshop,* July 28, National Academy of Sciences, Engineering, and Medicine.

Myers, C.W., Ball, J.T., Cooke, N.J., Freiman, M.D., Caisse, M., Rodgers, S.M., Demir, M., and McNeese, N.J. 2018. Autonomous intelligent agents for team training: Making the case for synthetic teammates. *IEEE Transactions on Intelligent Systems*. 1–1. doi: 10.1109/MIS.2018.2886670.

Nadeem, A. 2021. Human-centered approach to static-analysis-driven developer tools: The future depends on good HCI. *Queue, 19*(4), 68–95.

NASEM (National Academies of Sciences, Engineering, and Medicine). 2018. *Multi-Domain Command and Control: Proceedings of a Workshop–in Brief*. Washington, DC: The National Academies Press. doi: 10.17226/25316.

NASEM. 2021a. *Adapting to Shorter Time Cycles in the United States Air Force: Proceedings of a Workshop Series*. Washington, DC: The National Academies Press. doi: 10.17226/26148.

NASEM. 2021b. *Energizing Data-Driven Operations at the Tactical Edge: Challenges and Concerns*. Washington, DC: The National Academies Press. doi: 10.17226/26183.

Nass, C., and Moon, Y. 2000. Machines and mindlessness: Social responses to computers. *Journal of Social Issues, 56*(1), 81–103. doi: 10/cqzrs6.

National Security Commission on Artificial Intelligence. 2021. *Final Report*. Available: https://www.nscai.gov/wp-content/uploads/2021/03/Final_Report_Executive_Summary.pdf.

Nayyar, M., Zoloty, Z., McFarland, C., and Wagner, A.R. 2020. Exploring the Effect of Explanations During Robot-Guided Emergency Evacuation. *International Conference on Social Robotics,* Golden, Colorado, pp. 13–22.

Nelson, B., Biggio, B., and Laskov, P. 2011. Understanding the Risk Factors of Learning in Adversarial Environments. *Proceedings of the 4th ACM Workshop on Security and Artificial Intelligence*. Association for Computing Machinery, New York, NY, pp. 87–92.

Neville, K., Rosso, H., and Pires, B. 2021. A Systems-Resilience Approach to Technology Transition in High-Consequence Work Systems. *Proceedings of the Naturalistic Decision Making and Resilience Engineering Symposium,* Toulouse, France.

Northcutt, C.G., Athalye, A., and Mueller, J. 2021. Pervasive Label Errors in Test Sets Destabilize Machine Learning Benchmarks. *asXiv:2103.14749*.

Nourani, M., Kabir, S., Mohseni, S., and Ragan, E.D. 2019. The effects of meaningful and meaningless explanations on trust and perceived system accuracy in intelligent systems. *Proceedings of the AAAI Conference on Human Computation and Crowdsourcing, 7*(1), 97–105.

NRC (National Research Council). 1993. *Workload Transition: Implications for Individual and Team Performance*. Washington, DC: The National Academies Press.

NRC. 2015. *Enhancing the Effectiveness of Team Science*. Washington, DC: The National Academies Press.

NRC. 2007. *Human-System Integration in the System Development Process: A New Look*. Washington, DC: The National Academies Press.

NTSB (National Transportation Safety Board). 2020. *Collision Between a Sport Utility Vehicle Operating With Partial Driving Automation and a Crash Attenuator, Mountain View, CA, March 23, 2018*. (NTSB/HAR-20/01). Washington, DC: National Transportation Safety Board. Available: https://www.ntsb.gov/investigations/AccidentReports/Reports/HAR2001.pdf.

O'Neill, P.H. 2020. Hackers Can Trick a Tesla into Accelerating by 50 Miles Per Hour. Available: https://www.technologyreview.com/2020/02/19/868188/hackers-can-trick-a-tesla-into-accelerating-by-50-miles-per-hour/.

REFERENCES

O'Neill, T., McNeese, N., Barron, A., and Schelble, B. 2020. Human–autonomy teaming: A review and analysis of the empirical literature. *Human Factors,* 0018720820960865.

Oduor, K.F., and Wiebe, E.N. 2008. The effects of automated decision algorithm modality and transparency on reported trust and task performance. *Proceedings of the Human Factors and Ergonomics Society Annual Meeting, 52*(4), 302–306.

Olson, G.M., and Olson, J.S. 2001. Technology Support for Collaborative Workgroups. Pp. 559–584 in *Coordination Theory and Collaboration Technology* (G.M. Olson, T.W. Malone, and J.B. Smith, eds.). Mahwah, NJ: Lawrence Erlbaum Associates, Inc.

Olson, W.A., and Sarter, N.B. 1999. Supporting informed consent in human machine collaboration: The role of conflict type, time pressure, and display design. *Proceedings of the Human Factors and Ergonomics Society Annual Meeting, 43*(9), 189–193.

Onnasch, L., Wickens, C.D., Li, H., and Manzey, D. 2014. Human performance consequences of stages and levels of automation: An integrated meta-analysis. *Human Factors, 56*(3), 476–488.

Oppermann, R. 1994. *Adaptive User Support: Ergonomic Design of Manually and Automatically Adaptable Software.* Boca Raton, FL: CRC Press.

Oser, R.L., McCallum, G., Salas, E., and Morgan Jr., B.B. 1989. *Toward a Definition of Teamwork: An Analysis of Critical Team Behaviors.* Orlando, FL: Naval Training Systems Center. Available: https://apps.dtic.mil/sti/pdfs/ADA212454.pdf.

Owen, H., Mugford, B., Follows, V., and Pullmer, J. 2006. Comparison of three simulation-based training methods for management of medical emergencies. *Resuscitation, 71,* 204–11.

Panganiban, A.R., Matthews, G., and Long, M.D. 2020. Transparency in autonomous teammates: Intention to support as teaming information. *Journal of Cognitive Engineering and Decision Making, 14*(2), 174–190.

Papernot, N., McDaniel, P., Jha, S., Fredrikson, M., Celik, Z.B., and Swami, A. 2016. The limitations of deep learning in adversarial settings. *arXiv:*1511.07528.

Parasuraman, R., and Manzey, D. 2010. Complacency and bias in human use of automation: An attentional integration. *Human Factors, 52*(3), 381–410.

Parasuraman, R., and Riley, V. 1997. Humans and automation: Use, misuse, disuse and abuse. *Human Factors, 39*(2), 230–253.

Parasuraman, R., and Wickens, C.D. 2008. Humans: Still vital after all these years of automation. *Human Factors, 50*(3), 511–520.

Parasuraman, R., Molloy, R., and Singh, I.L. 1993. Performance consequences of automation-induced complacency. *International Journal of Aviation Psychology, 3*(1), 1–23.

Parasuraman, R., Sheridan, T.B., and Wickens, C.D. 2000. A model of types and levels of human interaction with automation. *IEEE Transactions on Systems, Man and Cybernetics, 30*(3), 286–297.

Parasuraman, R., Galster, S., Squire, P., Furukawa, H., and Miller, C. 2005. A flexible delegation-type interface enhances system performance in human supervision of multiple robots: Empirical studies with RoboFlag. *IEEE Transactions on Systems, Man, and Cybernetics-Part A: Systems and Humans, 35*(4), 481–493.

Parush, A., Hazan, M., and Shtekelmacher, D. 2017. Individuals perform better in teams but are not more aware – performance and situational awareness in teams and individuals. *Proceedings of the Human Factors and Ergonomics Society Annual Meeting, 61*(1), 1173–1177.

Paul, C., and Matthews, M. 2016. *The Russian "Firehose of Falsehood" Propaganda Model: Why It Might Work and Options to Counter It.* Santa Monica, CA: RAND Corporation.

Pearl, J., and Mackenzie, D. 2018. *The Book of Why: The New Science of Cause and Effect.* New York: Basic Books.

Premack, D., and Woodruff, G. 1978. Does the chimpanzee have a theory of mind? *Behavioral and Brain Sciences, 1*(4), 515–526.

Prince, C., Ellis, E., Brannick, M.T., and Salas, E. 2007. Measurement of team situation awareness in low experience level aviators. *The International Journal of Aviation Psychology, 17*(1), 41–57.

Prinzel, L.J., Freeman, F.G., Scerbo, M.W., Mikulka, P.J., and Pope, A.T. 2003. Effects of a psychophysiological system for adaptive automation on performance, workload, and the event-related potential P300 component. *Human Factors, 45*(4), 601–613.

Rabinowitz, N.C., Perbet, F., Song, H.F., Zhang, C., and Botvinick, M. 2018. Machine Theory of Mind. *Proceedings of the 35th International Conference on Machine Learning,* Stockholm, Sweden, PMLR 80.

Radloff, R., and Helmreich, R. 1968. *Groups Under Stress: Psychological Research in SEALAB II.* New York: Appleton-Century-Crofts.

Rajivan, P., and Gonzalez, C. 2018. Creative persuasion: A study on adversarial behaviors and strategies in phishing attacks. *Frontiers in Psychology, 9,* 135.

Ramakrishnan, R., Zhang, C., and Shah, J. 2017. Perturbation training for human-robot teams. *Journal of Artificial Intelligence Research, 59*, 495–541.

Ramchurn, S.D., Stein, S., and Jennings, N.R. 2021. Trustworthy human-AI partnerships. *IScience, 24*(8), 102891. doi: 10.1016/j.isci.2021.102891.

Rasmussen, J. 1983. Skills, rules, and knowledge; signals, signs, and symbols, and other distinctions in human performance models. *IEEE Transactions on Systems, Man, and Cybernetics, SMC-13*(3), 257–266. doi: 10.1109/TSMC.1983.6313160.

Reggia, J.A. 2013. The rise of machine consciousness: Studying consciousness with computational models. *Neural Networks, 44*, 112–131.

Reichenbach, J., Onnasch, L., and Manzey, D. 2010. Misuse of automation: The impact of system experience on complacency and automation bias in interaction with automated aids. *Proceedings of the Human Factors and Ergonomics Society Annual Meeting, 54*(4), 374–378.

Rensink, R., O'Regan, K. and Clark, J. 1997. To see or not to see: The need for attention to perceive changes in scenes. *Psychological Science, 8*, 368–373.

Reyes, D., Dinh, J., and Salas, E. 2019. What makes a good team leader?. *The Journal of Character & Leadership Development, 6*(1), 88–100.

Riegelsberger, J., Sasse, M.A., and McCarthy, J.D. 2005. The mechanics of trust: A framework for research and design. *International Journal of Human-Computer Studies, 62*(3), 381–422.

Riley, V. 1994. A Theory of Operator Reliance on Automation. Pp. 8–14 in *Human Performance in Automated Systems: Current Research and Trends* (M. Mouloua and R. Parasuraman, eds.). Hillsdale, NJ: Lawrence Erlbaum Associates.

Riley, J.M., Endsley, M.R., Bolstad, C.A., and Cuevas, H.M. 2006. Collaborative planning and situation awareness in Army command and control. *Ergonomics, Special Issue: Command and Control, 49*(12-13), 1139–1153.

Roethlisberger, F.J., and Dickson, W.J. 1934. *Management and the Worker: Technical Vs. Social Organization in An Industrial Plant*. Boston, MA: Harvard University Graduate School of Business.

Rosenman, E.D., Dixon, A.J., Webb, J.M., Brolliar, S., Golden, S.J., Jones, K.A. Shah, S., Grand, J.A., Kozlowski, S.W.J., Chao, G.T., and Fernandez, R. 2018. A simulation-based approach to measuring team situational awareness in emergency medicine: A multicenter, observational study. *Academic Emergency Medicine, 25*(2), 196–204.

Roth, E.M., and Pritchett, A.R. 2018. Preface to the special issue on advancing models of human-automation interaction. *Journal of Cognitive Engineering and Decision Making, 12*, 3–6.

Roth, E.M., DePass, B., Harter, J., Scott, R., and Wampler, J. 2018. Beyond levels of automation: Developing more detailed guidance for human automation interaction. *Proceedings of the Human Factors and Ergonomics Society Annual Meeting, 62*(1), 150–154.

Roth, E.M., DePass, B., Scott, R., Truxler, R., Smith, S., and Wampler, J. 2017. Designing Collaborative Planning Systems: Putting Joint Cognitive Systems Principles to Practice. Pp. 247–268 in *Cognitive Systems Engineering: The Future for a Changing World* (P.J. Smith and R.R. Hoffman, eds.). Boca Raton: Taylor and Francis, CRC Press.

Roth, E.M., Sushereba, C., Militello, L.G., Diiulio, J., and Ernst, K. 2019. Function allocation considerations in the era of human autonomy teaming. *Journal of Cognitive Engineering and Decision Making, 13*(4), 199–220.

Rouse, W.B. 1988. Adaptive aiding for human/computer control. *Human Factors, 30*(4), 431–438.

Rouse, W.B., Cannon-Bowers, J.A., and Salas, E. 1992. The role of mental models in team performance in complex systems. *IEEE Transactions on Systems, Man, and Cybernetics, 22*, 1296–1308.

Rouse, W.B., and Morris, N.M. 1985. On looking into the black box: Prospects and limits in the search for mental models. *Psychological Bulletin, 100*(3), 349–363.

Rudin, C. 2019. Stop explaining black box machine learning models for high stakes decision making and use interpretable models instead. *Nature Machine Intelligence, 1*, 206–215.

SAE International. 2013. *Requirements for Models of Situation Awareness (ARD 50050)*. Warrendale, PA: SEA International. Available: https://infostore.saiglobal.com/en-us/standards/sae-ard-50050-1997-1018481_saig_sae_sae_2370694/.

SAE International. 2019. *SAE6906 Standard Practice for Human Systems Integration*. Warrendale, PA: SEA International. Available: https://www.sae.org/standards/content/sae6906/.

Salas, E., Bowers, C.A., and Cannon-Bowers, J.A. 1995. Military team research: 10 years of progress. *Military Psychology, 7*(2), 55–75.

Salas, E., Cooke, N.J., and Rosen, M.A. 2008. On teams, teamwork, and team performance: Discoveries and developments. *Human Factors, 50*(3), 540–547.

Salas, E., Diaz Granados, D., Klein, C., Burke, C.S., Stagl, K.C., Goodwin, G.F., and Halpin, S.M. 2008. Does team training improve team performance? A meta-analysis. *Human Factors, 50*(6), 903–933.

Salas, E., Dickinson, T.L., Converse, S.A., and Tannenbaum, S.I. 1992. Toward An Understanding of Team Performance and Training. Pp. 3–29 in *Teams: Their Training and Performance* (R.W. Swezey and E. Salas, eds.). Norwood, NJ: Ablex.

Salas, E., Sims, D.E., and Burke, C.S. 2005. Is there a "big five" in teamwork? *Small Group Research, 36*(5), 555–599.

Salerno, J.J., Hinman, M.L., and Boulware, D.M. 2005. A situation awareness model applied to multiple domains. *Multisensor, Multisource Information Fusion: Architectures, Algorithms, and Applications, 5813*. Orlando, FL.

Salles, A., Evers, K., and Farisco, M. 2020. Anthropomorphism in AI. *AJOB Neuroscience, 11*(2), 88–95.

Salmon, P.M., Stanton, N.A., Walker, G.H., Jenkins, D., Ladva, D., Rafferty, L., and Young, M. 2009. Measuring situation awareness in complex systems: Comparison of measures study. *International Journal of Industrial Ergonomics, 39*(3), 490–500.

Sandberg, B. 2021. Artificial Social Intelligence for Successful Teams (ASIST). Presentation to the Committee on Human-System Integration Research Topics for the 711th Human Performance Wing of the Air Force Research Laboratory. July 29.

Samimi, A., Mohammadian, A., and Kawamura, K. 2010. An Online Freight Shipment Survey in US: Lessons Learnt and a Non-Response Bias Analysis. *89th Annual Transportation Research Board Meeting*, January 11–15, Washington, DC.

Sanders, T.L., Wixon, T., Schafer, K.E., Chen, J.Y., and Hancock, P.A. 2014. The Influence of Modality and Transparency on Trust in Human-Robot Interaction. *2014 IEEE International Inter-Disciplinary Conference on Cognitive Methods in Situation Awareness and Decision Support (CogSIMA)*, 156–159.

Sanneman, L., and Shah, J.A. 2020. A Situation Awareness-Based Framework for Design and Evaluation of Explainable AI. In *Explainable, Transparent Autonomous Agents and Multi-Agent Systems. EXTRAAMAS 2020*, Lecture Notes in Computer Science, vol. 12175 (D. Calvaresi, A. Najjar, M. Winikoff, and K. Främling, eds.). Springer, Cham. doi: 10.1007/978-3-030-51924-7_6.

Sarter, N.B., and Schroeder, B. 2001. Supporting decision making and action selection under time pressure and uncertainty: The case of in-flight icing. *Human Factors, 43*(4), 573–583.

Sarter, N.B., and Woods, D.D. 1994. "How in the World Did I Ever Get into That Mode": Mode Error and Awareness in Supervisory Control. Pp. 111–124 in *Situational Awareness in Complex Systems* (R.D. Gilson, D.J. Garland, and J.M. Koonce, eds.). Daytona Beach, FL: Embry-Riddle Aeronautical University Press.

Sarter, N.B., and Woods, D.D. 1995. "How in the World Did I Ever Get Into That Mode": Mode Error and Awareness in Supervisory Control. *Human Factors, 37*(1), 5–19.

Scerbo, M.W. 1996. Theoretical perspectives on adaptive automation. Pp. 37–63 in *Automation and Human Performance: Theory and Application* (R. Parasuraman and M. Mouloua, eds.). Mahwah, NJ: Lawrence Erlbaum.

Schaefer, K.E., Chen, J.Y.C., Szalma, J.L., and Hancock, P.A. 2016. A meta-analysis of factors influencing the development of trust in automation: Implications for understanding autonomy in future systems. *Human Factors, 58*(3), 377–400.

Schmidt, E., Work, B., Catz, S., Chien, S., Clyburn, M., Darby, C., Ford, K., Griffiths, J-M., Horvitz, E., Jassy, A., Louie, G., Mark, W., Matheny, J., McFarland, K., and Moore, A. 2021. *Final Report: National Security Commission on Artificial Intelligence*. Washington, DC: National Security Commission on Artificial Intelligence. Available: https://www.nscai.gov/wp-content/uploads/2021/03/Full-Report-Digital-1.pdf.

Schmitt, F., Roth, G., Barber, D., Chen, J., and Schulte, A. 2018. Experimental Validation of Pilot Situation Awareness Enhancement Through Transparency Design of a Scalable Mixed-Initiative Mission Planner. *Intelligent Human Systems Integration, Proceedings of the 1st International Conference on Intelligent Human Systems Integration (IHSI 2018): Integrating People and Intelligent Systems*, Dubai, United Arab Emirates, 209–215.

Schraagen, J.M., Barnhoorn, J.S., van Schendel, J., and van Vught, W. 2021. Supporting teamwork in hybrid multi-team systems. *Theoretical Issues in Ergonomics Science*, 1–22. doi: 10.1080/1463922X.2021.1936277.

Schroeder, N.L., Chiou, E.K., and Craig, S.D. 2021. Trust influences perceptions of virtual humans, but not necessarily learning. *Computers and Education, 160*, 104039.

Schünemann, B., Keller, J., Rakoczy, H., Behne, T., and Bräuer, J. 2021. Dogs distinguish human intentional and unintentional action. *Scientific Reports, 11*, 14967. doi: 10.1038/s41598-021-94374-3.

Sebok, A., and Wickens, C.D. 2017. Implementing lumberjacks and black swans into model-based tools to support human–automation interaction. *Human Factors, 59*(2), 189–203.

Sebok, A., Walters, B., and Plott, C. 2017. Integrating human-centered design and the agile development process for safety and mission critical system development. *Proceedings of the Human Factors and Ergonomics Society Annual Meeting, 61*(1), 1086–1090.

Seckler, M., Heinz, S., Forde, S., Tuch, A.N., and Opwis, K. 2015. Trust and distrust on the web: User experiences and website characteristics. *Computers in Human Behavior, 45*, 39–50. doi: 10.1016/j.chb.2014.11.064.

Selcon, S.J. 1990. Decision Support in the Cockpit: Probably a Good Thing? *Human Factors Society 34th Annual Meeting*, Santa Monica, CA.

Selkowitz, A.R., Lakhmani, S.G., and Chen, J.Y.C. 2017. Using agent transparency to support situation awareness of the autonomous squad member. *Cognitive Systems Research, 46,* 13–25.

Selkowitz, A.R., Lakhmani, S.G., Larios, C.N., and Chen, J.Y.C. 2016. Agent Transparency and the Autonomous Squad Member. *Human Factors and Ergonomics Society Annual Meeting,* Los Angeles, CA.

Seong, Y., and Bisantz, A.M. 2008. The impact of cognitive feedback on judgment performance and trust with decision aids. *International Journal of Industrial Ergonomics, 38*(7–8), 608–625.

Seppelt, B.D., and Lee, J.D. 2007. Making adaptive cruise control (ACC) limits visible. *International Journal of Human-Computer Studies, 65*(3), 192–205.

Sharif, M., Bhagavatula, S., Bauer, L., and Reiter, M.K. 2016. Accessorize to a Crime: Real and Stealthy Attacks on State-of-the-Art Face Recognition. *ACM SIGSAC Conference on Computer and Communications Security,* Vienna, Austria.

Sheridan, T. 1986. Human Supervisory Control of Robot Systems. *1986 IEEE International Conference on Robotics and Automation*, pp. 808–812. doi: 10.1109/ROBOT.1986.1087506.

Sheridan, T.B. 1988. Task Allocation and Supervisory Control. Pp. 159–173 in *Handbook of Human-Computer Interaction.* Netherlands: North Holland.

Sheridan, T.B. 1992. *Telerobotics, Automation, and Human Supervisory Control.* Cambridge, MA: MIT Press.

Sheridan, T.B. 2011. Adaptive automation, level of automation, allocation authority, supervisory control, and adaptive control: Distinctions and modes of adaptation. *IEEE Transactions on Systems, Man, and Cybernetics-Part A: Systems and Humans, 41*(4), 662–667.

Sheridan, T.B. 2019. Individual differences in attributes of trust in automation: Measurement and application to system design. *Frontiers in Psychology, 10,* 1117. doi: 10/gf4xk9.

Sheridan, T.B., and Johannsen, G. 1976. *Monitoring Behavior and Supervisory Control.* Boston, MA: Springer.

Sheridan, T.B., and Parasuraman, R. 2005. Human-automation interaction. *Reviews of Human Factors and Ergonomics, 1*(1), 89–129.

Sheridan, T.B., and Verplank, W.L. 1978. *Human and Computer Control of Undersea Teleoperators* (No. NR196-152). Arlington, VA: Office of Naval Research. Available: https://apps.dtic.mil/sti/pdfs/ADA057655.pdf.

Shively, R.J., Lachter, J., Brandt, S.L., Matessa, M., Battiste, V., and Johnson, W.W. 2017. Why Human-Autonomy Teaming? *International Conference on Applied Human Factors and Ergonomics,* Springer, Cham, pp. 3–11.

Shneiderman, B. 2020. Human-centered artificial intelligence: Three fresh ideas. *AIS Transactions on Human-Computer Interaction, 12*(3), 109–124.

Shneiderman, B. 2021. 19th Note: Human-Centered AI Google Group. In Human-Centered AI (September 12, 2021 ed.). Available: https://groups.google.com/g/human-centered-ai/c/syqiC1juHO.c.

Siau, K., and Wang, W. 2018. Building trust in artificial intelligence, machine learning, and robotics. *Cutter Business Technology Journal, 31*(2), 47–53.

Simon, H.A. 1955. A behavioral model of rational choice. *The Quarterly Journal of Economics, 69*(1), 99–118.

Simon, H.A. 1957. *Models of Man: Social and Rational.* New York: John Wiley & Sons.

Simpkiss, B. 2009. *Human Systems Integration Requirements Pocket Guide.* Falls Church, VA: Air Force Human Systems Integration Office.

Simpson, J.A. 2007. Psychological foundations of trust. *Current Directions in Psychological Science, 16*(5), 264–268.

Singer, S.J., Kellogg, K.C., Galper, A.B., and Viola, D. 2021. Enhancing the value to users of machine learning-based clinical decision support tools: A framework for iterative, collaborative development and implementation. *Health Care Management Review,* doi: 10.1097/hmr.0000000000000324.

Singh, K., Aggarwal, P., Rajivan, P., and Gonzalez, C. 2019. Training to detect phishing emails: Effects of the frequency of experienced emails. *Proceedings of the Human Factors and Ergonomics Society Annual Meeting, 63*(1), 453–457.

Slack, D., Hilgard, S., Jia, E., Singh, S., and Lakkaraju, H. 2020. Fooling LIME and SHAP: Adversarial Attacks on Post Hoc Explanation Methods. *Proceedings of the AAAI/ACM Conference on AI, Ethics, and Society. AIES '20 (Association for Computing Machinery),* pp. 180–186. doi: 10.1145/3375627. 3375830.

Smallman, H.S., and St. John, M.F. 2003. CHEX (Change History EXplicit): New HCI concepts for change awareness. *Proceedings of the Human Factors and Ergonomics Society Annual Meeting, 47*(3), 528–532.

Smith, P.J. 2018. Conceptual frameworks to guide design. *Special Issue on Advancing Models of Human-Automation Interaction, Journal of Cognitive Engineering and Decision Making, 12*(1), 50–52.

Smith, P.J. 2017. Making Brittle Technologies Useful. Pp. 181–208 in *Cognitive Systems Engineering.* Boca Raton, FL: CRC Press.

Sottilare, R.A., Shawn Burke, C., Salas, E., Sinatra, A.M., Johnston, J.H., and Gilbert, S.B. 2017. Designing adaptive instruction for teams: A meta-analysis. *International Journal of Artificial Intelligence in Education, 28*(2), 225–264. doi: 10.1007/s40593-017-0146-z.

Sreedharan, S., Chakraborti, T., and Kambhampati, S. 2021. Foundations of explanations as model reconciliation. *Artificial Intelligence, 301,* 103558.

Stanners, M., and French, H.T. 2005. *An Empirical Study of the Relationship Between Situation Awareness and Decision Making.* (DSTO-TR-1687). Edinburgh South Australia: Defence Science and Technology Organization, Land Operations Division.

Stanton, N.A., Baber, C., and Harris, D. 2008. *Modeling Command and Control: Event Analysis of Systematic Teamwork.* Hampshire, England and Burlington, VT: Ashgate Publishing Limited.

Stein, G.J. 1996. Information attack: Information warfare in 2025. *2025 White Papers: Power and Influence, 3,* 14–28.

Stevens, R., Galloway, T., and Lamb, C. 2014. Submarine navigation team resilience: Linking EEG and behavioral models. *Proceedings of the Human Factors and Ergonomics Society Annual Meeting, 58*(1), 245–249.

Stowers, K., Kasdaglis, N., Rupp, M., Chen, J., Barber, D., and Barnes, M. 2017. Insights Into Human-Agent Teaming: Intelligent Agent Transparency and Uncertainty. Pp. 149–160 in *Advances in Human Factors in Robots and Unmanned Systems: Proceedings of the AHFE 2016 International Conference on Human Factors in Robots and Unmanned Systems,* Walt Disney World, Florida.

Strater, L.D., Cuevas, H.M., Connors, E.S., Ungvarsky, D.M., and Endsley, M.R. 2008. Situation awareness and collaborative tool usage in ad hoc command and control teams. *Proceedings of the Human Factors and Ergonomics Society Annual Meeting, 52*(4), 468–472.

Su, J., Vargas, D.V., and Sakurai, K. 2019. One pixel attack for fooling deep neural networks. *IEEE Transactions on Evolutionary Computation, 23*(5), 828–841.

Sulistayawati, K., Wickens, C.D., and Chui, Y.P. 2011. Prediction in situation awareness: Confidence bias and underlying cognitive abilities. *International Journal of Aviation Psychology, 21*(2), 153–174.

Sundstrom, E., DeMeuse, K.P., and Futrell, D. 1990. Work teams: Applications and effectiveness. *American Psychologist, 45*(2), 120–133.

Swezey, R.W., and Salas, E. 1992. *Teams: Their Training and Performance.* Norwood, NJ: Ablex Publishing.

Takayama, L. 2009. Making Sense of Agentic Objects and Teleoperation: In-The-Moment and Reflective Perspectives. *Human-Robot Interaction Conference,* San Diego, CA, pp. 239–240.

Taleb, N.N. 2012. *Antifragile: Things That Gain from Disorder.* New York: Random House

Tambe, M. 2011. *Security and Game Theory: Algorithms, Deployed Systems, Lessons Learned.* Cambridge: Cambridge University Press.

Tannenbaum, S.I., and Cerasoli, C.P. 2013. Do team and individual debriefs enhance performance? A meta-analysis. *Human Factors, 55*(1), 231–245.

Taylor, R.M., and Reising, J. 1995. The Human-Electronic Crew: Can We Trust the Team? *Proceedings of the 3rd International Workshop on Human-Computer Teamwork,* Cambridge, United Kingdom. Available: https://apps.dtic.mil/sti/pdfs/ADA340601.pdf.

Topcu, U., Bliss, N., Cooke, N., Cummings, M., Llorens, A., Shrobe, H., and Zuck, L. 2020. Assured autonomy: Path toward living with autonomous systems we can trust. *arXiv*:2010.14443.

Toulmin, S.E. 1958. *The Uses of Argument.* Cambridge: Cambridge University Press.

Trapsilawati, F., Wickens, C., Chen, C.-H., and Qu, X. 2017. Transparency and Conflict Resolution Automation Reliability in Air Traffic Control. *19th International Symposium on Aviation Psychology,* Dayton, Ohio, pp. 419–424.

Tsifetakis, E., and Kontogiannis, T. 2019. Evaluating non-technical skills and mission essential competencies of pilots in military aviation environments. *Ergonomics, 62*(2), 204–218.

Turban, E., and Frenzel, L.E. 1992. Expert Systems and Applied Artificial Intelligence. MacMillan Publishing Company.

Turk, W. 2006. Writing requirements for engineers [good requirement writing]. *Engineering Management Journal, 16*(3), 20–23.

Tversky, A., and Kahneman, D. 1987. Rational Choice and the Framing of Decisions. *Rational Choice; The Contrast Between Economics and Psychology.* Chicago: University of Chicago Press.

Tversky, A., and Kahneman, D. 1974. Judgment under uncertainty: Heuristics and biases. *Science, 185*(4157), 1124–1131. doi: 10.1126/science.185.4157.1124.

USAF (U.S. Air Force). 2013. *Air Force Research Laboratory Autonomy Science and Technology Strategy.* Wright-Patterson Air Force Base, OH: Air Force Research Laboratory. December 2, 2013. Available: https://web.archive.org /web/20170125102447/http://www.defenseinnovationmarketplace.mil /resources/AFRL_Autonomy_Strategy_DistroA.PDF.

USAF. 2015. *Autonomous Horizons: The Way Forward.* Washington, DC: Office of the U.S. Air Force Chief Scientist.

USAF. 2020. *Department of the Air Force Role in Joint All Domain Operations (JADO)*. Air Force Doctrine Publication (AFDP) 3-99. Maxwell Air Force Base, AL. Available: https://www.doctrine.af.mil/Doctrine-Publications/AFDP-3-99-DAF-Role-in-Jt-All-Domain-Ops-JADO/.

van Dongen, K., and van Maanen, P. 2005. Designing for Dynamic Task Allocation. *Proceedings of the Seventh International Naturalistic Decision Making Conference (NDM7)*. Amsterdam, Netherlands.

Vered, M., Howe, P., Miller, T., Sonenberg, L., and Velloso, E. 2020. Demand-driven transparency for monitoring intelligent agents. *IEEE Transactions on Human-Machine Systems, 50*(3), 264–275.

Vicente, K.J. 1999. *Cognitive Work Analysis: Toward Safe, Productive, and Healthy Computer-Based Work*. Boca Raton, FL: CRC Press.

Volpe, C.E., Cannon-Bowers, J.A., Salas, E., and Spector, P.E. 1996. The impact of cross-training on team functioning: An empirical investigation. *Human Factors, 38*, 87–100.

Volz, K., Yang, E., Dudley, R., Lynch, E., Dropps, M., and Dorneich, M.C. 2016. An evaluation of cognitive skill degradation in information automation. *Proceedings of the Human Factors and Ergonomics Society Annual Meeting, 60*(1), 191–195.

Walker, G.H., Stanton, N.A., Salmon, P.M., and Jenkins, D.P. 2009. *Command and Control: The Sociotechnical Perspective*. London: CRC Press. doi: 10.1201/9781315572765.

Wang, L., Jamieson, G.A., and Hollands, J.G. 2009. Trust and reliance on an automated combat identification system. *Human Factors, 51*(3), 281–291.

Wang, N., Pynadath, D.V., and Hill, S.G. 2016. Trust Calibration Within a Human-Robot Team: Comparing Automatically Generated Explanations. *2016 11th ACM/IEEE International Conference on Human-Robot Interaction (HRI)*, pp. 109–116.

Wang, N., Pynadath, D.V., Rovira, E., Barnes, M.J., and Hill, S.G. 2018. Is It My Looks? Or Something I Said? The Impact of Explanations, Embodiment, and Expectations on Trust and Performance in Human-Robot Teams. *13th International Conference, Persuasive 2018*, Waterloo, ON, Canada, pp. 56–69. Springer, Cham.

Warm, J.S., Dember, W.N., and Hancock, P.A. 1996. Vigilance and Workload in Automated Systems. Pp. 183–200 in *Automation and Human Performance: Theory and Applications*. Boca Raton, FL: CRC Press.

Weaver, S.J., Salas, E., Lyons, R., Lazzara, E.H., Rosen, M.A., Diazgranados, D., and King, H. 2010. Simulation-based team training at the sharp end: A qualitative study of simulation-based team training design, implementation, and evaluation in healthcare. *Journal of Emergencies, Trauma and Shock, 3*(4), 369.

West, S.M., Whittaker, M., and Crawford, K. 2019. *Discriminating Systems: Gender Race and Power in AI*. AI Now Institute. Available: https://ainowinstitute.org/discriminatingsystems.pdf.

Wickens, C.D. 1995. The Tradeoff of Design for Routine and Unexpected Performance: Implications of Situation Awareness. Pp. 57–64 in *Experimental Analysis and Measurement of Situation Awareness* (D.J. Garland and M.R. Endsley, eds.). Daytona Beach, FL: Embry-Riddle Aeronautical University Press.

Wickens, C.D. 2008. Situation awareness: Review of Mica Endsley's 1995 articles on situation awareness theory and measurement. *Human Factors, 50*(3), 397–403.

Wickens, C.D. 2009. The Psychology of Aviation Surprise: An 8 Year Update Regarding the Noticing of Black Swans. *2009 International Symposium on Aviation Psychology,* Dayton, OH, pp. 1–6.

Wickens, C.D. 2015. Situation awareness: Its applications value and its fuzzy dichotomies. *Journal of Cognitive Engineering and Decision Making, 9*(1), 90–94.

Wickens, C.D. 2018. Automation stages and levels, 20 years after. *Journal of Cognitive Engineering and Decision Making, 12*(1), 35–41.

Wickens, C.D., Helton, W.S., Hollands, J.G., and Banbury, S. 2022. *Engineering Psychology and Human Performance, 5th ed*. New York: Routledge.

Widmer, G., and Kubat, M. 1996. Learning in the presence of concept drift and hidden contexts. *Machine Learning, 23*, 69–101.

Wiener, E.K., Kanki, B.G., and Helmreich, R.L. 1993. *Cockpit Resource Management*. San Diego, CA: Academic Press.

Wiener, E.L. 1985. Cockpit Automation: In Need of a Philosophy. *1985 Behavioral Engineering Conference,* Warrendale, PA.

Wiener, E.L., and Curry, R.E. 1980. Flight deck automation: Promises and problems. *Ergonomics, 23*(10), 995–1011.

Williams, K.D. 2010. Dyads can be groups (and often are). *Small Group Research, 41*(2), 268–274. doi: 10/d6msv6.

Wilson, G.F., and Russell, C.A. 2007. Performance enhancement in an uninhabited air vehicle task using psychophysiologically determined adaptive aiding. *Human Factors, 49*(6), 1005–1018.

Wimmer, H., and Perner, J. 1983. Beliefs about beliefs: Representation and constraining function of wrong beliefs in young children's understanding of deception. *Cognition, 13*(1), 103–128.

Wojton, H., Vickers, B., Carter, K., Sparrow, D., Wilkins, L., and Fealing, C. 2021. DATAWorks 2021: Characterizing Human-Machine Teaming Metrics for Test and Evaluation. IDA Document NS D-21563. Alexandria, VA: Institute for Defense Analysis.

Woods, D.D. 2015. Four concepts for resilience and the implications for the future of resilience engineering. *Reliability Engineering and System Safety, 141,* 5–9.

Woods, D.D. 2016. The risks of autonomy: Doyle's catch. *Journal of Cognitive Engineering and Decision Making, 10*(2), 131–133.

Woods, D.D. 2017. *STELLA: Report from the SNAFUcatchers Workshop on Coping with Complexity.* Columbus, OH: The Ohio State University. Available: https://snafucatchers.github.io/.

Woods, D.D., and Hollnagel, E. 2006. *Joint Cognitive Systems: Patterns in Cognitive Systems Engineering.* Boca Raton, FL: CRC Press (Taylor and Francis).

Wright, J.L., Chen, J.Y., Barnes, M.J., and Hancock, P.A. 2016. Agent reasoning transparency's effect on operator workload. *Human Factors: The Journal of the Human Factors and Ergonomic Society, 58*(3), 401–415.

Wynne, K.T., and Lyons, J.B. 2018. An integrative model of autonomous agent teammate-likeness. *Theoretical Issues in Ergonomics Science, 19*(3), 353–374.

Yadav, A., Patel, A., and Shah, M. 2021. A comprehensive review on resolving ambiguities in natural language processing. *AI Open, 2,* 85–92.

Yang, J.X., Schemanske, C., and Searle, C. 2021. Toward quantifying trust dynamics: How people adjust their trust after moment-to-moment interaction with automation. *Human Factors,* 00187208211034716.

Yeh, M., and Wickens, C. 2001. Display signaling in augmented reality: Effects on cue reliability and image realism on attention allocation and trust calibration. *Human Factors, 43*(3), 355–365.

Yeh, M., Wickens, C.D., and Seagull, F.J. 1999. Target cueing in visual search: The effects of conformality and display location on the allocation of visual attention. *Human Factors, 41*(4), 524–542.

Young, J.P., Fanjoy, R.O., and Suckow, M.W. 2006. Impact of glass cockpit experience on manual flight skills. *Journal of Aviation/Aerospace Education and Research, 15*(2), 27–32.

Young, L.R.A. 1969. On adaptive manual control. *Ergonomics, 12*(4), 635–657.

Young, M.S., Brookhuis, K.A., Wickens, C.D., and Hancock, P.A. 2015. State of science: Mental workload in ergonomics. *Ergonomics, 58*(1), 1–17.

Zaccaro, S.J., and DeChurch, L.A. 2011. Leadership Forms and Functions in Multiteam Systems. Pp. 265–300 in *Multiteam Systems.* New York: Routledge.

Zaccaro, S.J., Marks, M.A., and DeChurch, L.A. 2012. *Multiteam Systems: An Organization Form for Complex, Dynamic Environments.* New York, NY: Routledge Taylor and Francis Group.

Zacharias, G., Miao, A., Illgen, C., Yara, J., and Siouris, G. 1996. SAMPLE: Situation Awareness Model for Pilot-in-the-Loop Evaluation. *First Annual Conference on Situation Awareness in the Tactical Air Environment,* Patuxent River, MD: Naval Air Warfare Center.

Zhang, R., McNeese, N.J., Freeman, G., and Musick, G. 2021. "An ideal human" expectations of AI teammates in human-AI teaming. *ACM on Human-Computer Interaction, 4(CSCW3),* 1–25.

Zhang, T., Yang, J., Liang, N., Pitts, B.J., Prakah-Asante, K.O., Curry, R., Duerstock, B.S., Wachs, J.P., and Yu, D. 2020. Physiological measurements of situation awareness: A systematic review. *Human Factors: The Journal of the Human Factors and Ergonomics Society,* online November 26. doi: 10.1177/0018720820969071.

Appendixes

Appendix A

Committee Biographies

Mica Endsley (*Chair*) is president of SA Technologies and is the former chief scientist for the U.S. Air Force. She has also held the positions of visiting associate professor at Massachusetts Institute of Technology in the Department of Aeronautics and Astronautics and associate professor of industrial engineering at Texas Tech University. She was formerly an engineering specialist at the Northrop Corporation. Endsley is a fellow and past president of the Human Factors and Ergonomics Society. She is a recognized world leader in the design, development, and evaluation of systems to support human situation awareness and decision making, and the integration of humans and automation. She has published extensively on the effects of automation and AI on human performance and situation awareness. She has authored more than 200 scientific articles and is the coauthor of *Analysis and Measurement of Situation Awareness and Designing for Situation Awareness*. Endsley received the Human Factors and Ergonomics Society Jack Kraft Innovator Award and the Aerospace Medical Association Kent Gillingham Award for her work in situation awareness. She is currently a member of the Board of Human-System Integration of the National Academies of Sciences, Engineering, and Medicine and has previously served on the National Academies' Aeronautics and Space Engineering Board (2008 to 2013), as well as the Army Research Laboratory Technical Assessment Board Panel on Soldier Systems (1998 to 2000) and Panel on Human Factors in the Design of Tactical Display Systems for the Individual Soldier (1994 to 1996). She received her Ph.D. in industrial and systems engineering from the University of Southern California in 1990.

Barrett S. Caldwell is professor of industrial engineering (and aeronautics and astronautics, by courtesy) at Purdue University. His research team examines and improves how people get, share, and use information well in settings including aviation, critical incident response, healthcare, and spaceflight operations. He was named in 2008 as a fellow of the Human Factors and Ergonomics Society. Caldwell has served on multiple panels, and in a variety of projects, associated with the National Academies of Sciences, Engineering, and Medicine. He co-organized the National Academy of Engineering U.S. Frontiers of Engineering (FOE) 2008 session on cognitive ergonomics, participated in the 2003 U.S. FOE, the 2006 German-American FOE, and the 2016 Japan-U.S. FOE. National Academies' committee service has included panels on Human Factors Science at the Army Research Laboratory; Information Technology Automation and the U.S. Workforce; and Systems Engineering to Improve Traumatic Brain Injury Care in the Military Health System. During 2016 to 2017, Caldwell was a Jefferson science fellow at the U.S. Department of State, assigned to environment, science, technology, and health policy in the Office of Japanese Affairs. He received his Ph.D. in social psychology from the University of California, Davis, and B.S. degrees in aeronautics and astronautics and humanities from MIT.

Erin K. Chiou is an assistant professor of human systems engineering at Arizona State University and also directs the Automation Design Advancing People and Technology (ADAPT) Laboratory. The ADAPT Lab studies human-agent teaming in complex work environments, with a focus on social factors such as trust and accountability with automation. Recent projects have been supported by the U.S. Department of Homeland Security, the U.S. Department of Defense, and the National Science Foundation, and include applications in security, manufacturing, and healthcare. Chiou has served as a panelist on the National Academies of Sciences, Engineering, and Medicine panel on human factors science at the Army Research Laboratory (2019), and as an invited expert for workshops hosted by the Office of the Director of National Intelligence (2018), the U.N. Institute for Disarmament Research (2019), Trusted Autonomous Systems Defence CRC (2019), and the Computing Community Consortium (2020). She is also the coeditor of a recent volume titled *Advancing Diversity, Inclusion, and Social Justice Through Human Systems Engineering* (2019, CRC Press). Chiou received her Ph.D. and M.S. in industrial and systems engineering from the University of Wisconsin–Madison, concentrating in human factors and ergonomics, with a minor in health systems. Her B.S. was completed at the University of Illinois at Urbana-Champaign where she majored in psychology and philosophy.

Nancy Cooke is a professor of human systems engineering at Arizona State University (ASU) and directs ASU's Center for Human, AI, and Robot Teaming. She is past president of the Human Factors and Ergonomics Society and recently chaired a study panel for the National Academies of Sciences, Engineering, and Medicine on Enhancing the Effectiveness of Team Science. Cooke was a member of the U.S. Air Force Scientific Advisory board from 2008 to 2012. She currently serves on the Defense Advanced Research Projects Agency's Information and Science Technology Study Group and is a member of the National Academies' Committee on Risk Analysis for Nuclear War and Nuclear Terrorism. Her research interests include the study of individual and team cognition and its application to the development of cognitive and knowledge engineering methodologies and human-AI-robot teaming in defense operations, urban search and rescue, and distributed space operations. Her work is funded primarily by the U.S. Department of Defense. She received her Ph.D. in cognitive psychology from New Mexico State University.

Mary (Missy) Cummings is currently a professor in the Duke University Electrical and Computer Engineering Department and the director of the Humans and Autonomy Laboratory. A naval officer and military pilot from 1988 to 1999, she was one of the U.S. Navy's first female fighter pilots. She is an American Institute of Aeronautics and Astronautics fellow and a member of several technology-focused national committees. Her research interests include human supervisory control, explainable artificial intelligence, human-autonomous system collaboration, human-robot interaction, human-systems engineering, and the ethical and social impact of technology. Cummings received her B.S. in mathematics from the U.S. Naval Academy, an M.S. in space systems engineering from the Naval Postgraduate School, and a Ph.D. in systems engineering from the University of Virginia.

Cleotilde Gonzalez is a research professor of decision sciences and the founding director of the Dynamic Decision Making Laboratory at Carnegie Mellon University. Her main affiliation is with the Social and Decision Sciences Department and she has additional affiliations with many other departments and centers in the university. She is a lifetime fellow of the Cognitive Science Society and the Human Factors and Ergonomics Society. She is also a member of the governing board of the Cognitive Science Society. She is associate editor of *Cognitive Science* and part of the editorial board of *Decision*, the *Journal of Experimental Psychology-General*, the *Journal of Behavioral Decision Making*, *Human Factors*, and the *System Dynamics Review*. She is widely published across many fields deriving from her contributions to the Cognitive Science field. Her work includes the development of a theory of decisions from experience called Instance-Based Learning Theory, from which many computational models have emerged, including a run-up winner of a modeling competition focused on the prediction in repeated Market Entry Games. She has been principal or co-investigator on a wide range of multimillion dollar and multiyear collaborative efforts with government and industry, including current efforts on Collaborative Research Alliances and Multi-University Research Initiative grants from the Army Research Laboratories and Army Research Office. She has mentored more than 30 postdoctoral fellows and doctoral students, many of whom have pursued successful careers in academia, government, and industry. Gonzalez received a B.Sc. and an M.B.A. from the Universidad de las Americas-Puebla, Mexico, and her M.Sc. and Ph.D. from Texas Tech University.

John D. Lee is the Emerson Electric professor at the University of Wisconsin–Madison. He investigates the issues of human-automation interaction, particularly trust in automation. He has investigated trust in domains that include unmanned aerial vehicles, maritime operations, highly automated vehicles, and deep space exploration. His work also involves assessing interface and interaction methods to enhance trust calibration, as well as statistical approaches to assess trust and user state estimation. Lee helped to edit the *Handbook of Cognitive Engineering*, the *APA Handbook of Human-Systems Integration*, and the *Handbook of Human Factors for Automated, Connected, and Intelligent Vehicles*, and is also a coauthor of a popular textbook *Designing for People: An Introduction to Human Factors Engineering*. He has served on several National Academies of Sciences, Engineering, and Medicine committees including the Committee on Human Factors, Committee on Reducing and Preventing Teen Motor Vehicle Crashes, and the Army Research Laboratory Technical Assessment Board. Lee received a Ph.D. in mechanical engineering and an M.S. in industrial engineering from the University of Illinois, and a B.S. in mechanical engineering and B.A. in psychology from Lehigh University.

Nathan J. McNeese is an assistant professor and director of the Team Research Analytics in Computational Environments Research Group within the Human-Centered Computing Division in the School of Computing at Clemson University. He is also director of the university-wide Clemson University Data (Science) Lab. His research interests span across human-AI teaming, human-centered AI, and the development/design of human-centered collaborative tools and systems. He currently serves on multiple international/societal program and technical committees, in addition to multiple editorial boards including *Human Factors*. He is a previous member of the National Academies of Sciences, Engineering, and Medicine Panel on Human Factors Science, as well as previous member of the Army Research Lab HERD Technical Advisory Board. His research has received multiple best paper awards/nominations and has been published in top peer-reviewed human-computer interaction and human factors venues more than 90 times. In addition, he has acquired more than $14 million in research funding from agencies such as the National Science Foundation, the Office of Naval Research, the Air Force Office of Scientific Research, and the Agency for Healthcare Research and Quality. McNeese received a Ph.D. in information sciences and technology from Pennsylvania State University.

Christopher Miller is now the chief scientist and a co-owner of Smart Information Flow Technologies (SIFT), a small business doing human-systems integration research and development for more than 20 years. He is one of the co-creators of the Playbook® concept and has been involved in all phases of its development across multiple customers and applications. He has substantial project management experience, including leading more than 55 efforts in human-systems and human automation interaction for Defense Advanced Research Projects Agency (DARPA), the U.S. Navy, U.S. Army, U.S. Air Force, and the National Aeronautics and Space Administration—both as prime and subcontractor—as well as in medical, industrial processing, and commercial aviation domains. Prior to joining SIFT, Miller led a series of projects as the human factors fellow at Honeywell Technology Center where he was principal investigator for Honeywell's role in the U.S. Army's Rotorcraft Pilot's Associate ACTD Program and for Honeywell's effort in automated learning for task and information requirements for the U.S. Air Force and DARPA's Pilot's Associate Program. He won Honeywell's highest technical achievement award for his work in designing the intermodule and human communications aspects of the Abnormal Event Guidance and Information System—an associate-like system for use in oil refineries. He has also provided consulting services to Australia, Canada, and the UK on various defense research projects, and to the European Science Foundation in prioritizing research for autonomy support for deep space missions. Miller is the author of more than 140 publications in these fields and has served as chair of 17 conference sessions or symposia and has given invited addresses to NATO Research and Technology Organization advisory boards, the European Space Foundation, and the National Academies of Sciences, Engineering, and Medicine. He has previously served on multiple National Academies' activities including (most recently) helping to organize the Workshop on Human-Automation Interaction Considerations for Unmanned Aerial System Integration in 2018. Miller received his Ph.D. and M.A. degrees in cognitive psychology (with an emphasis on linguistics and language acquisition and use) from the University of Chicago and a B.A. from Pomona College.

Emilie M. Roth is owner and principal scientist of Roth Cognitive Engineering, a small company that conducts research and application in the areas of human factors and applied cognitive psychology (cognitive engineering). Her work involves analysis of human problem solving and decision making in real-world environments (e.g., military command and control; intelligence analysis; nuclear power plant emergencies; railroad operations; healthcare), and the impact of support systems (e.g., computerized procedures; alarm systems; advanced graphical displays; new forms of decision support and automation) on cognitive performance. Roth has supported analysis and design of first-of-a-kind systems, including design and manning of envisioned Army Future Vertical Lift; design and evaluation of next-generation nuclear power plant control rooms; and design of computer-based support systems for flight planning and monitoring for USTRANSCOM and the Air Mobility Command. She is a fellow of the Human Factors and Ergonomics Society, is an associate editor of the *Journal of Cognitive Engineering and Decision Making*, and serves on the editorial board of *Human Factors*. She participated in the National Academies of Sciences, Engineering, and Medicine's Committee on Human-System Design Support for Changing Technology (in 2006), and the National Academies' committee examining lessons learned from the Fukushima nuclear accident for improving safety and security of U.S. nuclear plants (2012 to 2016), and is currently a member of the Board on Human-Systems Integration at the National Academies. She received her Ph.D. from the University of Illinois, Urbana-Champaign, in cognitive psychology.

William B. Rouse is research professor in the McCourt School of Public Policy at Georgetown University, as well as senior fellow in the office of the senior vice president for research, and professor emeritus and former chair of the School of Industrial and Systems Engineering at the Georgia Institute of Technology. His research focuses on understanding and managing complex public-private systems such as healthcare delivery, higher education, transportation, and national security, with emphasis on mathematical and computational modeling of these systems for the purpose of policy design and analysis. He was chair of the Committee on Human Factors before it became the Board on Human-Systems Integration. Over the past four decades, he has served as chair, co-chair, or member of roughly 40 National Academies of Sciences, Engineering, and Medicine study committees, ad hoc committees, and other initiatives. He received his B.S. in mechanical engineering from the University of Rhode Island, and his S.M. and Ph.D., both in systems engineering, from the Massachusetts Institute of Technology.

Appendix B

Human-AI Teaming Workshop Agenda

July 28-29, 2021

MEETING OBJECTIVES

- Identify key human-systems integration design considerations, methods, approaches, and associated research aimed at warfighter systems that incorporate human-AI teaming
- Identify gaps in knowledge on effective human-machine teaming necessary to achieve future Air Force mission capability
- Identify promising human-systems integration and human factors research opportunities that would accelerate mission capability development.

WEDNESDAY, JULY 28, 2021

10:00 a.m. **Welcome and Introductions**
- Mica Endsley, *Chair*

10:15 a.m. **AI in Future DOD Operations**
Facilitated by Nancy Cooke (committee member)
- Mark Draper, *Human-AI Interaction in Future Joint All Domain Operations: Some Challenges and Opportunities*, Air Force Research Laboratory
- Robin Murphy, *Role of Autonomy in DOD and HADR*, Texas A&M University
- Greg Zacharias, *Human-Autonomy Test and Evaluation*, DOD-OSD

12:00 p.m. **Break**

12:45 p.m. **AI Status and Challenges**
Facilitated by Missy Cummings (committee member)
- Matt Turek, *XAI Program*, DARPA
- Joanna Bryson, *AI Ethics and Human Cooperation*, Hertie School

2:00 p.m.   **Break**

2:30 p.m.   **Human-AI Teaming Approaches**
Facilitated by Bill Rouse (committee member)
- Ben Shneiderman, *Human-Centered AI*, University of Maryland
- Jay Shively, *Human Autonomy Teaming*, NASA Ames
- Matthew Johnson, *Intelligent Teaming*, Florida Institute for Human and Machine Cognition

4:45 p.m.   **Adjourn**

THURSDAY, JULY 29, 2021

10:00 a.m.   **Welcome and First Day wrap up**
- Mica Endsley, *Chair*

10:15 a.m.   **Human-AI Team Design and Processes**
Facilitated by Emilie Roth (committee member)
- Jamie Gorman, *Modeling Human-Autonomy Team Coordination Using Layered Dynamics*, Georgia Tech University
- Brian Sandberg, *ASIST Program*, DARPA
- Thomas O'Neill, *Future Directions in Human-Autonomy Teams Research*, University of Calgary

12:15 p.m.   **Break**

12:30 p.m.   **Bias and Trust**
Facilitated by John Lee (committee member)
- Chris Wickens, *Black Swans, Complacency and Automation Bias*
- Peter Hancock, *Trust in AI Meta-Analysis*, University of Central Florida
- Joe Lyons, *Trust Research in AFRL*, Air Force Research Laboratory

2:00 p.m.   **Break**

2:30 p.m.   **Transparency and Explainability**
Facilitated by Chris Miller (committee member)
- Shane Mueller, *XAI*, Michigan Technology University
- Jessie Chen, *Transparent Communications for Effective Human-Autonomy Teaming*, Army Research Laboratory
- Tim Miller, *Transparency and Explainability*, University of Melbourne

4:30 p.m.   Conclusions/Discussion

5:00 p.m.   Adjourn

Appendix C

Definitions

Ad Hoc Teams—Teams that form rapidly and uniquely for short-term tasks and missions.

Adaptable Automation—Automation that can be activated or have its level of automation modified by the human in real time during system operation.

Adaptive Automation—Automation that automatically changes its performance or level of automation based on time, human performance or state, or other predefined characteristics of team performance.

Agile Software—An approach to software development that produces rapid iterative sections of software or "sprints," each of which works to define requirements for a limited set of functions, and then develop, integrate, and test the associated software. Agile software-development approaches feature a focus on (1) individuals and interactions over processes and tools; (2) working software over comprehensive documentation; (3) customer collaboration over contract negotiation; and (4) responding to change over following a plan (Abrahamsson et al., 2017; Beck et al., 2001; Cockburn, 2002).

Artificial Intelligence (AI)—Systems that seek to provide the intellectual processes characteristic of people, such as the ability to reason, discover meaning, generalize, or learn from past experience (Copeland, 2021). AI systems may be applied to parts of a task (e.g., perception and categorization, natural language understanding, problem solving, reasoning, system control), or to a combination. AI software approaches may involve symbolic approaches (i.e., rule-based or case-based reasoning), often taking form as decision-support systems; may apply other advanced algorithms such as Bayesian belief-nets, fuzzy systems, and connectionist or machine learning-based approaches (e.g., logistic regression, decision trees, or neural networks); or may incorporate hybrid architectures that include more than one algorithmic approach.

AI Auditability—The ability to document and assess the data and models used in developing an AI-embedded system.

AI Explainability—The ability to provide satisfactory, accurate, and efficient explanations of the results (i.e., recommendations, decisions, and/or actions) of an AI system.

Automation—A device that performs functions independently, without continuous input from an operator (Groover, 2020). Automation can be fixed (mechanical) or programmable (based on defined rules and feedback loops to ensure proper execution), either via a static set of software commands, or involving flexible, rapid customization by a human operator. Tasks may be fully automated (i.e., autonomous) or semi-automated, requiring human oversight and control for portions of the task. It is also often defined as "the execution by a machine agent (usually a computer) of a function that was previously carried out by a human. What is considered automation will therefore change with time" (Parasuraman and Riley, 1997, p. 231).

Automation Conundrum—"The more automation is added to a system, and the more reliable and robust that automation is, the less likely that human operators overseeing the automation will be aware of critical information and able to take over manual control when needed. More automation refers to automation use for more functions, longer durations, higher levels of automation, and automation that encompasses longer task sequences" (Endsley, 2017, p. 8).

Autonomy—Systems that have a set of intelligence-based capabilities that can respond to situations that were not explicitly programmed or were not anticipated in the design (i.e., systems that can generate decision-based responses). Autonomous systems have a degree of self-government and self-directed behavior (serving as a human's proxy for decisions) (USAF, 2013). Systems may be fully autonomous or partially autonomous (i.e., requiring human actions or inputs for portions of the task).

Bias—A preference toward certain information or options. Bias is created through systematic error introduced by selecting or encouraging one outcome or answer over others (Merriam-Webster, 2021). In the case of AI, bias may be introduced through a limited set of training data that fails to consider the wider range of circumstance where it may be employed, or by algorithms that focus on features in the datasets that may be incidental to performance.

Black-Box AI—AI systems in which the reasoning and processes are not transparent or observable.

Brittleness—The inability of automation to perform at the limits of its designed performance envelope, resulting in often unexpected system failures.

Common Ground—Mutual knowledge, beliefs, and assumptions required to support interdependent actions in teams (Klein, Feltovich, and Woods, 2005, p. 146) (see also shared situation awareness and shared mental models).

Context of Use—Includes characteristics of the users, the activities they perform, how the work is distributed across people and machine agents, the range and complexity of situations that can arise, as well as the broader sociotechnical environment in which the system will be integrated (NRC, 2007).

Cooperation—"Negotiating and aligning individual goals when they differ from a joint goal" (Chiou and Lee, 2021, p. 10), with individual teammates willing to give up individual benefit to achieve greater benefits for the team.

Coordination—Managing dependencies between activities (Malone and Crowston, 2001). This includes the timing or arrangement of joint decisions, or dependency management (Malone and Crowston, 1994).

Directability—"One's ability to influence the behavior of others and complementarily be influenced by others" (Johnson and Bradshaw, 2021, p. 390).

Distributed Teams—Teams that are distributed spatially (e.g., blocked from view by objects, in separate rooms, or separate geographical areas) or temporally.

Explainability—Support for understanding the logic, process, factors, or reasoning upon which a system's actions or recommendations are based.

Flexible Autonomy—Automation in which the level of automation can change dynamically over time for different functions, using either adaptive or adaptable approaches.

Granularity of Control (GOC)—The degree of specificity of control inputs that are required to interact with the system. GOC can range "from (a) manual control; to (b) programmable control, requiring the programming of each task parameter and specification; (c) Playbook control, selecting from a Playbook of preset, yet adaptable, behaviors (Miller, 2000); and (d) goal-based control, where only a high-level goal needs to be provided to the system (USAF, 2015)" (Endsley, 2017, p. 17).

Human-AI Team—A team consisting of "one or more people and one or more AI systems requiring collaboration and coordination to achieve successful task completion" (Cuevas et al., 2007, p. 64).

Human-Systems Integration (HSI)—Addresses human considerations within the system design and implementation process, with the aim of maximining total system performance and minimizing total ownership costs (Boehm-Davis, Durso, and Lee, 2015). HSI incorporates human-centered analyses, models, and evaluations throughout the system lifecycle, starting from early operational concepts, through research, design, and development, and continuing through operations (NRC, 2007). Within the DOD, HSI is divided into seven domains: manpower, personnel, training, human factors engineering, safety and occupational health, force protection and survivability, and habitability.

Ironies of Automation—The more advanced the automation, the more crucial the contribution of the human; the less likely the human is to have the manual skills necessary; and the more likely that workload will be high and more advanced cognitive skills will be needed when humans take over task performance (Bainbridge, 1983).

Level of Automation (LOA)—The amount of control or authority that is granted to the automation (or AI system) for a given task or function.

Lumberjack Effect—"More automation yields better human-system performance when all is well but induces increased dependence, which may produce more problematic performance when things fail" (Onnasch et al., 2014, p. 477).

Meaningful Human Control—"The ability to make timely, informed choices to influence AI-based systems that enable the best possible operational outcomes" (Boardman and Butcher, 2019, p. 7-1).

Mental Model—"Mechanisms whereby humans are able to generate descriptions of system purpose and form, explanation of system functioning and observed system states, and predictions of future states" (Rouse and Morris, 1985, p. 7).

Model Drift—Occurs when the relationship between input and output data changes over time, negatively affecting the accuracy of the model's predictions (Widmer and Kubat, 1996).

Multi-Domain Operations (MDO)—Dynamic and distributed combinations of actions across the traditionally separate air, land, maritime, space, cyberspace, information, and electro-magnetic spectrum domains to achieve synergistic and combined effects with improved mission outcomes.

Multi-Domain Operations Command and Control (MDC2)—Connected and "distributed sensors, shooters, and data from all domains to joint forces, enabling coordinated exercise of authority to integrate planning and synchronize convergence in time, space, and purpose" (USAF, 2020, p. 6). Also called joint all domain command and control (JADC2).

On-the-Loop Control—Operations in which people oversee a system that is operating at a high level of automation at very fast timeframes and/or volumes exceeding human capacity. There is no expectation that people will be able to monitor or intervene in operations prior to automation errors occurring, however, it may be possible to take actions to turn off the automation or change automation behaviors in an outer control loop.

Out-of-the-Loop (OOTL)—The tendency for people working with automated systems to be slower to detect a problem with system performance and slower to understand the problem once detected.

Playbook—A set of plays that are templates of behavior for automation, known to be effective at accomplishing specific goals (Miller, 2000).

Resilient Teams—Groups of people and/or automated agents that have the capacity to respond to change and disruption in a flexible and innovative manner to achieve successful outcomes.

Responsivity—"The input–output gain of a detector system, reflecting an ability to adjust to sudden, altered conditions in the environment and to resume stable operation" (Chiou and Lee, 2021, p. 6). Automation or AI responsivity refers to the "degree to which the automation effectively adapts to the person and situation" (Chiou and Lee, 2021, p. 6).

Shared Mental Model—A consistent understanding and representation of how systems work across teammates (i.e., the degree of agreement of one or more mental models). This includes models of the technology and equipment, models of taskwork, models of teamwork, and models of teammates (e.g., knowledge, skills, attitudes, preferences) (Cannon-Bowers, Salas, and Converse, 1993).

Shared Situation Awareness—"The degree to which team members possess the same SA on shared SA requirements" (Endsley and Jones, 2001, p. 48).

Situation Awareness (SA)—"The perception of the elements in the environment within a volume of time and space, the comprehension of their meaning and the projection of their status in the near future" (Endsley, 1988, p. 97).

Situation Structure—A 2 x 2 matrix that "specifies the choices available to each actor in a dyad, the outcomes of their choices, and how those outcomes depend on the choices of the other agent" (Chiou and Lee, 2021, p. 9).

Social Intelligence—An "aggregated measure of self- and social-awareness, evolved social beliefs and attitudes, and a capacity and appetite to manage complex social change" (Ganaie and Mudasir, 2015, p. 23).

Supervisory Control—Control by a human operator of automation, which, at a lower level, is controlling a dynamic system. The human operator handles higher-level tasks and determines the goals of the overall system, monitors the system to determine whether operations are normal and proceeding as desired, and diagnoses difficulties and intervenes in the case of abnormality or undesirable outcomes (Sheridan, 1986; Sheridan and Johannsen, 1976).

Taskwork—Activities, skills, and knowledge associated with carrying out the tasks required for a job (i.e., the functioning, operating procedures, and capabilities and limitations of equipment and technology; task procedures, strategies, constraints; relationships between components; and likely contingencies and scenarios). Taskwork is directly related to the goals of a team (Cannon-Bowers et al., 1993), and is often contrasted with teamwork.

Team—A "distinguishable set of two or more people who interact dynamically, interdependently, and adaptively toward a common and valued goal/objective/mission, who have each been assigned specific roles or functions to perform, and who have a limited lifespan of membership" (Salas et al., 1992, p. 4).

Teammate—A fellow member of a team. Teammates may be human or non-human (e.g., an animal, bird, robot, or autonomous software agent).

Teamwork—An interrelated set of knowledge, skills, and attitudes that facilitate coordinated, adaptive performance in teams. This includes an understanding of roles, responsibilities, interdependencies and interaction patterns, communications, and information flow (Cannon-Bowers et al., 1993). Teamwork is often contrasted with taskwork.

Team Mental Model—A mental model of one's teammate(s) that provides an understanding of teammates' capabilities, limitations, current goals and needs, and current and future performance (Cannon-Bowers, Salas, and Converse, 1993).

Team Situation Awareness—"The degree to which every team member has the SA required for his or her responsibilities" (Endsley, 1995, p. 39).

Theory of Mind—The mental capacity to understand other people and their behavior by ascribing mental states to them.

Transparency—The understandability and predictability of the system (Endsley, Bolte, and Jones, 2003), including its "abilities to afford an operator's comprehension about an intelligent agent's intent, performance, future plans, and reasoning process" (Chen et al., 2014a, p. 2).

Trust—The attitude that an "agent will help achieve an individual's goals in a situation characterized by uncertainty and vulnerability" (Lee and See, 2004, p. 2). Trust can mediate the degree to which people rely on each other as well as on a technology, such as AI.

White-Box AI—AI approaches that can explain how they behave, how they produce predictions, and what the influencing factors are (i.e., transparent approaches).